D1563202

WAYS *of*
THINKING

WAYS *of*

THINKING

The Limits of
Rational Thought
and
Artificial Intelligence

LÁSZLÓ MÉRŐ

*Department of
Experimental Psychology
Loránd Eötvös University
Budapest, Hungary*

English translation by Anna C. Gősi-Greguss
English version edited by Viktor Mészáros

World Scientific
Singapore • New Jersey • London • Hong Kong

Published by

World Scientific Publishing Co. Pte. Ltd.
P O Box 128, Farrer Road, Singapore 9128
USA office: 687 Hartwell Street, Teaneck, NJ 07666
UK office: 73 Lynton Mead, Totteridge, London N20 8DH

Library of Congress Cataloging-in-Publication Data

Merő, László.
   Ways of thinking: the limits of rational thought and artificial intelligence/
László Merő; English translation by Anna C. Gősi-Greguss; English version
edited by Viktor Mészáros.
   p. cm.
Includes bibliographical references and index.
ISBN 9810202660. -- ISBN 9810202679 (pbk.)
1. Thought and thinking.   2. Artificial intelligence.
I. Mészáros, Viktor.   II. Title.
B105.T54M47   1990
153.4'2 -- dc20   90-36036
                                                        CIP

Original Hungarian text © László Merő
English version © 1990 by World Scientific Publishing Co. Pte. Ltd.

Typeset by TYPOTEX Ltd., Budapest

Printed in Singapore by JBW Printers & Binders Pte. Ltd.

Acknowledgments

For their contribution I would like to thank everybody who helped me in writing this book with his or her professional, personal, technical or stylistic pieces of advice, remarks, sensible incomprehension or patience in tolerating the tension going together with writing. My first thanks are due to my wife, Éva Kovácsházy and my colleagues at the Department of Experimental Psychology of Eötvös Loránd University of Budapest: Sándor Illyés, Éva Bányai, István Czigler, Zoltán Vassy, Csilla Greguss, Péter Vágó, Róbert Horváth, Katalin Varga, Andrea Dúll, Irén Murányi, and Judit Bokor. My thanks are also due to Tibor Vámos, Ferenc Bródy, György Csaba, Éva Gartner, János Herczeg, János Pataki, Erika Kovács, István Fekete, Csaba Pléh, Ilona Barkóczi, János Geier, András Vargha, Anikó Kónya, András Joó, Csaba Andor, István Síklaki, Zsuzsa Votisky, László Vekerdi, and the students attending my university courses for their valuable comments and reflections. Special thanks must go to Ágnes Fraller for the hundreds of objective, factual, stylistic and sometimes vitriolic remarks, Anna C. Gősi–Greguss for her more than professional translation and Viktor Mészáros for his help in editing the English version.

Contents

Contents

0. Chapter Zero

There are as many ways of thinking as persons. There is no thought,
kindness or insult two persons would react the same way to. "You who read
me, are you sure of understanding my language?" — asks Jorge Luis Borges
in one of his short stories, stepping out from within the strict frame of his
fable for a moment. The well-defined frame and its deliberate breakdown
are both means of expression.

Some people will nod in agreement with the last sentence, others will
argue about it. Still others will just shrug at best. All those reactions are
very human. Those who agree probably react to something I was not even
thinking of when I was writing that sentence. The same is true for those
who disagree. Those who shrug are left unaffected by this sentence: they
watch the issue from the outside. They may be of the scientific breed that
would first want to see a well-built system of concepts around a statement
like this, in which they can decide the validity of the statement. Or they
want it to be proven to them by the usual scientific methods.

The phenomena of thinking and intellect are studied by several branches of science — all from different points of view. Biologists, philosophers,
psychologists and even mathematicians interested in logic, or engineers
wishing to build artificial intelligence, all pry into the essential nature of
reason. Nevertheless, they have hardly anything to say to each other, for
their frames of investigation are so different. Which should then be the
branch of science whose methods and system we will accept as competent?

I would like to start by admitting that you are not holding a so-called
interdisciplinary book in your hands. Such books perhaps do not even
exist, as will be expounded in greater detail later, in Chapter 12. If you
wish you may read this book as an interdisciplinary study till then, for we
are going to use the results of several branches of science indeed.

I would also like to avoid mislabeling: this is not a popular scientific
book either. We will talk about science, the book may possibly propagate
public knowledge, even unintentionally, but not within the frame of popular
science. This time I am not against the genre. It is a justified and

nice undertaking for someone to try and familiarize outsiders with his profession's way of thinking. This book, however, goes right into the causes and reasons of the diversity of ways of thinking.

I have written this piece of reading — or if you wish to switch to Latin: this legend — to provoke readers' minds. This is a legend or a tale about the tricks of how our thinking works and about the efforts and failures of artificial intelligence. Rather than any special previous education, I hope some mental effort will be necessary during reading. In order to facilitate continuous reading, I do not interrupt the text with exact citations or notes. But if the reader wants to dig deeper into the subject, look up some of the scientific results or simply check what the author means, it is necessary to make the sources available to him even in such a book. The detailed Index helps him in that, with the references also indicated. Instead of footnotes, the sources of quotations can be found under Sources at the end of the book.

Let us start with the statement: there are a lot of ways of thinking. However, we do know some guiding principles along which the ways of thinking can be classified into types. It can be seen day by day how differently specialists and laymen think within any profession. We can talk about common and scientific ways of thinking, and we feel that the artists' way of seeing things radically differs from both. Abstract and concrete ways of thinking can also be differentiated. We also talk about rational and irrational thinking. What do these expressions actually mean?

In fact, we can now even talk about artificial intelligence that is created with the help of computers. Is it of the same form of reason as natural thinking, or is it basically different? Can this distinction also be listed among the above, not necessarily exact but commonly used, categories?

Meeting a young man

Artificial intelligence still owes us the fulfillment of its greatest promises. Sometimes one cannot help confronting "his young self" who impertinently asks the questions: What about the translator program? What about the dictaphone that types a text from a tape recorder at least as correctly as an average secretary? What about the World Champion chess-program? What about the visual form perception, poetry and music?

The answers are similar to those Frigyes Karinthy, the father of satire in Hungary, gave to a young man who — as his own former self in a short story — sprang the questions on him: "What about your flying machine?" "What about your great symphony? Your awe-inspiring play about the grey horizon and the vibrations and convolutions of the proud gods beyond the horizon?" "What about Hungary, proud and independent?" Karinthy answers in embarrassment: "We are working towards that goal, I and other people. Still, it isn't something you can achieve overnight. After all, one's got to make a living, too." Today the commercially successful practical products of artificial intelligence give a wide berth to the unexpectedly difficult basic questions, and embark on solving only simple partial problems.

Nobody has been able so far to solve the above great problems through artificial intelligence, albeit they are surely not theoretically unsolvable, since man's natural intelligence can solve them. That is why the investigators of artificial intelligence have become increasingly interested in the results of psychology. If man's thinking mechanisms were understood better, then somehow it would also become possible to model and simulate them by artificial means.

I have also met the above young man and repeated Karinthy's excuses almost word by word: "Well, you see... It was no go... The Grey Horizon — that isn't something an actor can play... But I have written a pretty good sonnet on the theme... It appeared in print in a distinguished review... People liked it... And I've been a better-paid writer ever since..." Today I am not quite sure any more that the great promises of artificial intelligence can be realized at all (although I am not convinced of its opposite either), but I am certain that we are on a much longer and more difficult road than was originally thought by the enthusiastic founders of artificial intelligence some twenty or thirty years ago, who were encouraged by the initial spectacular successes.

When the library comes to life

There are libraries where the elaborately and spaciously arranged shelves invite one for a kind of browsing instead of absorbed reading. Having borrowed the book one wanted, one may spend even hours there, rambling frivolously among the books, dipping into some of them, reading a couple of pages in the theory of relativity, then five pages about the habits of primitive people. There is something interesting in each of them, and one feels it would be nice to read them all thoroughly. Not as thoroughly, though, as to spend too much energy on it: they are just pleasant passing adventures.

Then there comes a time when the visitor to the library becomes deeply interested in something: e.g. he receives eye-glasses, she gets pregnant or becomes possessed by a scientific problem. He or she goes to the same library and starts browsing. He/she is astonished to find that every book is meant for him/her: every book has something to say about seeing, birth, or the scientific problem he/she is interested in. Even the radio programmes are talking about the topic, i.e. it is all over town. The library comes to life.

As time passes, one gets accustomed to wearing spectacles, bringing up a child, or investigating a scientific problem. The picture becomes complete and one forgets its components. Or at least one sees the problems within a quite different system. One reorganizes those incidences that were not forgotten: probably there is a reason for keeping them in memory. And, of course — as it will be discussed abundantly — the whole is more than the sum of its parts.

> Logic is doubtless unshakable, but it cannot withstand a man who wants to go on living.
>
> (Franz Kafka)
>
> A happiness that often madness hits on, which reason and sanity could not so prosperously be delivered of.
>
> (William Shakespeare)
>
> Reason is a harmonizing, controlling force rather than a creative one. Even in the most purely logical realm, it is insight that first arrives at what is new.
>
> (Bertrand Russell)
>
> Reason is a good tool, in fact, it is an essential tool, yet, it is a subordinate tool. We must not believe in it, we ought to believe only in description and reality — but it is our duty to be sceptical by the aid of reason.
>
> (Géza Ottlik)
>
> Our washing up is just like our language. We have dirty water and dirty dishcloths, and yet we manage to get the plates and the glasses clean. In language, too, we have to work with unclear

concepts and form a logic whose scope is restricted in an unknown way, and yet we use it to bring some clarity into our understanding of nature.

(Niels Bohr)

He had two characteristic features, two passions: an unusual power of clear and logical reasoning, and a great moral purity and sense of justice: he was ardent and honorable.

But he would not have made a scientist of the sort who breaks new ground. His intelligence lacked the capacity for bold leaps into the unknown, the sudden flashes of insight that transcend barren, logical deductions.

And if he were really to do good, he would have needed, in addition to his principles, a heart capable of violating them — a heart which knows only of particular, not of general, cases, and which achieves greatness in little actions.

(Boris Pasternak)

The heart has its reasons which reason does not understand.

(Blaise Pascal)

My smartest sayings are those that even I had not expected.

(Jules Renard)

In the beginner's mind there are many possibilities, but in the expert's there are few.

(Shunryu Suzuki)

A few puzzles

The following puzzles also help to provide some idea of what this book is about. It is no wonder if they seem to be quite different from the above quotations: they show the other side of the coin. Some of them are easy, some are difficult, but — except for Puzzle 7 — they are genuine puzzles, i.e. they can definitely be solved, and solving them induces a feeling of intellectual excitement. The puzzles will serve the purpose of illustration at one part of the book or another. If you feel like solving them, go ahead. For the sake of fairness the page number of where the given puzzle will be discussed, together with the solution, is given in parentheses. (This way you do not have to read the whole book for the solution.)

5

Puzzle 1. Some definitions for crossword puzzles:
- Everyone shakes hands with it (5 letters)
- Sees through the fog back and forth (5 letters)
- It can be numerous and innumerable (4 letters)
- Speedy Irish poet known for his prose (13 letters)(page 37)

Puzzle 2. Six matches must be assembled to form four congruent equilateral triangles, each side of which is equal to the length of the matches. (page 44)

Puzzle 3. There is a refrigerator operating in a well-insulated, closed room. Will the temperature of the room decrease, increase or remain the same after you have left the door of the refrigerator open for some period of time? (page 46)

Puzzle 4. The structure of the third question of Puzzle 1 is quite strange. Look for similar examples where a word or expression and its formal opposite may define the same thing. (page 56)

Puzzle 5. Three travelers go into a hostel. Each of them pays 10 thalers for the accommodation. Later, however, the innkeeper remembers that three persons in a room should pay only 25 thalers, so he sends 5 thalers back to them by his servant. The servant, however, thinks that this is an unexpected stroke of luck for the travelers anyhow, and it is enough to give only 1 thaler to each of them. So he can slip 2 thalers into his own pocket. Now, each of the guests ends up having paid 9 thalers and the servant put 2 into his pocket. This amounts to $3 \times 9 + 2 = 29$ thalers. Where is the thirtieth thaler? (page 66)

Puzzle 6. Put as many cigarettes as possible on the table so that any two of them touch each other. How many cigarettes can you use? (page 130)

Puzzle 7. Why do mirrors reverse the left and right sides, without reversing the upper and lower sides? How does the mirror "know" where upside is? (page 140)

Puzzle 8. Examine the following sentence:
There are three error in this sentense.
Is this sentence true or false? Is it correct? (page 166)

Puzzle 9. Nine dots are arranged in a square as in the figure below. The problem is to connect them by drawing four continuous lines without lifting pencil from paper. (Please ignore tricks like parallel lines meet in infinity.) (page 221)

Puzzle 10. There is a country where two types of people live: the clearheaded and the dimheaded. The clearheaded people always perceive the world as it is, and they always tell the truth. The dimheaded always perceive the opposite of everything, but always lie. If, for instance, you ask a clearheaded person if the grass is green, he will see that the grass is green and tell the truth, so he will answer "yes". If you ask a dimheaded person the same question, he will not see that the grass is green, but will lie and say "yes". It is clear that the clearheaded persons will always give the same answer as the dimheaded ones to questions requiring a yes or no answer. Thus, it is *impossible* to tell who the clearheaded and who the dimheaded persons are in this country.

Let us see, however, what happens if you ask someone whether he himself is clearheaded. If he is clearheaded, he sees himself correctly and tells the truth, answering "yes". If he is dimheaded, however, he sees himself as clearheaded, perceiving the opposite of everything, but will lie, saying "no". Accordingly, it is *possible* to differentiate the clearheaded and the dimheaded persons by the aid of this question. But where is then the error in the previous reasoning? (page 221)

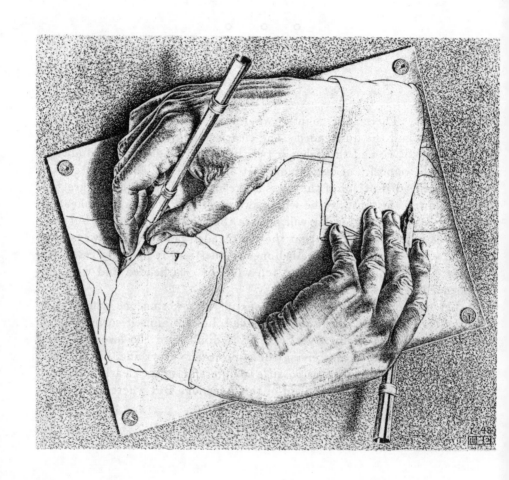

Drawing Hands © 1990 M. C. Escher Heirs / Cordon Art – Baarn – Holland

PART I

THE DIVERSITY OF THINKING

1. Logical thinking

Logic is the science of correct reasoning. This definition seems to be quite unambiguous, but it soon turns out to leave open the possibility for a great variety of interpretations. A standard problem in logic is how the logical explication of logic can be started before having explicated it.

If there is no fuel in a car, it will not start. We consider this reasoning completely logical, and by our definition we do it justly, since it is correct. It seems so natural to us but we do not really examine why we consider it correct. Rather, we immediately turn our attention to the next step: how to get some fuel or how to get to our destination without the car. In this example we have accepted that the occurrence of certain events necessarily causes other events to happen, the investigation of which is useless, for they are true due to the nature of things. In this case we can talk about the *logic of things*.

If the car does not start, its fuel tank is empty. We do not consider this reasoning logical, because we know very well that there can be a thousand other reasons why the car will not start. Such a conclusion cannot be drawn from the logic of things. In fact, it happens even to an experienced driver that only after having long tried to repair it does he find the indeed rare reason of the car's refusal to start: the fuel gauge has stuck, and the car does not start because there is no gasoline in the tank. Furthermore, this type of mistake is made almost exclusively by experienced drivers, who know so many typical reasons why a car would not start. They may feel a little embarrassed when realizing what the problem is, but do not feel that they were thinking illogically: somehow the defect was "illogical".

Such a driver's thinking is really logical, even if logical thinking delays him in finding the simple defect this time. He understands the structure of the car and is looking for the cause of the defect in accordance with the logic of things. This is the reason why he finds it with such difficulty. However, he does find it because, with several "logical" causes of troubles eliminated, no other possibility remains for him. The way our driver finally reaches the cause of the trouble can justly be called logical, since it is based

11

on correct principles and necessarily leads to the solution. It leads to a solution that may be simple but by no means obvious. The expression "logical" is commonly used in this sense, too, when it means the methods of correct thinking, i.e. the ability to find the real connections between things and to recognize their consequences. We are going to call this type of interpretation *everyday logic*.

Already the ancient Greeks recognized that in the course of correct thinking certain elements are used regularly and repeatedly. The following is a classical example: if we know that every man is mortal and if we know that Socrates is a man then we may consider the statement "Socrates is mortal" true. In other words: *if* we accept the following two sentences to be true: "It follows from the fact of being a man that he is mortal" and "Socrates is a man", *then* we may conclude that "Socrates is mortal". Similar conclusions are drawn moment by moment. Generally, and independently of the particular content, it seems very logical (because of the logic of things, for the time being) to consider the following type of reasoning correct:

If we know that from A follows B, and A is true, then we accept the statement "B is true" without further examination of the facts.

This form of reasoning is called *"modus ponens"*. Even today we consider it correct and feel it convincing if someone builds his train of thoughts through a series of similar type of statements.

There are forms of reasoning we are unwilling to accept. See how the equation 4×7=32 was proved. An elderly lady hit all the five numbers drawn out of 90 in the state lottery, thus winning a large sum of money. Someone asked her how she had done it. "Well," she said, "the night before I dreamed of flying sheep whose backs were spotted, like those of ladybirds. The sheep had four legs and seven spots on their backs each. So I marked 4 and 7 on the lottery ticket. Together they can be read as 47, so I also marked this number. Their sum is 11 — it was my fourth number — and if you multiply them you get 32, so I marked it as my fifth number."

"But 4×7 is only 28, not 32!" objected the questioner. "But of course it's 32, haven't I won with it?" the old lady retorted.

It would be a very difficult task to convince our lady that her reasoning was not correct, as her argument is quite powerful. The questioner will probably never hit all the five numbers, however good he may be in arithmetic. Why are we so reluctant then to accept her reasoning that 4×7=32?

Formal logic

The least convincing argument against the lady's train of thoughts is that back in school we had learnt that $4 \times 7 = 28$, and not 32. There is no book without misprints. Why could it not be possible that there was a misprint just there in our arithmetic book? The probability of this event is not less than that of hitting 5 numbers out of 90, which is the lady's argument. All tables of multiplication in the world could have a misprint there.

After all, our problem is not with 4×7 being 32 or not, but with the way of reasoning. The result of 4×7 can be deduced in theory by a given system of rules: it is either 32, or not. But this system of rules contains no dreams or flying spotted sheep. Thus, finally our objection is primarily not against the content, but against the form. We do not accept this form of reasoning, regardless of the accuracy of the result. We would not accept this demonstration if it were for $4 + 7 = 11$, although the lady was correct about the result of this addition.

The forms of arguments and reasoning that can or cannot be accepted in general meant a fundamental problem for the ancient Greek philosophers. In the books of his "Organon", Aristotle defines the forms of conclusions that can be considered correct in his opinion. It is known from experience that philosophical disputes (especially those that discuss the general questions of existence rather than the narrow problems of philosophical systems) tend to result in disputes on the correct ways of argumentation. The Greeks tried to overcome this difficulty by limiting the forms of reasoning that could be used in disputes. The forms of reasoning accepted as correct were called *syllogisms*. It was proper for decent philosophers to bring up arguments and conclusions in such forms only.

Naturally, further and necessarily correct forms of reasoning can also be deduced from the individual syllogisms. The organization of these forms developed into a separate branch of science, giving rise to the *systems of formal logic*. The plural form is justified, for various systems can be developed, depending on the applied initial basic syllogisms. Traditional logic deals only with true or false statements. Separate branches of logic deal with forms of reasoning that wish to handle ideas like necessity, possibility, probability, temporal order, etc. too.

We have every right to expect that a logical system results in no contradiction and that the truths of the world can be expressed by its aid. These two expectations are, on the one hand, undoubtedly logical (in the sense of the logic of things, i.e. from the aspect of why a complex formal system should be built, had this not been our aim). On the other hand, however, the aim is very ambitious, for what could our reason possibly be in supposing that the complex and perplexed things of the world can be expressed with the aid of such simple building blocks? The weight of the problem can be demonstrated by the fact that even the most complex formal logical systems are set out from no more than 5–20 initial syllogisms. They do so not because they do not wish to over-complicate things, but because no matter how much they search, they cannot find more forms of reasoning they could accept with a clean conscience as generally valid and which do not result from the previous ones.

The totality of thinking, thus, correct thinking too, can certainly be expressed with the aid of formal logic. Syllogisms can be produced easily by simple basic elements, either by natural elements like reflex arcs, or by easily producible artificial elements like circuit elements. What else could our brain consist of than neurons transmitting physical or chemical impulses? If this is true, then it must be possible to describe the activity of the brain with the aid of syllogisms. This train of thought seems to be in contradiction with the fact that we cannot be certain whether our brains can actually perform really correct thinking or not. Undoubtedly, we are able to handle a lot of situations well, or even without error, but it is also known that we can become confused very easily in new, previously unknown situations. As a first step, however, we may be contented if we can describe the forms of correct thinking achievable by (or somewhat superior to) the human brain with the aid of formal logic. This alone would already be a great accomplishment; its possibility is guaranteed by the previous train of thought.

Yet there are various arguments against the possibility that the totality of our thinking can be expressed with the aid of formal logic. Mystic counter-arguments will be discussed in Chapter 16; a few rational counter-arguments are indicated here. The development of artificial intelligence seems to have encountered great difficulties, the reason of which could be not only practical, but also theoretical. Another system of counter-arguments can be built upon the results of psychology. To make a long story short: various psychological experiments and theoretical constructions indicate that our thinking is quite reluctant to put its self-developed, excellent means of formal logic into practice.

A third sytem of counter-arguments was put forward by formal logic itself: as soon as we not only apply it to the esoteric world of formal

14

conclusions, but also take into consideration what the conclusions are about (although we still remain behind the shield of mathematics), we meet sudden restrictions again. It turns out that the system of formal logic is even theoretically unable to fulfil our great hopes. This negative result seems to do nothing less than express the doubt — previously brushed aside so easily — as to whether or not our brain can actually carry out really correct thinking. However, it does say more, because — as we shall see later — these seemingly purely negative mathematical theorems of impossibility are in close connection not only with the structure of our thinking, but perhaps also with the deeper rules of nature. This will be expressed in more detail in Chapter 18.

A lot of reasons have been listed for and against whether or not formal logic (or more generally, artificial intelligence) is possibly able to realize intellect that reaches the level of human thinking. I must say in advance that I cannot decide whether one of the systems of arguments is correct or not. I hope it will become clear by the end of the book that even each reasoning may be correct within its own system, while independently of this, artificial intelligence either can or cannot be realized.

An unexpectedly unpleasant simple problem

There are four cards lying in front of us. We know that there is a letter on one side of each card, and a number on the other. On the visible sides of the four cards we can see the following signs:

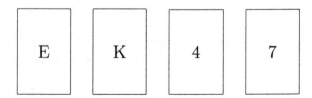

The task is to decide whether or not the following statement is true of these cards: If the letter is a vowel on one side of the card, the other side has an even number on it. Evidently, one has to turn and see the other side of certain cards, but it is also a task to turn as few cards as possible.

Which cards would you, dear reader, turn and check for the correctness of this statement? It is worth pondering a while, for the problem proves to be unexpectedly catchy. It might as well have been included in Chapter Zero, but it is not very conspicuous for a puzzle, although it is tremendously informative in a psychological experiment.

P.C. Wason and P.N. Johnson-Laird received the following results in the experiment with psychology students at Sussex University (i.e. with intelligent people who were not very familiar with formal logic). 46% of the students turned cards E and 4, 33% turned only E. Only 4% turned cards E and 7, and nothing else, which is the correct answer. The remaining 17% gave other incorrect answers.

It is quite easy to see that turning the card E cannot be avoided, for we cannot see whether the number on the back side is even or not. If it is odd, it will contradict our statement. It is evident that card K should not be turned, for it is quite indifferent for the veracity of our statement what the other side shows. Now comes the difficult part. What are the possibilities if we turn card 4? If there is a consonant on the back, again it will be indifferent for us. If there is a vowel, it will back up our statement. Whatever we find on the back cannot contradict our statement, thus, it is useless to turn it. Card 7, however, must be turned, for a vowel will contradict our statement, while a consonant will not.

This train of thought does not seem very difficult. The great problem is why such a great percentage of intelligent people do badly on it. Even of students of programming mathematics, quite at home in formal logic, only 50% arrived at the correct solution within the first one or two minutes.

Syllogisms then do not seem to be uniformly obvious for us. There is practically no problem with *modus ponens*: almost everyone turned card E. There is another syllogism called *modus tollens*. It says that if we know that A causes B, and that B is false, then it can be concluded that A is false. This is the "if there is no fuel in the car, it will not start — therefore if the car starts, there is fuel in it" type of reasoning. This rule should have been applied upon the examination of the card showing a numeral. This seems to have caused difficulties.

It was also studied how generally valid we feel certain forms of reasoning to be. Table 1 shows the result of such a study.

Table 1.

Form of reasoning	Percentage of people saying when the statement is valid		
	always	sometimes	never
$A \Longrightarrow B$, A is true therefore: B is also true	100	0	0
$A \Longrightarrow B$, A is false, therefore: B is true	5	79	16
$A \Longrightarrow B$, B is false, therefore: A is also false	57	39	4

Many other forms were studied, but it can be seen even from this table that *modus ponens* really seems to be free of problems for us. *Modus tollens*, however, was considered generally true by barely more than half of the experimental subjects. The middle formula, which is obviously not suitable for a syllogism, also caused problems to a surprising lot of people. Particularly many people consider the following two candidates for syllogism correct:

Some of the things with "A" characteristics are also of "B" characteristics,

some of the things with "B" characteristics are also of "C" characteristics,

therefore, some of the things with "A" characteristics are also of "C" characteristics.

And the other one, in a shorter form:

No A is B,

no B is C,

therefore, no A is C.

It is worthwhile to think it over why these two forms of reasoning cannot be accepted as generally true. (An effectively simple counter-argument for the second example is received if A=C is imagined.) Still, somehow we feel that these conclusions are very obvious and friendly. It cannot be immediately seen that they are false. Are we really so illogical and stupid?

Everyday logic

There are four cheques lying in front of us, with the following visible sides:

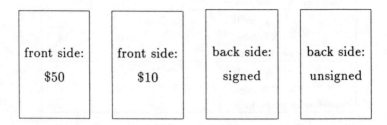

| front side: $50 | front side: $10 | back side: signed | back side: unsigned |

We know that one side of a cheque shows the value, while the place of the signature is on the back. Cheques under $30 are valid without a signature, those over this value are valid only with a signature. Which ones should be turned to see the validity of the cheques?

Most people soon realize that they have to turn the $50 cheque and the unsigned one, and it is useless to turn the other two, because they are valid as they are. We are not surprised at how easy it is to solve this problem, for we feel that the solution is evident.

But this problem is formally very similar to the previous one with the letters and numbers, which proved to be so unexpectedly difficult! It is not only very similar, but its structure is *exactly* the same: if sums above $30 meant consonants and those under $30 were vowels, while the presence of the signature stood for an even number, and its absence for an odd number, then the two problems would turn into each other. In this case the two problems are called *logically isomorphous*. Once we accept *modus ponens* and *modus tollens* as correct syllogisms and solve one of the problems with their aid, then we have already solved the other problem as well.

Thus, two totally rational arguments can be set against each other: one says that the two problems are logically equally complex, the solution of neither of them is more difficult than that of the other, requiring no

18

deeper thinking on either of them. On the other hand, the experimental results show that the first problem is more difficult psychologically than the second, for most of the people solve the first one incorrectly, while they solve the second one correctly. Even those who solve both of them correctly finish the second task faster.

The investigator of logic is not required to notice this experimental result: it is outside the scope of his investigation. The form of reasoning can be correct, regardless of the fact that it may be difficult for outsiders to use it, or that it may be incorrect even if there are people who successfully convince each other with such arguments. The correctness, completeness, consistency and expressiveness of formal logical systems are not influenced by these facts of everyday life.

A psychologist, however, is more sensitive to these facts, as he aims at describing the mechanisms of human thinking as clearly as possible. It would be temptingly comfortable for him to receive a complete, clear and relatively simple tool for this purpose from the science of formal logic. It is a two thousand-year-old belief that our thinking is of a logically closed character, and that the basic rules of its mechanism can be described by the rules of logic, and all we have to do is find the system of logic suitable for this purpose. This belief is undermined by experimental results like the above, forcing the science of psychology either to limit the circle of validity of formal logic within its own sphere of use, or to look for other explanations.

The investigator of artificial intelligence is in an intermediate position. His working tool is the computer, which is based exactly on formal logic, thus it is not easy for him to sweep formal logic under the carpet by saying, "In my field, this is not the way things work." Naturally, a psychologist does not like to do it either, because it is difficult to figure out another mechanism, but at least he could do it in theory. The situation of artificial intelligence will be analyzed in more detail in Chapter 13. Now let us return to the studies of psychology.

What makes the second problem so much easier than the first one? We may sense that the key to the mystery might be somewhere around the fact that the second problem is not "in thin air", it is not independent of the real things of the world as the first one is, but concerns something we know quite well from daily experience. Certainly, this is not a clear, well circumscribed explanation yet; anyway, it is only a hypothesis for now, and not a fact. In order to discover the more exact structure of the phenomenon, the experimental conditions were further varied.

In one of the wittiest experiments a variation of the problem with the cheques was used. On one side an envelope was affixed with either a 40 or a 50 lira stamp, and on the other, it was either sealed or unsealed. The rule was that a 40 lira stamp was sufficient for an unsealed envelope, but a 50 lira stamp was needed for a sealed one. Indeed, some 30 years ago this rule really existed in Italy. In this experiment the performance of young people was almost as bad as in the vowel–consonant problem, while older people performed almost as well as in the problem with the cheques. In other tasks there were no significant differences between the performances of the two age-groups. The reason of this great difference could be that for the older people it was a real experience that the mail was more expensive for the sealed envelopes than for the unsealed ones, while for the younger generation it was only an abstract, meaningless possibility alien to life. Other experiments resulted in similar conclusions.

Of course, the situation is not as clear as that. The performance of those who received the problem with the cheques with the condition that cheques with a value over $30 are valid without a signature, and those under $30 are valid only with a signature was just as good as that of those who received the opposite instruction. They were not bothered by the silly condition of the task: it is evidently nonsense that cheques with high values are accepted without a signature, while those with low values are accepted strictly with a signature. Since the circumstances and material of the task were familiar to the participants, the little nonsense element which was just the opposite of what common sense would demand did not hinder the consistent performance of reasoning. This phenomenon may be in the root of the fact that children's silly, nonsense rhymes do not disturb their intellect (as adults sometimes believe in irritation); on the contrary, because of their curiosity and humor they even stimulate them.

Another strange phenomenon came to light in the course of these experiments. When a lot of similar problems were given to people, with abstract and concrete tasks mixed, most of the subjects consequently solved the concrete problems taken from life correctly, but did not solve the abstract ones well, i.e. no learning effect could be shown, at least in the course of 5–8 tasks.

As time passed, a kind of mass sport developed among psychologists working in this field: let us construct logically isomorphous problems whose solution times differ from each other as much as possible. The aim is to compose tasks that are solved by many people sooner or later, although some might solve them much slower than others. This game was not done for its own sake, although it is exciting just to engage in sports and break records. But the best results are achieved by those who have the best grasp of how man's reasoning mechanism can be triggered or hindered. The investigators succeeded in figuring out pairs of (I repeat, logically totally isomorphous) problems where the solution time of the more difficult task was 10–12 times as long as that of the easier one.

A general conclusion of these experiments was that *formal logic is disregarded in arriving at those conclusions that can be perfectly well described by means of formal logic.* We try to apply everyday logic in these cases, too. We can draw conclusions easily and well if we know the inner logic and structure of things, when we have a correct idea about the mechanism of the thing in question. But then, what is formal logic good for? Why has it proven to be so effective in the course of centuries? This will be discussed in Part II of the book, but I want to say just a sentence about it in advance. Rather than a primary tool of thinking, formal logic, as an efficient framework of communicating knowledge, is indispensable on a level between the two extreme stages of cognition.

Male and female logics

If we made our everyday conclusions on the basis of the rules of formal logic, the expression "female logic" would obviously have no meaning at all. Gender differences — similar to flying sheep — have no place within the frame of formal logic. If, however, our reasoning depends upon our previous experiences and knowledge, it will come as no surprise that characteristic differences can be found between the ways men and women think. Although they are far from showing sexual differences with the accuracy of sex tests, on the average they do come out quite definitely.

It is characteristic at the dawn of a great love that the man looks at his mate with sheep's eyes: "Gee! What a funny way you squeeze the toothpaste! In the middle of the tube...!" Then, about ten years later he is grumbling: "Damn it! You cannot squeeze even a tube of toothpaste well! Half of it remains in the tube!" From the woman's aspect, the same goes for the cigarette butts floating in the flower vase. But me no butts...

Men and women consider different things to be important in the world around them. Often, something that is an abstract possibility for a woman is a real, everyday experience for a man, and vice versa. Accordingly, it happens quite often that drawing a logical conclusion in a certain situation is almost self-evidently easy for one of them, but presents a nearly unsolvable problem to the other, just like the problems with the consonants and with the cheques. Thus, it is evident to talk about male and female logics without the slightest discriminative overtone. Of course, we must carefully stress that we are talking about the typical or average, allowing for enormous individual differences — just as there are female weight-lifters and male nursery school teachers.

All the same, the question remains open whether or not there are differences between the purely formal logical abilities of men and women. The answer to this question is that it can be measured so as to find such differences, and it can be measured so as not to find such differences. I do not want to say, however, that either of the measurements is the result of cheating or conscious distortion.

Let me start from a little further away. Intelligence tests show no differences between the two sexes. The main reason for this is that they are constructed that way — this is in accordance with the social and cultural expectation. The questions showing gender differences are either left out at the very beginning, or are carefully balanced so that the number of questions favoring men is the same as those favoring women. More refined studies do show differences, once in favor of men, then in favor of women. In general, women's verbal expression and vocabulary develop faster and remain better even in adulthood than men's. The visual–spatial orientation of men, however, is better than that of women. For instance, among the puzzles of Chapter Zero women do better in Puzzles 1 and 4, but men are favored by Puzzles 6 and 9.

It is difficult to answer the question of whether these differences can be traced back to biological or socio-cultural reasons — probably both play their parts. Definite differences can be shown between the sexes in the development of the two cerebral hemispheres and in their division of labor — this is probably biologically determined. It was also demonstrated that the verbal abilities of those boys *and* girls who mature sooner will be better than those of them who mature later. The development of visual abilities, however, is just the opposite. Girls' maturing sooner than boys' may also play a role in the differences in abilities.

It is also easy to find differences that can be traced back to socio–cultural reasons. Boys' games stand closer to the logic of physical things, or are even directly abstract, while the games of girls are more closely connected to the logic of human relationships, to society. This may also explain why boys are somewhat better at purely abstract logical or geometrical problems, while girls do better at textual mathematical problems. Which should be considered as a correct measure of formal logical abilities?

As we have seen, it can be demonstrated by correct measurement that there is no difference between the two sexes in formal logical abilities, and that there is a difference in favor of either of the sexes. But if our mechanisms of reasoning are not based on the fundamentals of formal logic anyway, then perhaps the question itself has no meaning. We may talk about mathematical ability (for this is already a kind of experience, even though in an abstract sphere), chess-playing ability, or persuasive ability, but the abstract formal logical ability may be only a secondary phenomenon, a so-called *epiphenomenon* beside the others.

Trance logic

Some particularly interesting phenomena regarding the mechanisms of reasoning can be observed in altered states of consciousness. Altered states of consciousness are situations where the system and organization of one's sensation, thinking and behavior differ considerably from those of the normal waking state. Dreams, (eastern) meditation, hypnosis, drugged states and sometimes love may serve as examples. This is not a very exact definition, but we do not need a more detailed analysis. It is hypnosis that can be studied best experimentally and within controlled conditions.

A great question is whether the hypnotized person really gets into some kind of an altered state of consciousness as a result of the hypnotist's effort, or merely conforms to the expectations of the hypnotist obediently, and plays the role given to him. The experiences of those who have sometime or another been in hypnosis unanimously support the first hypothesis. But, after all, we cannot tell if a person is lying. What if he only continues playing his role after hypnosis, saying what the hypnotist expects him to, i.e. if he is willy-nilly lying. How is it possible to set outwardly observable criteria that definitely show whether or not the person is in hypnosis (or at least in an altered state of consciousness)? Having been able to pose the question, we have an obvious solution: let us train people not to go into hypnosis, but to act as if they did, in order to deceive the hypnotist. Will the latter notice somehow that the hypnotic state is only simulated, or not?

It was not an easy task for the hypnotist to decide whether he was dealing with an innocent experimental subject or with a well-trained fake.

(Naturally, he did not know the truth.) Even quite rude tests failed: Having given the suggestion: "Your left arm feels no pain", the hypnotist held a lighted match to the subject's arm (so as to cause pain without injury), but the simulators never turned a hair. After hypnosis, when relating their experiences, there appeared an all important difference between the really hypnotized and the playacting subjects: the real ones really felt nothing, while the simulators reported having felt considerable pain. But this is still no proof, as it fails to prevent the possibility of a hypnotic subject's unwilling lie.

The most unerringly recognizable signs could be found in the reasoning mechanisms of the hypnotized persons, e.g. in Martin T. Orne's following experiment: there was an assistant sitting in a chair beside the subject at the beginning of the hypnotic session. When the subject was already in hypnosis, the assistant silently got up and sneaked behind the subject. The hypnotist gave the suggestion to the subject that the assistant was still sitting in the chair. The subject was to open his eyes and have a look. Up to this point there was no difference between the real and fake subjects' behavior: "Okay, he is there, I can see him." Then the hypnotist asked the subject to turn around and tell whom he could see. This was the moment when the real and the fake subjects' behaviors were astonishingly (and, what is most important, observably) different.

The simulators declared they could see nobody or they could see a stranger. The really hypnotized subjects calmly recognized the assistant behind them. Then they looked at the empty chair, then looked back and forth between the assistant and the chair. Finally they announced that they could see the same person in duplicate. Asked by the hypnotist how it was possible, the subjects said it must have been done by mirrors or by some magician's trick. They might have found it a little curious but were not confused at all. They felt at ease, were under hypnosis, and undisturbed by trifles like that.

We cannot say that the really hypnotized subjects behaved illogically. As soon as the hypnotist asked them, they gave some kind of a totally logical and believable reply. But the situation did not really engross their attention. If their spheres and their peaceful hypnosis were not especially disturbed, they found no fault with the obvious logical contradiction. Their current everyday logic was not disturbed by the contradiction, because the contradiction fell outside the sphere of their current logic. This phenomenon is called *trance logic.* The simulators applied another logic, i.e. normal everyday logic. They imagined that being in the situation and having lied about seeing the assistant in the chair they should not get into a contradiction. The experiment was successful: the investigators discovered something that can be observed well and surely cannot be explained by the possible unwilling role-playing of the hypnotized subjects.

There was no way to teach simulators how trance logic works. Naturally, they could be trained in concrete situations, but as soon as the situation changed the simulators got caught because of their erroneous trance logic.

In another experiment there were two chairs on each side of the hypnotized subject at the beginning of the hypnotic session. The assistant sat on the right side, while the chair on the left side was empty. During hypnosis the assistant silently changed his seat and sat in the left chair. The hypnotist suggested that the assistant still sat on the right side and that the left chair was empty. Until this point the real and the simulating subjects agreed: they hallucinated the assistant to be in the right chair and saw nobody in the left chair as a result of negative hallucination. Then the hypnotist asked the subject to sit in the left chair (which the subject thought to be empty). At this moment the simulators were bewildered for a moment, then they sat in the assistant's lap. The really hypnotized persons reacted in either of two ways. Those who had no objection against sitting in the assistant's lap (i.e. if they did not consider the assistant sexually repulsive, or if they did not care whether the assistant was of the same or of the opposite sex) sat there without thinking, and knew nothing of not sitting on an empty chair. Those who had no liking for sitting in the assistant's lap slowly stood up, turned around and sat down on the empty chair which was now to the subject's left. If the hypnotist asked what they had done, the reply was something like they had thought the hypnotist had meant the chair left to himself.

Again we cannot say that the hypnotized subjects acted illogically. Trance logic worked consistently, although far differently from normal everyday logic. Had formal logic worked automatically, it would have indicated the contradiction immediately, for the results showed that the really hypnotized subjects somehow also knew all along that in reality somebody was sitting in the chair to their left. This triviality did not bother trance logic, or if it did, the hypnotized person immediately found a way out.

2. Common sense

In the 1970s farming regulations were changed too often and too roughly in Hungary. Accordingly, even those products showed tremendous fluctuations that were not exposed to the rigors of weather. The farmers reacted with astonishing accuracy to what and how much was profitable for them to produce on the basis of the momentary regulations. People not very educated in formal thinking were able not only to make the inconsistent revisions of the regulations tolerable in a few years, but also to avoid jeopardizing seriously the future food supply. For example, according to the statistical yearbooks, the pig population was rapidly decreasing in the years when the regulations made pig-breeding non-profitable for most of the breeders. Under similar circumstances the decrease of the cattle population was much slower, although it was just as threatening. The reason is simple: the pig population can be increased quickly, while the cattle population is difficult to grow once it has decreased considerably.

The farmers' so rational behavior was not due to exact rentability calculations. Experience had taught them what the consequences of their behavior and those of the regulations would be. Everyone undertaking an enterprise will soon develop a real gain–loss evaluation, otherwise he will leave the field. With lack of sufficient information there is often no possibility for exact, formal calculations at all. In these cases a sober common sense based on experience becomes significant: does the present situation resemble those which turned out to be successful, or is it similar to those that were unprofitable?

Every concrete situation is different from the previous ones. The logic of things can be applied to yet unseen cases, so that known examples resembling the present situation in some respects are looked for: then we mentally enact what would happen in those situations under the present conditions. The chosen analogous situations are used as if they were the *models* of the present situation. We assume that, in their basic characteristics, structure and important consequences, they agree with the current problem to be solved. A model is a model because we know its structure.

We know it either because we have had a lot of experience with it, or because at the very beginning we determine it to have a simple and clear-cut structure.

Sometimes a model is really more complex than what it is modeling, but we know much better how the model works. An experienced mystery book reader tells in ten minutes who the murderer is in a poor Friday night television film, because he knows the real classics of the genre and will certainly be reminded of one of the classical problems by the current simple setup. Most of the time, however, the model is deliberately and consciously made more simple than the real situation. In order to decide if an egg is rotten or not, one does not have to be able to lay an egg. A few simple signs are enough to begin to suspect that something is wrong. In lucky cases it is not necessary even to crack the egg. The strength of common sense lies in the art of choosing the correct analogy.

The more one has seen, the more analogies one has and the more models are available for choosing the most suitable one from. The method of choosing is one of the most living and still unsolved problems of both psychology and artificial intelligence. The question can also be put this way: how are we making associations? Naturally, in many cases simple formal features and outstanding stereotyped similarities are sufficient.

A conversational program

One of the earliest and most spectacular successes of artificial intelligence was Joseph Weizenbaum's program called ELIZA in 1966. The program contained two components: with the aid of one (the learning component) of them, the phrases to be used during the conversation could be taught to the program, while the other component carried out the conversation itself. The program was named after Eliza in G.B. Shaw's *Pygmalion*, for its style is somewhat rude, but if anyone is willing to devote a lot of time to the learning component, ELIZA's behavior can be made more civilized.

The learning component of ELIZA contains a collection of patterns and a collection of answers corresponding to the patterns. The answering component analyzes the text written by the conversational partner, and tries to fit it to one of the elements of the collection of patterns. When the program has finished that, it replies to the partner with one of the answers belonging to the given pattern.

The pattern collection contains standard sentences, certain elements of which are fixed, while others can be replaced by anything. The following could be an example of such a pattern:

(*1st anything* you *2nd anything* me *3rd anything.*)

Thus, the sentence "I feel you are bored with me lately" fits the above pattern just as much as the sentence "I think you have been angry with me recently."

In the collection of replies there are rules to create, out of the sentence fitting the given pattern, such a sentence that — at least in theory — answers the given sentence. For example, the following reply-rules could be made for the previous pattern:

(Why do you think that you *1st anything* I *2nd anything* *3rd anything*).

Or, according to another possible rule, the program does not react at all to the part standing in the place of the *1st anything*:

(Let us suppose that I *2nd anything* you *3rd anything*. Would that make a difference?)

Naturally, the conjugation of words must be taken into consideration. In English it is very simple. In my native Hungarian it would probably cause some difficulties. As far as I know no Hungarian version of ELIZA has been made yet, but there exist German, French and Spanish ELIZA programs. This difficulty has been overcome in these languages. It is a very unpleasant obstacle in making the Hungarian version that the word order in Hungarian is very free. Linguists say that it is the most difficult thing to find the correct word order in a language whose word order is free. Replies like the following ones may be sufficient to keep a conversation going:

— Why do you think that you feel I am bored with you lately?

— Let us suppose that I am angry with you. Would that make a difference?

There are some further possibilities of making rules in ELIZA. Since ELIZA stores the whole conversation in its memory, a rule can be made that becomes active only if a word that has already occurred in the course of the conversation can be found at a given place. This is about the essence of the program. But the most important rule has not been mentioned yet: if the partner's sentence does not fit any of the patterns, i.e. if ELIZA finds no cue from which it could build up its reply, it will give some ready answer from a set of pre-stored answers. In cases like this it may say: "Please, continue." or "This is very interesting." or simply "I see." This is ELIZA's cutest feature: when it understands nothing of what is said to "her", it is likely to say "I see." Experience shows, however, that this encourages the partner very much: this is when he really gets warmed up.

When researchers started to play with ELIZA, they soon noticed that the conversation of the program definitely had some kind of a style. Sometimes it is exasperatingly meaningless (but why would it have any meaning?), yet it does have a style. It mostly resembles the style of psychotherapists who — because of the peculiarities of their situation — deliberately want to avoid disturbing the patients with their own thoughts. This is especially true of certain schools of psychotherapy (particularly of the followers of Carl Rogers). Having recognized this, the programmers altered the replies of ELIZA so as to resemble the usually stereotyped answers of psychotherapists as much as possible. Thus, a new program called DOCTOR was written.

DOCTOR worked astonishingly well. It fooled even real psychiatrists: shown different parts of conversations, they could not decide which ones were from real conversations and which ones from the program. It was raised seriously that (after some slight further developments in the program) the time has come to change the expensive sessions with the psychotherapists to computer services that are available to everyone. The computer often produced real direct hits like this:

DOCTOR: What's your problem?
Patient: My mother drinks too much.
DOCTOR: Who else drinks too much in the family?

This is a very intelligent question. For if a mother drinks too much, she is not able to attend to her family duties satisfactorily, which may lead to further tension. But it is also possible that it is family tensions that lead to the mother's drinking. Thus, it is worth leading the conversation in this direction. Naturally, DOCTOR had no idea of this. It had no idea even that "drinks" does not only mean that someone swallows liquid. You could say that it is sufficient that the programmer knew it, but why then is the program called intelligent? By the way, the program did not even react to the word "drinks": DOCTOR's reply was based on the recognition of the words "mother" and "too much". The program would have used the same pattern if someone had complained that his brother was playing too much snooker.

The DOCTOR program may prove surprisingly intelligent just because people like to open their hearts to a really neutral but attentive listener. The author of DOCTOR was astonished when once his secretary began to talk to the program and after a few sentences she asked him to leave the room. Incidentally, Weizenbaum did not intend to write a program that was the product of artificial intelligence: he designed it only as a jolly good game to demonstrate what the computer networks developed in those times could do: even thirty people could have simultaneous conversations with the machine. He was fully aware of the fact that the machine understood nothing of what was happening around it, and he was most astonished when he saw to what extent people could project into this simple program.

Even today Weizenbaum is one of the toughest and most sceptical critics of artificial intelligence. In his opinion ELIZA behaves as a man who has sensitive ears and minimal language skills, wanting to keep the conversation going at any price. Sometimes he recognizes a word or two but has no idea why the partner has uttered it, and urgently reacts to it by saying something neutral. Such a conversation can be kept going for a considerable period of time to the full satisfaction of the partner — especially if the partner wants nothing more than to be listened to and have someone to talk to.

A friendly conversation could be important for us, too: we can get accommodation in a foreign country, or we can study the gestures and mimic of our partner, etc. It is an exciting game, like the conversation of Kornél Esti with the Bulgarian conductor in the Hungarian poet Kosztolányi's novel. But there is always something at stake in human affairs. Unwittingly, Kornél Esti first outraged the Bulgarian conductor, then conciliated him, while he deeply felt and understood the affair, although at a level that was quite different from where the conductor's story took place. Kornél Esti would certainly have had a very bad feeling if he could not have conciliated the Bulgarian conductor. There is no such understanding and feeling in ELIZA. It cannot be found in any of the present artificial intelligence programs either. Not only is this level unattainable, but even direct understanding, which is much simpler, leaves much to be desired, even if the program (or rather its author) aims at mastering only a very narrow field.

Artificial paranoia

Kenneth Colby made another twist in his program called PARRY. He attempted to simulate the insane mind rather than normal intelligence, aiming at creating artificial paranoia. He hoped on the one hand to understand real paranoia better this way, and thought we could also learn more about intact intelligence on the other hand. (Paranoia is a mental disorder where the patient loses contact with reality in some areas of life, sets up a false reference system, but within this system and in other areas of life he behaves completely logically. He lives in a system of delusions, referring things to himself that do not refer to him.)

Artificial paranoia is a promising experimental field to make a program understand the context of a narrow but everyday domain. Similarly to ELIZA, PARRY reacts normally — from its point of view — to everything that is not related to its own system of delusions, although sometimes it is a little insolent. However, as soon as it perceives the faintest indication of its delusion it will refer the received text to this delusion and will answer accordingly (in a hurt, nervous or aggressive way).

PARRY could deceive even practicing psychiatrists. In a carefully arranged and controlled study, psychiatrists could correctly guess exactly 50% of the times whether they were talking to a computer or to a real patient. Can we draw the conclusion from the above results that an experienced observer cannot tell the difference between PARRY's paranoid reactions and those of a real paranoid patient? And can the mechanisms of paranoia be studied efficiently with the help of PARRY? And can we consider the problem of at least artificially insane minds to be solved?

DOCTOR treating PARRY

If we already have an artificial psychiatrist program and an artificial paranoia program, why not bring the two together. This time PARRY is an enthusiastic punter at horse races, and his delusion is that a Mafia at the horse-races is after him and wants to rob him (to tell the truth, the nature of his delusion makes no difference in this case, as you will see). Let us see a part from the middle of the conversation. If you are not interested in my comments, simply skip the remarks in the brackets.
DOCTOR: Would you like to discuss your nerves?
PARRY: I guess so.
DOCTOR: What does that suggest to you?
    (I think DOCTOR reacted to the cue "guess", misunderstanding, of
    course, the whole situation.)
PARRY: What are you getting at?
DOCTOR: What answer would please you most?
PARRY: It is not a matter of like or dislike.

DOCTOR: What else would you like to discuss?
(Pass. It is a standard reply, for DOCTOR has nothing to hang on to.)
PARRY: I am getting tired of answering the same questions over and over.
(PARRY's memory is also working!)
DOCTOR: What resemblance do you see?
(Reaction to the word "same")
PARRY: Why do you need to know that?
DOCTOR: What do you think?
PARRY: I don't understand your motives.
DOCTOR: Why don't you understand my motives?
PARRY: Shouldn't I be?
DOCTOR: Why do you say that just now?
(Finally a direct hit. The word "should" was beneficial.)
PARRY: That's just the way it is.
DOCTOR: Suppose that's just the way it were not.
PARRY: So?
DOCTOR: I am not sure I understand you fully.
(This is neither a confession, nor a bluff. He gives this standard reply because lately he has often been unable to hang on to anything.)
PARRY: You harp on the same question too much.
(They are birds of a feather: he has not understood the other for a long time, either. But this is *his* standard reply.)
DOCTOR: What does that similarity suggest to you?
(The word "same" is a sure starting point.)
PARRY: I don't get you.
DOCTOR: Do you wish that you did get I?
PARRY: It is about time you showed some interest in my feelings.
DOCTOR: Oh! I showed some interest in your feelings?

Let us leave DOCTOR and PARRY to themselves at this little mishap. Are *they* the two programs that fooled trained psychiatrists, and to whom mature and intelligent secretaries opened their hearts? Yes, they are. Their human partners unwillingly brought their intellect to the conversation, thus giving meaning to the conversation itself.

In spite of ELIZA's and PARRY's similar styles there is an essential difference between their philosophies. As we have mentioned, ELIZA was not intended for a product of artificial intelligence, it was rather written as a demonstration, as a game. Its author may have justly counted on the fact that the player will bring meaning to it. This program was used for artificial intelligence purposes against his intention, only to be dropped disappointedly when it turned out that the program could not be improved considerably. ELIZA did not attempt to simulate intelligence; it rather attempted to dissimulate the lack of intelligence — with considerable success. PARRY was not written for dissimulation purposes. It was written to simulate insane minds sensibly — but the result was quite unsuccessful. An important lesson could be learnt, however: it showed with an overwhelming force how easily we can see meaning in something which has none. It seems to be an important characteristic of our intellect that we project it to anything we possibly can.

How much there is in a simple text

ELIZA's and PARRY's incomprehension barely touches the depths which our common sense cannot help comprehending even in the most simple texts. The problems arose primarily in the course of investigating the possibilities of computer translator programs. The following are two nightmares from the folklore of computer translation:

Original English text	*Russian translation, put back into English*
The spirit is strong but the flesh is weak.	The vodka is good but the meat is rotten.
Out of sight, out of mind.	Blind idiot.

The following joke is also a product of computer folklore: The chief of staff asks the superintelligent computer the following question: "Will the first man be sent to Mars by the USSR or the USA?" After a short pause the computer prints out the reply: "Yes." The chief gets into a fury and asks: "Yes, who?". After another short pause the computer prints out the reply: "Yes, sir."

Though jokes are not to be explained, it is worth pondering over why the computer's way of thinking does not notice that the *first* "Yes" reply is silly. Well, today it is almost certain that either the USSR or the USA will send the first man to Mars. *Yes*, who else would send man there? The answer is not silly, it is correct. How on earth should this poor computer know that this was not the question it was asked? If, for instance, a Canadian correspondent asked the President of the United States, "Will the first man be sent to Mars by the USA or Canada?", a simple "Yes" answer would only mean a promise that the USSR will be outrivaled in this matter. And if the superintelligent computer is asked: "Will the first man be sent to Mars by Sweden or Norway?", and the answer is "Yes", we will be surprised not at the silliness of the reply, but at the boldness of the prognosis.

It is evident in common sense how the word "or" is meant in the different situations, but how can we let the computer know it, too? Perhaps we could invent a few rules for this special case, and the computer would then give sensible answers — although this does not seem to be an easy task. For one thing, even the word "first" can quite easily be misunderstood. Furthermore, it also has to be known that the USA and Canada are to a certain extent related to each other, just as Sweden and Norway are, while the USA and the USSR could not be considered related at all. Several thousands, or maybe several millions of special rules should be made up if we did not want to receive nonsense answers like the above all the time. Or is there a more elegant, a more general solution? Is there a kind of formal logic that would help with its comprehensive generality?

Animal fables written by computers

J.R. Meehan attempted to write a program that could write animal fables with snappy endings in Aesop's style. He included dozens of rules of reasoning that are taken into consideration by common sense even if they are not stated openly. For example, one of the rules was that if participant A moves object B to place C then we can conclude not only that object B is at place C, but also that participant A is at place C, too. He also provided the different animals with their usual characteristics. He also included some general principles like if someone is in the river he will want to get out, otherwise he will sink. (No fish was present in his fables.) Those who have legs can crawl to the riverside. Those who have wings can fly away. Those who have friends can ask for help. The instance "X fell" was represented as "gravity moved X", because this fit the increasingly complex system best. Besides, it is logical.

At this moment the author of the program had an unpleasant surprise. The computer created the following story without blushing:

"Henry Ant was thirsty. He walked over the river bank, where his good friend Bill Bird was sitting. Henry slipped and fell in the river. Gravity drowned."

Well, according to the rules, Henry Ant did have a friend there, so he was saved. But since it was gravity that moved Henry into the river, according to the rules of syllogism, gravity was there, too. But gravity has no legs, no wings and no friends. Therefore, gravity had to sink.

This concrete blunder could be eliminated by a few additional complex rules, but the number of similar — although not so striking — mistakes would not decrease. It is here where the strength of laymen's common sense — as it treats these simple, everyday situations with such obvious ease — can be seen well.

3. Puzzles and science

The point of puzzles is that they have solutions. Those who sit down to solve riddles may rest assured that, if they are witty and clever enough, they can reach their goal. Someone has made up that puzzle, therefore he must know the solution. But why strain ourselves and not ask him what the solution is? The author does not even have to be hunted up, the solution can usually be found a few pages later. In gross social measures huge wasted efforts are made. There is a riddle published in a newspaper with — let us say — half a million copies. Suppose that only every tenth reader solves it, each spending half an hour on it. This is 25,000 hours of work, just to solve one riddle. This is more than one full year's working hours of ten people. And we have not multiplied this by the amount of crossword puzzles yet.

If this huge wasted effort had no concrete use in the preservation of the human race, a new race that solves no puzzles would have developed long ago, and with the utilization of the energy saved this way it would have swept away *Homo sapiens* who wastes his energy on re-discovering with much work solutions that can be found easily. What could be the use of puzzle solving for the survival of mankind? This question itself looks like a puzzle. It must have a solution, for we have just shown that, if this puzzle had no solution, we would be quite different now. Still, magazines contain different types of puzzles — our question belongs rather to the sphere of scientific essays.

The frames of puzzles

All the same, let us suppose that a quiz question in a puzzle magazine reads like this: What is the significance of puzzle solving in the survival of mankind? We would perhaps muse over the question and interesting thoughts would come to our minds. But we would certainly turn to the key of the puzzles with scepticism. We would be sure to find a solution different from our thoughts. A question like this requires no direct answer; it urges us to dispute the matter. But puzzles bear no dispute. Puzzles are based upon a kind of silent agreement that definite and clear-cut answers can be given to each of the puzzles. The question itself may be as obscure and mysterious as it wishes to be, but with knowledge of the solution it must become evident that of all things in the world this and only this answer fits the question and its surroundings.

The questions of Puzzle 1 in Chapter Zero are good examples to this. We can see in the television programme that everyone shakes hands with the President, but something is still missing. A solution like this is not real. Furthermore, it is more than 5 letters. Maybe the trick is that it is not human. There are some who soon find the right answer, but some will find it only when they already know a few letters. But as soon as the solution: LATCH flashes in, it will immediately become unambiguous that this is the only solution. Sees through the fog back and forth — 5 letters. What could this mysterious "back and forth" mean? Experienced puzzle solvers will soon suspect that it may be a word that reads the same backward and forward. But if inexperienced puzzles solvers know the solution (RADAR) they will also see clearly what the mysterious "back and forth" meant. It can be numerous and innumerable. If we know the answer: MANY, the strange question will become clear immediately.

The fourth puzzle is more elaborate, frankly, it is not very good for a crossword puzzle definition. Not because it is not a good riddle (it would be an excellent question in a quiz), but because it is not clearly evident from the solution (JONATHAN SWIFT) why this is the only correct one. Most of his elaborate poetry is obscure today, he is remembered only for *Gulliver's Travels*. The cue is the adjective reminding one of the name. Such an explanation is nigh impossible in the genre of crosswords, though it is perfectly all right in a quiz; also while solvers must take some minor thought-steps to understand the link in that one as well, it is really not too difficult. *Nota bene*, it would be for today's artificial intelligence software.

Well-designed puzzles

The frame of puzzles is common sense, i.e. the system of knowledge and reasoning of our everyday culture. A Soviet psychologist, Rubinstein, says, "The so-called riddles are not some kind of curios where the general laws of thinking do not apply. On the contrary, they are in a special, but inseparable relationship with the general rules of thinking. As a matter of fact, the designers of riddles and puzzles are empirical specialists of these laws." Well-designed puzzles make our minds take natural, but rarely used, paths of thinking. They prompt us to make unusual, but sensible associations; they require the drawing of logical but rarely occurring conclusions. They mobilize our knowledge in an unusual structure, preparing the ground for accepting new knowledge, too.

Puzzle designers strive to do just that. But in Chapter 1 the car whose fuel gauge stuck and whose failure to start had, despite all appearances, been caused by the simplest of reasons, i.e. the lack of fuel, also produced a good puzzle. The environment and the objects around us often produce problems that could be considered as well-designed puzzles. To be more precise: only some of the problems have puzzle characters, otherwise we would think of the solution immediately and they would not prove to be good puzzles. But even if only one thousandth of the problems proved to be good puzzles we would already find the experience gained through puzzle solving useful.

The case with the repairer of clocks is well-known: he repaired an expensive Swiss watch by a slight hit with a small hammer, then charged $100 for it. When the customer found the price too high the specialist gave an account of the fee: he asked $1 for the hit, and $99 for knowing where to hit. If this repairer was the fifth who attempted to repair the watch, as the first four had failed, then our specialist evidently solved a difficult puzzle; he will be given work to do in the future as well. If any repairer knows this trick of the hit with the hammer, then our specialist will soon find no work if he continues to charge so high.

Our material and social environments present a lot of puzzles, but the brain-teasers originally designed to be puzzles have a different style. Puzzles have a characteristic jargon. An example of this is the mysterious expression "back and forth" in the puzzle with the radar. Those who know this jargon are more successful with the riddles in magazines. The style of the language, however, does not belong to the essence of puzzles. It looks strange only because puzzles willfully avoid the most frequent stereotypes of thinking, thus, the otherwise less frequently used paths become more frequent in the world of puzzles.

If puzzles are related to everyday logic, why are puzzles that purposely try our abilities in formal logic so frequent? Because the use of syllogisms has been an accepted and legitimate way of reasoning and persuasion since the ancient Greeks. This is how formal logic is linked to everyday logic, this is why problems provoking formalized thinking are interesting for us. But these problems are not detached from daily reality to the extremes, either. They do not state conditions like: "if A is true then the negation of B and C are also true", but say: "The Norwegian has a red shirt and does not keep giraffes." These riddles create a miniature world and we live in that world while we solve the problem. Any other type of puzzles from jigsaw puzzles to crossword puzzles do the same.

A well-designed puzzle does not disturb this miniature world with superfluous participants. The natural participants of the puzzle divert our thinking by behaving in an unusual way in the correct solution. In a well-designed chess problem there are no surplus figures; it mars the beauty of a chess problem considerably if the only role of a figure is to prevent a secondary solution. The aesthetic conditions of other puzzles are not always so strict, but it always mars the beauty of the puzzles if the only role of something is to make it more difficult to solve.

When we are solving a puzzle the significance of all the partial data is not clear at the outset. This is why puzzle solvers are so glad to find what the role of an additional datum is, e.g. in a chess problem when the player suddenly realizes that a hitherto seemingly unnecessary knight does have a meaningful function, or in reading a mystery it suddenly becomes significant why the heroine needed two parlormaids. We can justly feel the mobilization of each new datum as a step toward the solution; in high probability it is really so.

The frames of science

It was mentioned at the beginning of this chapter that the question of what the use of puzzle solving means for the survival of mankind is not suitable for a puzzle. We can already see that it is not suitable because the question does not fit the frames of common everyday sense; it is meaningful almost only within the framework of science. But why should science be interested in questions like this? Half the answer is that we can know right at the beginning that there exists an answer to it. As we have stated previously, our train of thought is based on scientific evidence, i.e. on the Darwinian theory of evolution. For the other half of the answer we first have to take a look at what science is dealing with.

As Thomas Kuhn writes in his book *The Structure of Scientific Revolutions*: "The scientific enterprise as a whole does from time to time prove useful, open up new territory, display order, and test long-accepted belief. Nevertheless, *the individual* engaged on a normal research problem *is almost never doing any one of these things.* Once engaged, his motivation is of a rather different sort. What then challenges him is the conviction that, if only he is skillful enough, he will succeed in solving a puzzle that no one before has solved or solved so well. Many of the greatest scientific minds have devoted all of their professional attention to demanding puzzles of this sort. On most occasions any particular specialization offers nothing else to do, a fact that makes it no less fascinating to the proper sort of addict."

Natural science is primarily nothing but solving puzzles, for it is willing to study a given problem only if a solution to it is known at the very beginning to exist. This is why science does not study the problems of the existence of God or the ethical problems of world peace. The existence of a solution, however, does not alone guarantee that the problem is suited for the purposes of riddles. As we have seen, puzzles operate within well-defined frames where it can be definitely determined whether a solution is correct or not. These frames appeal to common sense in the cases of puzzles and riddles. Scientific problems also have their proper frameworks within which it can be decided whether or not a given scientific result can be accepted. Just as the frame of puzzles is common sense, the frame of science is the system of rules arising from the generally accepted *Weltanschauung* of the scholars concerned.

It seems to be nonsense to talk about the generally accepted *Weltanschauung* of the scholars concerned, for there are as many world concepts as people. There are religious, atheistic and indifferent persons among scientists as well. This is a private matter of each scientist. Regarding the narrow professional problems of the given branch of science, only those are accepted as of the same profession (*therefore* only those are accepted as scientists), who share the current world concept of the given branch of science. Only those who accept the common system of rules have the right to exist in the field. The situation is similar to that of crossword puzzle solvers who also organize competitions, but they would indignantly reject the participant who filled the frame with A's faster than anyone else and demanded to be announced as the winner for producing a full frame with no squares left empty.

The generally accepted system of rules is called the *paradigm* of the given scientific field. The order of the facts and knowledge are coordinated by paradigms; they also offer guidance to further possible directions of research. Pieces of knowledge and the direction of an investigation turn into science when a paradigm generally accepted by the participants develops around it, thus the whole direction of research acquires meaning as a system.

The syllogisms of formal logic have been accepted uniformly by all branches of science as the only correct way to publish conclusions and results. If something happens to be inexpressible this way, it will fall outside the frames of science. It is the firm conviction of every scientist that no substantial message can be lost (at least in his field of interest) with the above restriction. Without this conviction his colleagues could not consider him a scientist.

By this approach, science naturally separates itself from a lot of things and becomes an intensive ensemble of small communities evaluating themselves. On the other hand, this approach has proved to be undoubtedly successful. Just think of the rapid development of science in the past 200–300 years, leading to a lot of technical achievements that have made life definitely more comfortable.

Basically, science behaves as the drunkard who is intensely looking for something under the street lamp. Asked by a policeman what he is looking for, he says he has lost his keys further up in the dark alley, and is looking for them. "But why are you looking for them here?" — asks the policeman. "Because only here are the lights on!"

Still, the behavior of science is not illogical. Several times we have seen in the history of science that when the brightly lit areas are sufficiently scrutinized, quite good conclusions can be drawn regarding the characteristics of the dark areas as well. As a matter of fact, these conclusions are often better than groping about in the dark.

Well-designed scientific questions

Let us return to the question of whether or not science should be interested in what the use of solving puzzles could be for the survival of mankind. The first half of the answer was yes, because the question surely has an answer. For the second half of the answer it has to be studied whether or not the question fits the paradigm of any branch of science.

The branch of science to be considered must deal with the theory of evolution; the question falls outside the paradigms of other branches at the very beginning. Thus, mainly biology must be concerned with it, though usually it seems to study quite different problems.

Our question resembles the problem of whether the time- and energy-wasting habit of courting before mating is useful for the survival of the species or not. Maybe it is useful because the male loses so much energy by courting that he will have no energy left to leave the female after mating, and together they will have better chances of bringing up their offspring. But once all the males have learnt that it is worth being faithful, those females who do not demand courting will suddenly gain enormous advantage over the others, because their mates will save a lot of energy, and so will themselves. Subsequently, unfaithful males will reappear sooner or later. Is it possible that an equilibrium will develop where a certain percentage of the females demand long courtship, while others do not, and a certain percentage of the males will be faithful, while others will not?

A biological paradigm that studies similar questions has evolved in the past twenty years. This new branch of science is called *sociobiology*. It is worth asking our question within this framework, although not exactly in its original form. For the question "What is the use of solving puzzles?" falls outside the paradigm of this branch, too. It also fails to answer what the use of courting is. Anyone who wishes may give an answer to it, but this branch is not interested in that; rather, it is interested in the quantitative chances of the occurrence of the concerned feature in cases of given model hypotheses. When setting up the model, we alluded to the role of courting, but that disappears in the quantitative study. The real use of courting may be quite different, as long as the consequences conform to the above described mechanism.

Let us re-phrase our question. Imagine that people who do not solve puzzles can solve a lot of relatively easy problems because they have time to do it. Those who usually solve puzzles have less time to solve real problems, but will be able to solve more difficult ones as well. Difficult problems occur with a certain probability in everyone's life to be solved, so as to avoid perishing. On the other hand, if someone has no time to solve all his easy problems, he will be at a disadvantage. In this form (with conditions made a little more complex) the question is already meaningful: will the puzzle solving species perish or will a certain percentage survive? Or will the non-puzzle-solvers perish? We are not going to detail the methods of studying the problem, but you can already feel that in this form we have already conformed to a system of rules: we are within the stronghold of the science of sociobiology. If we find a species of animals that has both puzzle solving individuals and non-puzzle-solvers (which is possible, as it will be seen in Chapter 5), then in theory we can test our hypothesis experimentally too, by increasing and decreasing the frequency of the occurrence of difficult situations.

Thus, we have arrived at a well-designed scientific question. To tell the truth, our question went through a kind of metamorphosis: a popular question was changed into a scientific one. If someone does not find the question interesting enough in this form, he may ponder further over what the use of puzzle solving could be, but in that form it remains outside the frame of science.

Well-designed scientific questions operate similarly to puzzles, but the role of the concepts and rules of common sense is taken by the current paradigm of science. However, there is a basic difference between a well-designed puzzle and a well-designed scientific question: the designers of puzzles set out from the solution, while a scientific question is already justified if the existence of a solution is guaranteed by the paradigm. Since in science we cannot ask the designer what the solution is, some promising partial results — e.g. steps that mobilize new data or fit new facts into the system — are also significant.

A well-designed scientific question is similar to a well-designed puzzle in that unnecessary figures and omissible conditions are not easily tolerated. *Occam's razor* is the name of the time-honored principle which states that of several scientific theories the one that is based on the least number of preconditions should be accepted.

Scientists and puzzle solvers

Puzzle solving is a good school for scientific work. The work of the student solving exercises in mathematics is a transition between problem solving and studying science. He is working within the paradigm of mathematics, but he can be sure that there is a solution he can achieve, otherwise he would not have been given the exercise. Still, there is a difference between the work of a student and that of a scholar of mathematics. Psychologically they are in a completely different situation. Only those will become successful scholars who can bear the tension that even though they are sure the problem can be solved, they are not at all sure if the problem is as complex as to necessarily go beyond their comprehension.

Solving puzzles teaches us to work within a given frame and — if necessary — to leave the system and arrive at a higher level of solution, but remaining still within the frame of the paradigm. Puzzle 2 of Chapter

Zero is a good example. Most people have seen a lot of similar tasks in their lives and were usually successful after more or fewer trials in arranging the matchsticks on the table in the desired order. Here it does not work: one has to leave the plane of the table. Once this idea occurs, the solution is ready: arrange three sticks to form an equilateral triangle on the table, then build a *pyramid* over it from the remaining three matchsticks. You already have the four equilateral triangles.

The following is only for mathematicians: let us complicate matters further. How can you make ten equilateral triangles from ten matchsticks? If you want to ponder over the problem, stop reading: I give you the answer. Maybe some will consider it revolting. For a fourth dimension is needed. We cannot show the fourth dimension, but it is easy to imagine it (at least for mathematicians ...). A four-dimensional tetrahedron has exactly ten edges and ten equilateral sides. The genre of this latter problem is no puzzle at all, but is no science yet, either.

4. Ways of thinking in different cultures

In Saltikov–Shtchedrin's satire the Russian horse knows the whip. The German horse does not know the whip, but knows the cultural history of whips very well. The ways of thinking in different cultures differ considerably from each other — probably this is the reason why they can be so easily caricatured. Where the policemen are British, the engineers are German, the organizers are Swiss, the cooks are Hungarian and the lovers are French, life is Paradise there. But where the policemen are German, the cooks are British, the engineers are French, the organizers are Hungarian and the lovers are Swiss, life is a nightmare.

There are considerable differences among the nations' cultures, their relationships to their environments and their orders of values; they have deep historical experiences in widely different areas of life. As we have seen in the case of male and female logics in Chapter 1, this difference makes it probable that even drawing some conclusions in the field of *formal logic* may be natural for members of one culture, while posing enormous difficulties for those of another culture. Thus we may talk about different ways of thinking in different cultures, and we may justly expect essential differences.

What we have said above is especially true of the different subcultures of different professions. There are things considered logical in every profession that are far from being evident for outsiders.

Robert Schumann, the composer, wrote the following at the beginning of one of his works: "To be played as fast as possible." A few lines later he wrote: "Faster!" The story became well-known and it is perfectly justifiable from the viewpoint of everyday humor, albeit it was absolutely logical: a few lines later the notes may have become easier to play, thus it really may have become possible to increase the speed.

The engineer calculates the parameters of the planned construction to six places of decimals, then multiplies the result by the required safety factor. This factor may be as much as nine, but it is rarely less than one and a half. Of course, this multiplication makes the determination of even the first decimal useless, not to talk about the sixth. Still, no engineer would do differently, because otherwise he would not conform to the rules of his profession.

Puzzle 3 of Chapter Zero serves to gain practice in the law of the conservation of energy. Since the refrigerator is consuming electric power continuously when its door is open in the insulated room, the end result should be extra heat, therefore the temperature of the whole room will gradually increase. To tell the truth, an eccentric theoretical physicist may find fault with this, saying that all is not finished yet. Theoretically, it should also be proven that opening the door of the refrigerator does not start other energy absorbing processes in the room. For example, everything might gradually turn green because of the open refrigerator.

Since each profession has its own characteristic way of thinking, they can be splendidly caricatured: The person who removes the legs of the flea one after the other until the flea does not react to the command "Jump!", then concludes that, with all its legs removed, the flea will become deaf, is called a biologist. The person who heats a pan of water so that first he pours out the water, reducing the task this way to the well-known water-heating task with an empty pan, is called a mathematician. The person who captures a lion by sifting the sand of the Sahara, and says that it is the lion that remains in the sieve, is an experimental physicist. It is a jurist who can see subjects of law when looking around in a crowd, although in a taxman's opinion he should see subjects of taxation there. A politician is the one who, finding any number of people marching in one direction, will rise above his principles and take their lead. Artificial intelligence — as we have seen in Chapter 2 — has unwillingly created its own parodies.

Approaches of artificial intelligence

On the one hand, artificial intelligence is a technical science whose task is *to create a given function* by artificially realizable and reproducible (as well as possible) means. For lack of better means, computers are used for this purpose today.

A technical creation may function perfectly well without our having the slightest idea of how Nature solves similar problems. If an engineer wants to realize translational motion he will be thinking in the world of wheels, propellers and jet engines. He will not design galloping or jumping cars with strange articulated apparatus. In realizing artificial intelligence we do not have to know necessarily how the mechanisms of the human brain work. It is conceivable that there exists a better solution with the aid of mathematical algorithms or electric circuits; computers may prove to be at least as revolutionary an invention as wheels and propellers were in the realization of smooth translational motion.

If, for instance, the aim of artificial intelligence is to realize certain of man's memory functions (e.g. the storage and retrieval of phone numbers according to name, address and number), we can say that man's similar abilities are already surpassed by the aid of computers and programming techniques. They are perfectly satisfactory technically, even if they are organized in a totally different way from man's memory.

On the other hand, artificial intelligence can also be considered as a new tool in scientific cognition, as it provides a possibility *to model* our knowledge about man's thinking mechanism. The primary aim of such models is to resemble man's functioning as much as possible: their virtues and imperfections should be similar. For example, when evaluating a chess program made for technical purposes, the only thing that counts is the results it achieves at competitions. A chess program intended for modeling thinking may be esteemed higher than the one that beats it regularly — if its principle of operation is closer to our knowledge about man's thinking, i.e. if we are more apt to believe that the games played by it could have been played by a human being.

However well a model resembled our thinking processes, a technical man would never follow them exactly in building an expedient system. Man would never restrict himself by his own biological limits if no technical reasons forced him to. Nevertheless, the performance of artificial intelligence programs, prepared so far purely on the basis of technical ways of thinking, have stubbornly failed to surpass a certain limit, although there are people capable of going far beyond that limit. This fact prompted several investigators of artificial intelligence to study the thinking mechanisms of man more thoroughly. It is this point where artificial intelligence research meets the so-called cognitive trend of psychology.

Cognitive psychology, cognitive science

The investigation of human thinking is one of the classical areas of psychology. Its fundamental questions are how and in what form we store our knowledge about the world, and what means we have to mobilize this knowledge to solve the continually emerging problems. What is it that organizes our knowledge into thinking and problem-solving ability? What do the concepts of memory, learning, retrieval, association, creativity and intelligence mean in general? What processes take place in us when we learn something about the world? The trend of cognitive psychology was named after this latter question (cognition = acquiring knowledge), but it was not the question that was something new in psychology (there are several thousand-year-old questions), rather its attitude, methods and means of investigation, or in short: its paradigm was new.

The cognitive trend of psychology studies those *active* processes with the aid of which man processes the incoming stimuli and information: he transforms them into different forms while he is most likely to modify them as well. When we read a text, many types of transformation, coding and recoding take place in our heads. Cognitive psychology strives at demonstrating these processes as really existing and showing them in as exact models as possible, while preserving as much of the millennial concepts about thinking as possible. Cognitive psychology would, perhaps, rate it as total success if it succeeded in describing the units, structures and the almost incessantly changing frames of thinking in the form of mathematical objects and constructions.

Looking from the outside, the products of artificial intelligence and those of the models of cognitive psychology are barely distinguishable: they are computer programs; they work with man-made tools and analyze their functioning. The fruits are similar, but the roots and aims are quite different. The prompting of cognitive psychology was *description*, i.e. to describe and model really existing and natural functions, while the prompting of artificial intelligence was *construction*, i.e. the creation of functions.

In order to reach their aims, both branches of science may need to understand the naturally existing functions; this is why the two branches are interwoven nowadays. If they reach their goal, their paths will separate again: subsequently, the investigators of artificial intelligence will be interested in the technical possibilities of the artificial realization and improvement of the functions, while psychologists would rather continue to study the reasons and roles of individual differences within the general principles. Cognitive psychologists search for the good models of human thinking because, for them, this may be a means of *understanding*. For artificial intelligence researchers these models may serve as means of *creating* similar or even better functions.

The immediate tasks and methods of the two branches of science are very similar nowadays, but as their motivations, attitudes and aims are radically different, they arrived at their meeting point with different dowries. This is why they have something to say to each other. Both branches have reached significant results that could be of interest to each other. Naturally, with full recognition of the aforesaid, both branches exist independently of each other as well, and live their separate lives. Artificial intelligence — as a technical branch of science — develops new methods and algorithms to solve its problems; cognitive psychology — as a psychological branch of science — discovers new relationships within human thinking.

Although the models of cognitive psychology and artificial intelligence resemble each other from the outside, the order of values and ways of thinking cannot be reconciled. They work on the basis of different paradigms. This is why a new, independent branch called *cognitive science* has developed. This branch deals with certain kinds of abstract objects: the models of human cognition and thinking.

Cognitive science inherited its model-building attitude from artificial intelligence: the model's functioning and quality present independent values by themselves, regardless of the concrete procedure of the realization. The points of view used to evaluate the models come from cognitive psychology: our knowledge about the functioning of human thinking is the reference for evaluating the models. As opposed to artificial intelligence, cognitive science is not interested in the technical parameters of the realization; it does not appreciate the possibility of the same function created by a much simpler and faster algorithm. As opposed to cognitive psychology, the models for cognitive science do not suggest experiments that would discover new phenomena; cognitive science is interested purely in the models themselves.

The basis of the *Weltanschauung* or paradigm of cognitive science is the firm belief that every aspect of man's thinking can be grasped by suitable computer programs. This belief is the one that distinguishes it from its sources. The scholars led by this conviction gathered under the new flag of cognitive science. Artificial intelligence does not consider it automatically guaranteed that its basic aims can be realized; it considers finding the methods and procedures useful in this direction, and regards its task to be the organizing and further developing of the well-proved methods of their use. This is a typical technical branch of science. The investigators of cognitive psychology do not believe that their models are suitable for the perfect realization of any aspect of human thinking: they only help to understand them better and discover the inter-relationships among them.

Thus cognitive science is based on a paradigm totally different from its predecessors. It is rightfully called a new branch of science, because it bears all the characteristics of science. Its investigators are more and more organized in independent, self-evaluating and closed communities, and solve well-definable types of puzzles. A new discipline, its basic ideas were conceived in the 1960s, primarily upon the basis of the works of the Nobel prize laureate economist Herbert Simon and Allen Newell. It is an abstract science, though its characteristic way of thinking has not developed totally yet.

Holism and reductionism

The question of holism and reductionism played a central role in the 20th century's philosophical debates on sciences. *Holism* is a trend proclaiming that "the whole is more than the sum of its parts". Up to this point it is self-evident: a tune is naturally more than the sequence of its notes, a cathedral is more than the sum of the constituent stones. This is not contested by even the most extreme reductionists. *Reductionism* is the belief according to which, although the whole may be another quality than the sum of its parts, it can still be understood perfectly if we know the constituent parts and the way, principles and motifs of its construction. This is the belief that is rejected by holism which says that new principles and qualities, about which neither the components nor the way of their construction can say anything essential, may arise in the whole.

Both philosophical trends are far more detailed than our brief summary here. European science (which naturally means American science as well) has strictly committed itself to the philosophy of reductionism; still, from time to time, it procures radically new principles that would be considered holistic, had we not known the route that led to them. The principle of the conservation of energy and matter, the law of equal weight relations, Dollo's law (that ontogenesis roughly repeats phylogenesis), Darwin's theory of evolution, the discovery of the unconscious, the theory of relativity, are just a few of the best-known examples.

Thus, reductionism does not exclude that, by carefully studying the components of the whole and the way of their construction, we can recognize relationships and general rules which do not apply to details any more, but do apply to the whole. On the other hand, holism does not deny that these general rules come about through the careful study of the parts: it only denies that *every* important characteristic of the whole could be understood that way.

Cognitive science extends the principle of reductionism to the extreme and thus makes it the basis of its functioning. It sets out from the conviction that it is guaranteed to know everything about the components and the ways of composition of its models, for it created them artificially. Cognitive science hopes that the study of the models as a whole may lead to new and more general knowledge, and on the basis of functioning models we can discover rules that can describe such characteristics of the relationship between the whole and its parts that do not follow from the way of composition. The basis of science is reductionism, but no branch has brought it to such logical extremes as cognitive science.

According to holistic thinking, we do not know everything even about an artificially created model: e.g. every model has a trace of its designer's motivations, ambitions and way of thinking. Thus, it is not necessarily true that cognitive science knows everything about its models' components and the way of composition. This is no counter-argument against the models of the other branches like physics, biology or cognitive psychology, for their interests are artificially narrowed down to certain types of questions. Cognitive science argues, however, by asking: once the model is ready, which component, where, in which program-part could be contained something that cannot be learned from the model itself? And which of our neurons or synapses may contain such things?

★   ★   ★

"Asterisks too are a refreshment for the eye and mind of the reader. One does not always need the greater articulation of a Roman numeral..."

(Thomas Mann: Doctor Faustus)

The author should probably take sides with one of these trends. I am not going to do this now, or later. In my everyday scientific (i.e. puzzle solving) work I naturally adhere strictly to the norms of science — primarily not because otherwise the scientific community would expel me from among them, but because it is worth making science and solving puzzles only within the strictly given frames. This, however, does not prevent us from trying to look at our daily work from the outside of science occasionally — like at the moments of meeting a young man, as in Chapter Zero. On these occasions a more holistic approach may be helpful. This cannot be expressed by the methods of science, although there are generally accepted methods by which it can be expressed, such as the arts, for instance. Karinthy's work is a piece of literary art rather than a scientific work or case history about the unfulfilled hopes of a genius. I do not know whether science will ever be able to grasp the essence of literature, but at present it is far from it.

An atheist could also build a good cathedral. It is enough to understand the religion whose cathedral he is entrusted to build. It is the employer who needs the belief to concentrate his resouces just on this goal. The situation is the same in science. All the scientific community requires of its members is to work according to the appropriate paradigm; in the meanwhile, the members may think of the paradigm as they like.

I can see no more trustworthy method than science to study thinking, either. My native language is rationality; my everyday logic cannot accept conclusions that contradict scientific results. Yet at the same time I clearly feel that there are many fields that slip out of the present range of science — and I do not deem them unworthy of reflection. I cannot and do not find it important to decide where — if they exist — are the boundaries of the fields that can ever be possessed by science. This is why I do not take sides on the question of reductionism versus holism.

On the other hand, I feel that boundaries have been outlined by now that perhaps can be reached through the foreseeable methods of artificial intelligence, but that can hardly be exceeded. I would like to draft these boundaries, and also to show the areas where science may be competent (whether you like it or not), as well as those areas where we justly look for (and find) other means of expression and presentation.

Psychology as natural science

Man's everyday thinking is holistic, rather than reductionist. We immediately see cathedrals, not stones; it is easier for us to remember a whole tune than a few separate notes. We can easily recognize our acquaintances even if certain things have changed about them since we last met them. Psychology's way of thinking is also traditionally holistic. Psychology was a partial area within philosophy for centuries, trying to draw a whole and uniform picture of man.

Only around the middle of the 19th century did psychology reach the point where it could conceptualize its object like the natural sciences did: there is a function existing in Nature, let us learn about it as much as possible. Let us experiment and think.

In psychology's way of thinking the two approaches still live together: on the one hand it is a uniform, comprehensive human science that is building a holistic system of cognition, while on the other hand it is a branch of reductionist natural science that builds its theories on the basis of strict experiments and carefully controlled partial results. The two attitudes are incompatible within one paradigm, therefore the scholars of psychology have formed different schools. Psychoanalytic schools conduct no experiments, but build their systems of ideas on the basis of case studies. This does not convince the scholars of the experimental trends because the scarce cases do not provide sufficient control; the clinical cases are too complex and so many effects are mixed in them that it is impossible to rely on them in building a well-founded theory. For the holistic schools, however, studying experimental subjects who sit in the laboratory and apathetically press buttons is boredom itself: they can say hardly anything valuable about the human psyche.

Experimental psychologists have the history of physics in view, where the complex holistic (scholastic) systems of thought had achieved relatively little regard, e.g. the analysis of falling or flying tendencies of objects. Much more was achieved by those who spent their whole lives constructing boring and sophisticated falling machines and devices with springs, pulleys and spirals that are totally useless in themselves — just to demonstrate satisfactorily the foundations of some radical theoretical generalization.

Still, we cannot say that the two trends are independent of each other. Their subject — man — is the same. If one branch succeeds in saying something really definite, the other will acknowledge it even if it will not fit the finding into its own system directly. Holistic schools are not irrational either: if an experimental result shows something very different from what would follow from their holistic world view, they will alter their conceptions so as not to oppose the exact facts. On the other hand, scholars of the experimental trends are also well acquainted with and take into consideration the holistic and comprehensive world views. In solving puzzles it is allowed to use means that do not belong to the puzzles. Who cares why and what experiences helped me in finding the solution to 43 across: the name of the Old French poet (12 letters)? No one can tell the answer to that from the solution.

Sigmund Freud started off as a normal, reductionist neurophysiologist, but when he felt he understood much more of the inherences of neuroses than what could be hoped to be expressed by means of the science of his time, he broke with science spectacularly. Psychoanalysis became a world view outside academic science, or a kind of movement — which it still is. Yet, even the scholars of academic science feel that, relying on the world view of psychoanalysis, such truths can be grasped that at present have significance far beyond the inherences that can be studied within the frames of science. That such truths exist is more general than this concrete case: they will always exist. Let us see the other side of the coin for the time being: how can truths outside the terrain of science influence research?

Freud says, for instance, that a hidden message can be read from every slip of the tongue. Slips of the tongue express the hidden motivations and anxieties. This is too general a statement, impossible to be grasped experimentally. The scientists who studied the mental processes of language and speech within the paradigm of cognitive psychology did not pay attention to slips of the tongue for a long time. They studied speech mostly as a more or less autonomous process and did not care much about motivations, anxieties or other factors that were indifferent from the aspect of what one had to or wanted to say. The process of speech, however, proved to be so complex even beside this highly restricted sphere of questions that its components could not be found and studied in isolation from each other.

Seeing the difficulties, the investigators' interest turned towards studying mistakes and slips of the tongue. Hundreds of collected anecdotal examples indicated that through mistakes and slips of the tongue an important phase of speech production can be grasped almost as a still picture. However, slips of the tongue are rare and improbable to occur just when the experimental subject is right in the laboratory. It is even more difficult to get them produced under controlled experimental conditions.

Michael Motley and his colleagues found an elegant solution. In most of the cases of slips of the tongue only one mound is mistaken. (What is the hidden purpose of this error? Is the author perhaps an amateur archeologist?) This mistake is so typical that it promises to prove a good field for experimentation. If pairs of words are flashed on the screen of a computer in rapid succession so that the first members always start with e.g. letter T and the second with R (e.g. tiny ring, two roads, text read, etc.), and subsequently a pair like "right tail" is flashed, then it is quite likely that we will misread the pair as "tight rail". Under these circumstances the experimental subject would make a mistake in reading about every fifth or sixth critical pair, where the words remain sensible even with the first letters interchanged. Thus, the occurrence of the slips of the tongue could be increased so as to provide the necessary controlled conditions for their investigation.

The study was carried out under three conditions. In the first group electrodes were fixed to the arms of the subjects and the subjects were told they would receive a painful electric shock at some point in the experiment. Although it never came, the experimenters hoped that this possibility might cause some anxiety. (It did — as will be seen from the results.) In the second group a very attractive, flirtatious young woman conducted the experiment, while in the third the conditions were purposely neutral. In all the three groups the same series of pairs of words were shown on the computer screen. There were pairs related to electric shock, to sexual excitement, and there were totally neutral ones, too, among the critical pairs.

The subjects in the neutral condition made mistakes in cases of pairs related to electric shock or sexual desire as often as in the neutral cases. They were just as likely to say CURSED WATTAGE instead of WORST COTTAGE, or FAST PASSION instead of PAST FASHION, as SHRED HINKER instead of HEAD SHRINKER.

The subjects who were promised an electric shock were more than twice as likely to make mistakes in the word pairs related to electric shock. For instance, they made a mistake in reading the pairs VARIED COLTS, or SHAM DOCK far more often than in reading other pairs.

Those subjects whose experiment was conducted by the attractive flirtatious lady made mistakes twice as often with pairs of words related to sexuality than the other pairs. These subjects usually misread the following pairs: SAPPY HEX, SHARE BOULDERS, etc.

The experiment clearly shows that even if there is no hidden meaning behind each of our slips of the tongue, our hidden motivations are really manifested in our mistakes and slips of the tongue. Thus, Freudian slips marched into the group of phenomena that can be studied by the methods of normal science.

Antonyms changing into each other

Exchanging letters, or in a more general form: turning around situations and relationships is an important characteristic of dream-work, too, in Freud's theory. *Dream-work* is a process by which the *manifest dream* is produced from our latent and secret wishes and fears into a form that is acceptable by our consciousness. Dream-work has several typical methods. Let us cite Freud himself:

"Among the most surprising findings is the way in which the dream-work treats contraries that occur in the latent dream. We know already that conformities in the latent material are replaced by condensations in the manifest dream. Well, contraries are treated in the same way as conformities, and there is a special preference for expressing them by the same manifest element. Thus an element in the manifest dream which is capable of having a contrary may equally well be expressing either itself or its contrary or both together: only the sense can decide which translation is to be chosen. This connects with the further fact that a representation of 'no' — or at any rate an unambiguous one — is not to be found in dreams.

A welcome analogy to this strange behavior of the dream-work is provided for us in the development of language. Some philologists have maintained that in the most ancient languages contraries such as 'light — dark', 'big — small' are expressed by the same verbal roots. (What we term 'the antithetical meaning of primal words'.) Thus in Ancient Egyptian '*ken*' originally meant 'strong' and 'weak'."

This opposition has not disappeared yet from the English language, either. Puzzle 4 of Chapter Zero emphasizes a characteristic like this: it occurs even in our rational and logical age that something can be defined in one way and also by its formal opposite. Maybe, numerous is not exactly as many as innumerable, but the same word MANY can be recalled by two expressions that are formally opposites.

If someone helps me, I can thank him saying: "Your services were invaluable to me" or "Your services were valuable to me", and still mean that I received services of GREAT VALUE. If someone says that there were MANY people at the party he can express it by saying "There were quite a few people there", or "There were quite a lot of people there". When you WALK ALONG Oxford street you may walk up Oxford street or you may walk down Oxford street and still go in the same direction! To be sure, the pairs of expressions do not mean exactly the same thing, but it is hardly accidental that in certain contexts they can be exchanged — without disturbing our thinking or causing logical contradiction.

Western and Eastern thinking

The previous paragraph can probably be expounded logically in any language (at least in Hungarian it is possible), although it necessarily has different connotations. Translation necessarily means distortion as well. Let us recall the 27th koan of the classical collection of Zen Buddhism "Mumonkan" ("No-gate barrier", "The gateless gate") in two translations, together with the attached verse and comments:

Translation by Paul Reps:
A monk asked Nansen: "Is there any teaching no master ever taught before?" Nansen said: "Yes, there is." "What is it?" asked the monk. Nansen replied: "It is not mind, it is not Buddha, it is not things."
MUMON'S COMMENTARY: Old Nansen gave away his treasure-words. He must have been greatly upset.
MUMON'S POEM:
Nansen was too kind and lost his treasure.
Truly, words have no power.
Even though the mountain becomes the sea,
Words cannot open another's mind.

Translation by Katsuki Sekida:
A monk asked Nansen, "Is there any Dharma that has not been preached to the people?" Nansen answered, "There is." "What is the truth that has not been taught?" asked the monk. Nansen said: "It is not mind, it is not Buddha; it is not things."
MUMON'S COMMENT: At this question, Nansen used up all his treasure and was not a little confused.
MUMON'S VERSE:
Talking too much spoils your virtue;
Silence is truly unequaled.
Let the mountains become the sea;
I'll give you no comment.

It would be senseless, and even Zenless to subject the two translations to a comparative analysis. Not because of our lack of linguistic competence, but because both translations may be authentic, even if they are different or even outright opposites. It is the essence of the koan that the essence cannot be expressed by words, while silence is not the appropriate means of expression, either. This is why the original text is probably sufficiently obscure as well. The author of the koan is visibly vexed with master Nansen because he is trying to express something that can only be felt, experienced or rather be united with.

Zen Buddhism is holism brought to the extremes. Not only is there no sense in talking about the whole as being more than the sum of its parts, it is also altogether meaningless to talk about parts at all. There exists no differentiation, no distance, no categories, no words, no me and no not-me: everything is one, everything is the same as the universe. But these are only words, of course: how would it feel to get rid of them? What could there be beyond words?

To get beyond words finally and completely is an experience that cannot be described by words, and is said to be wonderful. The feeling may be similar to the feeling described by those who are able to get into really deep hypnosis: they unanimously state that it is an extremely good feeling and is totally different from their normal state. But the peak experience of Zen is an even more altered state than the others. In hypnosis people remain in some kind of a connection with the everyday world. They perceive the changes, processes and relationships, but ignore them. Through Zen one can get over many things, and according to those practicing Zen it is worth sacrificing many things (actually: everything) for this experience. In fact, everything must be sacrificed — otherwise it does not work.

Zen (and Buddhism in general) calls this experience *satori*. A Zen koan is one of the means of the long and complex path preparing the ability to reach the state of satori. Koans could be translated as cautionary tales, but they caution against nothing. The meaning of koans is that they have no meaning for our daily common sense. We might as well consider them as puzzles, for they are guaranteed to have a solution, otherwise the Zen master would not give it to us. The frame of the koan puzzle, however, is not that of common sense (as in the case of normal puzzles), nor the paradigm of a branch of science (as in the case of scientific questions), but it is a Zen way of thinking intended to be achieved. Koans, naturally, have no solution in the common sense. The solution is not that they have no solution, as is the case with some mathematical problems. The solution is to go beyond or transcend the range of thinking where the things of the world have solutions and insolubilities; the aim is to approach the ability to get into a kind of altered state of consciousness.

A Zen koan perhaps resembles the rosary: it is a tool that has no meaning by itself. It has to be kept going, because this way it is easier to do the daily ritual. This way everyday matters are less likely to distract one's attention from the essence.

A lot of similarities can be found between Buddhist and Christian mysticisms. The Jesuit Father Enomiya-Lassalle, who spent years in Japan studying Buddhism, seriously suggested that perhaps it would be worth adapting certain physical and mental techniques into Catholic training, for some Zen meditation techniques are considerably more efficient and they can also be easily adapted to Catholic principles. Certain techniques may be easy to adapt, but the radical difference between the two *Weltanschauungs* is highlighted by the very first sentences of the Bible: "In the beginning God created the heaven and the earth." "And God saw the light, that *it* was good: and God divided the light from the darkness." Everything starts with a separation, a distinction between good and bad, something that the Buddhist world concept considers earthly casualties, without the transcendence of which the experience of satori is unreachable.

Perhaps this is one of the reasons why European thinking started in the direction of categorization and reductionism. There can be other reasons as well, e.g. in Europe the worldly and religious powers separated, while in the East the Emperor was looked upon as a god. We have seen that the ways in which different European nations think differ; it is evident that there are differences in the ways Eastern nations think, too. History and determining experiences are different there as well. The first sentence of a Japanese primary school reading book says: China is a big country, Japan is small. This is what some Japanese children first read; the Chinese read something else first. It is an interesting (although perhaps not very important) consonance that the first sentence of a Hungarian primary school reading book is: The Turk and the cows. (For 200 years, Turks were for Hungarians what China was for Japan.) Still, the differences between Eastern and Western ways of thinking are much more profound than those among the different European nations.

Eastern thinking is more holistic. When a battle is described in a Chinese history-book, it is not the military potentials of the opposing parties that are outlined primarily. The weather, the different omens and simultaneous events — even things like a wedding of two common persons at the time proving to be a good match — are described. European thinking sets out from the logic of things, while Eastern thinking starts from the logic of the thing (i.e. the uniform order of the world) as much as possible. The latter is exemplified in the following story of a Chinese rain-maker:

It had not been raining for a long time in a Chinese village when the rain-maker was sent for. The rain-maker occupied his lodgings and did nothing special, performed no magic, did not even move from his place, when eventually it started to rain. When the villagers asked how he did it, he said one did not make things like that. The rain comes when things are in natural harmony. When he arrived at the village he registered that disharmony prevailed in the village, thus the processes of Nature could not go on in their normal ways. But he also noticed that the disharmony of the village created disharmony in him too, so he withdrew to his lodging to restore harmony within himself. When his own inner harmony was restored it started to rain as it should according to the harmony of the world.

The story is undoubtedly unrealistic, but the legends of our culture complex are no less unrealistic, either. Our legends talk about wonderful individual deeds. They reflect the stressed importance of the individual in our culture, as the story of the rain-maker stresses the inseparable unity of the individual and nature, of the inner and outer world. Radically different experiences, therefore radically different ways of thinking, characterize the two types of cultures.

The peak performance of reductionist European thinking is manifested in the accomplishments of science from nuclear energy to gene technology. The peak performance of Eastern thinking is probably the achievement of the state of satori: this is probably an immensely sensational experience (though I cannot be sure, of course). But working at the peaks of science is granted only to a few in Western cultures, just as satori is reached only by a few in Eastern cultures. The driving force of the Western way of thinking is advancement, and it gives the comfort produced by technical achievements to its members. Eastern thinking offers the inner harmony of the individual, his harmony with the universe.

This recognition directed the attention of Western cultures toward Eastern philosophies (simultaneously with the mini skirt, the hippie movement, LSD, bio-foods, and the music of the Beatles) in the 1960s. I should explain here why I mention the children of flowers together with *I Ching* and Zen Buddhism (and I do not think I could argue convincingly). Temporal concurrence is not a sufficient argument in our sphere. This mentality has led to our scientific achievements, but this is also the reason why we should not even hope that Eastern philosophies will ever be rooted more deeply in our thinking. Concrete techniques may be taken over for concrete aims — as the East has accepted our technical achievements. But Western thinking has to find the way to its own inner harmony in agreement with its own logic and way of thinking.

5. Levels of thinking

Certain digger wasps provide for their offspring once and for all when the time comes for laying eggs. They look for a suitable little hatching chamber somewhere, lay their eggs there and put a cricket beside them as food. First they immobilize the cricket by a sting so that the cricket stays alive but cannot move any more. Subsequently, the mother wasp buries the hatching chamber and flies away for ever. When the grub hatches it finds the preserved cricket right there. By the time it has eaten the whole cricket it will be grown up so that it can further take care of itself.

The behavior of the mother wasp represents a nice, logical chain of action. This is what investigators interfered with, in order to study how consciously the wasp does what it does. At a certain moment the wasp puts the cricket down at the opening of the hatching chamber, leaves it there for a while and adds the finishing touches to the inside of the chamber before laying the eggs. With a blade of grass the wicked investigators now push the cricket preserve a little further off. Some of the digger wasps are not bothered by this maneuver: when everything is ready in the chamber, the wasp comes out, flies about a little confused, then finds the cricket and carries it into the chamber to finish laying the eggs.

Other digger wasps are totally stunned by this slight intervention. When they finally find their cricket preserve after flying about confusedly, they pull it again to the opening of the chamber, leave it there, and go inside again to add the finishing touches. But the investigators push the cricket off again. The wasp comes out, flies about confusedly, finds the cricket, leaves it again at the opening of the chamber to add the finishing touches. These digger wasps can never recognize that they are already through with this step and could peacefully take the cricket right into the chamber. Sometimes the investigators pushed the cricket off forty times in a row, and the wasp added the finishing touches forty times.

It is possible that when the investigators got bored with annoying the female wasp, she encoded somehow (e.g. on the cricket) a message for her offspring that man is an animal that stops harrassing after the fortieth trial. But biologists — characteristically — did not start looking for such codes, instead they studied whether the higher intelligence of the smarter digger wasps is manifested or not in other areas as well. Strangely enough, in other situations the smarter digger wasps did not prove to be more intelligent than the others. Probably they could disregard the disorder caused by the investigators not because of some intelligence in the human sense; perhaps this particular biological program of theirs was somewhat more general, it had more degrees of freedom. But it resulted in no higher intellect to solve other problems.

The hierarchy of our concepts

Higher intellect could have been expected of the smarter digger wasps in other tasks, because they behaved as if they were seeing through the maneuvers of the scientists. As if they knew what the reason of their chain of behavior was, independently of the routine work of the actual laying of eggs; as if they had drawn some conclusion on the basis of the logic of things. Unfortunately, even the smarter digger wasps lack this capacity: they are unable to see through the relationships of their actions and to handle the whole process as a larger unit under different circumstances.

This is the moment of concept formation. Man is capable of handling a whole series of actions as a whole, and also to analyze it, to reduce it to its components. At first the moment of analysis seems to be more important, for the digger wasp also saw the unit of the chain of actions; in fact, it was the only thing she saw — she could not see the meaning of the components. Still, we cannot say that the digger wasp has any idea about the process of egg laying, because, for her, the process does not mean that independently meaningful actions are combined into one unit meaningful by itself. For the more stupid digger wasps the partial actions (at least leaving the cricket at the opening and adding the finishing touches) had no meaning by themselves.

Concepts can be formed only of independently meaningful elements, because only in this case can we talk about things that belong to one another in a certain respect, and only in this case can we handle their combination together as one unit of thought. There can be quite a few aspects. A concept may summarize elements of a series of actions, or it may summarize components belonging to one another according to certain characteristics or features (like the concepts of mammals or inert gases),

63

but a concept may combine concepts that combine elements according to a similar system (like a branch of science or the concept of puzzles).

If that is the case, there must be complex hierarchies of concepts present in our heads. It would be nice to study experimentally whether such things really exist or whether they are just our fabrications. Here is another nice puzzle for cognitive psychology.

Investigation is made especially difficult by the fact that, in order to talk about concepts, one has to have concepts. How can we find any starting point then?

First of all: can we give a sure sign of having concepts? V.D. Volkova used Pavlov's technique to study similar questions. For example, she put some drops of delicious cranberry juice into the mouths of small schoolchildren while saying "good". When the conditioned response was already established and the children started salivating upon simply hearing the word "good" without the cranberry juice, she started saying different things. Salivation started when the children heard "Leningrad is a nice city" or "A pioneer helps his comrade". Salivation did not start after sentences like "The child was impudent with his teacher" or "My friend is severely ill".

Thus, our concepts work even if we do not consciously make them work. And are they really organized into hierarchies? We need to have some previous idea about the organization of concept hierarchies to study them, but there is a danger of thinking in circles here. A reference was needed from the outside — and it was found in the time factor. It was studied how long it took the experimental subjects to answer questions like "Are robins animals?" "Are canaries birds?" "Are tits fish?" "Are fishes fish?"

In order to analyze the data, a quite handy concept hierarchy was outlined, like "animal — bird — canary" and "animal — fish — shark". The researchers said: let us consider the distance between two concepts to be the number of steps that lead from one concept to the other within this hierarchy. The principle is very simple, but the results confirmed the hypothesis: it turned out unexpectedly uniformly that about 75 milliseconds are needed to take any step between the units. Thus, e.g. it takes about 75 msec longer to answer the question whether the shark is an animal than to decide whether the shark is a fish. Stepping over two levels takes 150 msecs, etc. In cases of more complex questions ("Do canaries breathe?" "Do wild ducks swim?") the picture becomes too complex, but the basic phenomenon, namely, the necessity of a fixed period of time for taking the steps between the levels of the hierarchy remains quite stable.

A sceptical reader may not be convinced by these results. The ground is marshy, the danger of reasoning in a roundabout way is not warded off. The hierarchy of concepts by which the distances are measured is quite accidental; we might as well draw another one (e.g.: animal — yellow animal — feathered yellow animal — canary). In this case, however, we would not receive the nice and stable 75 msec intervals when stepping over to the next level. Whatever the temporal data show, however, in cases of similarly simple questions it is easy to find corresponding hierarchies (or models, rather) where the interval of stepping from one level to the next is stable — the worst that could happen is that the model has to be made a little more complex.

Although they are justified questions, we do have to find some point to start from. This field of cognitive psychology developed a paradigm for itself by accepting two hypotheses. First, somehow our concepts are organized in our heads, and either there is, or there is not, a direct link between two concepts. (Thus, we have already relaxed the hypothesis of a strict hierarchic organization — which really does not stand the test in the cases of rather complex systems of ideas.) Second, the period of time necessary for making a connection between two concepts is proportional to the number of steps necessary to take between them within the given organization. Well, this is the starting idea. We can believe in it because in the simplest of cases, when organization is easily imaginable, the expected result is always obtained — and always with the model closest at hand.

Once we have accepted this starting position, we already have a paradigm: we can build models of complex concept organization about which we can decide whether or not they are the solution of the puzzle or what kind of structures the studied concepts are organized into. Do the methods of making the decision, i.e. experimentation and the measurement of reaction times, conform to what the model predicted?

Tangled hierarchies

Naturally, in this paradigm the decision about whether or not a model conforms to the results of measurement is only a theoretical possibility. In cases of somewhat more complex models no experimental subject had the patience of Job of whom all the possible connections of the model could be asked. Even if a model had only a few hundred convergences, thousands of life spans would be necessary.

This alone would be no trouble: science is built by creating concepts on the basis of discovered phenomena, followed by the construction with the aid of the existing system of concepts. The paradigm governs the construction even if the original thought can barely be recognized after the development of a few new concepts. This is the case here, too. The complex system of exceptions makes the models more varied: e.g. are whales fish? Unexpected cross-connections, possibilities of short circuits between seemingly distant concepts appear in the systems. Concepts postulating each other had to be introduced and the related reaction times had to be measured.

It soon turned out that the nice idea of the concepts in us being organized in a simply describable order had to be given up. But the main problem is not that the picture becomes very tangled: it also produces some strange phenomena. It regularly occurs that a concept proves to be at a higher level, i.e. more general than another one, which in turn is more general than a third, etc. until eventually an even-lower-level concept proves to be more general in a certain sense than the first. Of course, in cases like this the reference system also changes a little between levels of the hierarchy. Task, work and learning each has somewhat different connotations when a task is more general than work, work is more general than learning and learning is more general than a task.

The paradigm seems to have slipped: it should be either changed or defined more exactly. However, the problem lies deeper: several facts indicate that such strange, self-closing loops constitute the basis of the thinking function. Whatever is mentioned in this chapter are only the first signs. It can already be seen that, on the one hand, there is a strong hierarchic element in the organization of our concepts while, on the other hand, these hierarchies become hopelessly tangled in the course of changing the different points of view and reference systems until they can barely be called hierarchies. This strange structure will be called a *tangled hierarchy*. The name itself shows the basic contradiction in the structure.

Man easily changes the reference system even accidentally. In Puzzle 5 in Chapter Zero, the accounting sounds very logical; suspicion arises only when it turns out that a thaler is missing. The mistake is that, although each of the guests paid 9 thalers, this includes everything they spent in the hostel, from the accommodation to the servant's tip. Why add the servant's tip once more? They spent 3×9 thalers and were given 3 thalers back: we accounted for all the 30 thalers.

Those who spent a few minutes solving the puzzle are justly disappointed a little: they had accepted a meaningless reference system for a while. How come they did not immediately pounce upon *what* it was we had added the servant's tip to?

In the next example we make a barely visible shift between two fully sensible reference systems. Look at the following two statements:

(*a*) The uglier a woman the more cosmetics she uses.

(*b*) The more cosmetics a woman uses the more beautiful she looks.

From the rules of formal logic it follows that:

(*c*) The uglier a woman the more beautiful she looks.

The conclusion is ridiculous, of course. The mistake is not in the original statements. They might not be true, but they are not inconceivable. Statement (*a*) could even be the result of a survey — in this case its validity cannot be easily doubted. Statement (*b*) is also realistic, at least within certain limits.

The mistake is that in this context the first statement is absolute: here the form "the more ... the more" means that the person who is uglier will use more cosmetics. This meaning also implies that the person who uses more cosmetics is also uglier. In statement (*b*) the form "the more ... the more" is clearly relative: in this context it only means that those persons who use cosmetics will look more beautiful than *their own former self*. Thus the form "the more ... the more" does not imply that the person who looks more beautiful also uses more cometics. Yet, formal reasoning is valid only if the form "the more ... the more" is used in an absolute sense in both statements.

In language, the form "the more ... the more" is justly used in both meanings. Still, it may cause problems if we are not fully aware of this duality. And now remember how ridiculous we felt the computer to be in Chapter 2 when it intepreted the word "or" in the wrong reference system and answered "YES" (in a formally logical way). Because of our tangled hierarchies and conceptual loops ending in the beginning, we are not safeguarded against similar mistakes either, although we justly feel superior to the present performances of artificial intelligence. But our superiority is due exactly to our tangled hierarchies and to our loops of thinking and concepts that end in their beginnings.

Gödel, Escher, Bach

The three heroes of Douglas R. Hofstadter's book seemingly make a strange group. How are the German mathematician Kurt Gödel, the Dutch painter Maurits Cornelis Escher and Johann Sebastian Bach brought together in a book? These three creators were not brought together through some incalculable free association test. The main question of their *oeuvres* was what kinds of means of expression were made possible by the characteristics of our conceptual organization.

When I tried to sum up the common essence of the three life-works in the previous sentence, I combined three radically different systems of reference. Still, the sentence does not sound meaningless. One feels there is some reason for the existence of a thought like this; this is what makes it possible in Hofstadter's book for the three main themes (and several subthemes) to be combined into a whole, like the melodies of a Bach fugue. Let us have a brief look at the three main themes.

Gödel proved a theorem in the field of mathematical logic that has far-reaching consequences. The theorem is the first one in the history of logic that would have seriously surprised the great Aristotle himself. All the other results of the past two thousand years of logic would evoke only a nod from him, saying "Nice work, this is how things should be done." He would also approve the proof of Gödel's theorem with a nod: it remains strictly within the sphere of logic. The significance and consequences of the theorem, however, reach far beyond mathematical logic — which would make Aristotle reconsider his system of ideas radically.

Gödel's theorem, discovered in 1931, proves the following (as expressed in a single informal sentence leaving out the technical details): If in a mathematical system every truth that can be expressed by the means of the system can also be proven somehow within the system, then the system is necessarily contradictory.

In other words: if a formal system contains no contradictions, then a statement can be phrased which cannot be either proven or disproven. This sentence means the same thing as the previous one, because if a statement cannot be proven or disproven then the same must hold true of its opposite as well. But either the statement in question or its opposite must be true, because in formal logic we are dealing only with statements that are either true or false: there is no third case. Regardless of which is true, the statement or its opposite, we have a truth that cannot be proven within the frame of formal logic.

Even less formally we may also phrase Gödel's result as follows: if we want to stay open for every truth with our logic then it is necessary to make shifts among reference systems.

The *oeuvre* of Maurits C. Escher explores the possibilities of changing the reference systems subtly by means of painting and graphics. In his pictures you can find constantly rising staircases which return to their starting points, waterstreams returning to their points of origin by waterfalls, and strange metamorphoses: birds changing almost imperceptibly into insects that turn into frogs that turn into fish that turn into leaves that turn into houses that turn into birds again. We feel the constant metamorphoses totally harmonious — somehow they do not contradict our view of the world, our system of concepts. Perhaps we are sensitive to Escher's self-closing loops because our thinking is also based upon similar loops. But Escher's pictures are not only intellectually exciting and thought-provoking but also simply *beautiful*, independently of the tricks used in their production or the way they were used.

Let us recall only one of Johann Sebastian Bach's works, namely, the part "Canon per Tonos" of the *Musikalisches Opfer*. The melody of the lower voices starts in C minor, and in the continual variations of the theme we do not even notice that we are already in D minor when the melody returns gradually to the starting point — just to start again and arrive in E minor. We hear Bach juggle the reference systems without our having any idea how on earth we got into another key. As it goes on, finally we get back, of course, to C minor. This is again a strange, self-closing loop, made this time with the aid of music: and it is also simply harmonious and beautiful.

If a fugue becomes compact it will become more than the sum of its parts because it will become a concept by itself: it will find a place in the organization of our tangled hierarchy as an independent unit. Hofstadter lists the sparklingly witty variations of the topic on 777 pages in his book. And the fugue becomes compact. The casually raised thought becomes meaningful as an independent concept by its own right: the life-works of Gödel, Escher and Bach show the means of expression made possible by the tangled, self-closing loops of the organization of our concepts.

Concept-forming programs

In parallel with cognitive psychology, artificial intelligence also traversed the path leading from the hypothesis of simple hierarchic models to complex, confused models with self-closing loops. The paradigm of artificial intelligence was again different here. It did not build its models on the basis of measuring reaction times, but on construction principles that promised to produce well-operable systems.

The first steps produced spectacular successes here, too. For example, Pat Langley's program called BACON was destined to rediscover classical physics. This system looks for relationships between concepts from a huge amount of numerical data ("measurement results") and forms new concepts. At the outset some very simple concepts like distance, time and weight were defined for the system, and a large mass of data were given: more or less exact results of various imagined measurements.

The basic idea behind the BACON system was that if it can show a stable relationship between two of its existing concepts then probably there is another interesting concept behind this relationship. Thus, it is worth defining a third concept with the aid of the two.

The program searched for the relationships on the basis of a few very simple principles. For instance, it took two variables (two already existing physical concepts) and examined how the two variables were related to each other. If it found that the increase of one of the variables was usually accompanied by the increase of the other then it examined whether the ratio of the two variables was constant or not. If it was constant, the ratio of the two variables was included as a new concept in the program's memory. If it found a negative correlation between the two variables, then it examined their product.

Program BACON could apply the previous procedure many times; this principle proved to be very efficient. This way it managed to discover Kepler's third law (the squares of the revolution times of planets are to each other as the cubes of their mean distances from the sun). It discovered the Snellius–Descartes law, on the basis of which it formed the concept of refraction coefficient. In electrotechnics it discovered Ohm's and Kirchhoff's laws.

There was another rule built into BACON, namely, that it should try to consider every datum as a unit: it might perhaps turn out that other data are always its integral multiples (at least with a certain exactness). If it finds such cases, it should form a new concept from the appropriate unit. This principle also proved to be useful, as the program recognized Dalton's law and formed the concept of molecular weight.

BACON discovered no concept or relationship physicists had not known for a long time. If a child or a layman discovered them he would be considered very creative. BACON and similar artificial intelligence programs taught us an important lesson: it is probably not necessary to postulate special psychological mechanisms in explaining creative thinking.

★   ★   ★

Douglas B. Lenat's AM (Automated Mathematics) program was made to discover mathematical concepts. At the outset relatively little mathematical knowledge was built into the program: the concepts of set, equality, smaller than, greater than, union of sets and forming their common part, and a few other basic definitions. The development of new concepts was served by several rules that can be classed into two groups.

The first type of rules served to form new concepts. Every mathematical concept is defined by a formula, thus, these rules served to generate new types of formulae on the basis of the already existing concept-formulae. For example, if there is a formula for which it is easy to find numbers to satisfy, then the program should make it more special. If it is difficult or impossible to find such numbers, the program should make the formula more general. If there are two formulae that are difficult to satisfy, the program should make a new one by connecting the two by "or". If there are two easily satisfiable formulae, a new formula should be made by linking them with "and". A few dozen similar rules were included in AM.

The other type of rules evaluated whether a newly generated formula was to be considered interesting or not, and whether to be included in the existing group of concepts or not. A concept is interesting if, e.g. examples of it are not very easy to find, but not impossible, either. A concept is also interesting if the program can ask difficult questions about it. The questions of this examination are generated by the other set, the formula-generating rules.

Program AM contained no theorem-proving apparatus. Its only means of examining the concepts and relationships was testing their functioning with a lot of numbers.

Program AM included altogether 115 rules. When it was ready, its author left it to itself and waited to see what it could discover. AM found a lot of interesting concepts: it soon formed the concept of integers, then defined the four arithmetic operations and the concept of prime numbers. It arrived at the prime numbers in an interesting way: it noticed that the numbers that have three submultiples are all square numbers, then noticed that the square root of such numbers always have exactly two submultiples (1 and the number itself). Then it found the fundamental theorem of the number theory (every number can be definitely produced by the product of prime numbers). Later it also guessed Goldbach's famous conjecture (every even number is the sum of two prime numbers — this theorem has not been proven or disproven yet.)

Program AM discovered many concepts that mathematicians consider really interesting. It also created a concept that the mathematicians at Stanford University did not know, but said was quite interesting. Later it turned out that a lesser known Indian mathematician had analyzed it in several papers.

Heuristics

Program AM aimed primarily at examining the behavior of *heuristics*. The name heuristics applies to every rule, conclusion, evaluation, and principle that works in certain situations most of the time, *but not always*. The word comes from Archimedes' famous exclamation when in the bath it suddenly struck him how he could decide whether King Hieron's crown was made of real gold or not. Screaming "heureka" (I got it, I found it), Archimedes ran naked along the main street of Syracuse to make the test as soon as possible.

The realization achieved by heuristics justly make us happy, for the essence of the thing is just that we cannot be sure of the success. At every moment man applies heuristic procedures in almost all his trains of thought, as this is the only way he can act appropriately within a reasonable time without thinking over the host of possibilies with all their consequences and all the possible consequences of the consequences. Artificial intelligence cannot do without heuristics either, because thinking over all the branches of the chains of reasoning is mostly impossible even by the fastest computers.

In the case of a game of chess it is theoretically possible to count all of the chains of consequences, but let us have a look at how much work it would take. The astounding result makes it worth calculating a little. Experience shows that in an average chess situation 30 to 40 proper moves can be made. As a reply to each of the moves, the opponent could also make the same amount of moves, in turn I could also make the same amount of moves, etc. If we carry this through only through 25 pairs of moves we will have to consider at least 30^{50} cases. Suppose that each atom of the Earth is a computer that examines only chess positions and can examine one position in the time that it takes light to travel one millimeter. After some short calculation it will turn out that this rather well-developed computer would need several million years to examine so many cases.

We cannot hope to have such a computer or so much patience. This is why even artificial intelligence cannot do without concept formation and heuristics even in a well-defined area like chess.

Neumann's principle

Douglas Lenat developed program AM further in a daring and radical way. EURISKO, in addition to being able to produce concepts by using certain heuristic rules, is also able to modify its own heuristics. In order to understand how it can do it, let us go a few levels deeper and have a brief look at the essence of today's computers: why they are such efficient tools.

Hitherto we have spoken of a computer as a whole being, as a member of another species that can produce various types of behavior (although sometimes it is somewhat stupid). We were not surprised that it could conduct discussions and write snappy tales, because we are used to its writing different messages to us daily. Seeing it around us, we also know that it can do all these things with the aid of suitably made programs. We are not dealing with it in more depth, because it lies as much outside our field of interest as the question of whether a cow has an appendix or not.

The operating principle of present-day computers was introduced in practice by John von Neumann. There had been calculating machines before Neumann too. They could carry out arithmetic operations by pushing, say, four buttons. The first two button pushings indicated the two numbers to work with. The third defined where to put the result. The fourth push defined the arithmetic operation. Then the machine carried out the appropriate operation, putting the result in the defined place. And the buttons could be pushed again for the next operation. Or a separate button-pushing machine could also be built, which was told well in advance what buttons to push — the two machines together already constituted a fully automatic calculating machine.

Neumann's idea was astoundingly simple, yet it opened up radically new possibilities. The only idea was: why use two machines? The memories of the calculating and the controlling (=button-pushing) units both contained only numbers, the latter coded the places of the subsequent button pushes. In the computers based on Neumann's principle, the controlling part (i.e. the program) and all the data are located in the same memory, for they are made of the same material: they are numbers. To tell the truth, the absurdity that the program accidentally uses itself as a datum may also happen. Perhaps it may as well rewrite itself, because it says that the result of an operation should be put in a place where the code of the next button-push is placed. But, as Neumann said, let that be the programmer's problem to take care that no such oddities occur.

It was this simple principle that founded the lightning development of computer technology. It became possible to give orders not only in the simple language of pushing buttons as to what man wanted to have the computer do. Higher levels of programming languages, closer to man's way of thinking, became imaginable. The text of the programs written in a high level language is transformed by another, the so-called compiler, program into data that finally, acting as a program, carry out the procedure conceived in the higher level language. This is how programming languages developed. It is interesting that as soon as the possibility arose that man did not have to make himself understood by the computer on its direct and ponderous level of pressing buttons, he immediately created another perfect Babel. Today there are already over two thousand essentially different programming languages.

The programmers, usually, really do take care that the programs do not rewrite themselves. But program EURISKO is written so that occasionally it deliberately changes its own program. Let us skip a few levels again on our way back, omitting the technical description of how one can write a program that changes itself, how one has to write programs in LISP language (by the way: a few words are sufficient). Let us return to the level of what EURISKO does.

Program EURISKO

Certain heuristics of EURISKO work not only with formulae representing concepts, but by other heuristics as well. These special heuristics are called *metaheuristics*. One heuristic, for instance, watches the operation of the other heuristics and continuously analyzes how often and which ones lead to successful concept formation. The less successful heuristics' conditions of applications are automatically eased: the metaheuristic rewrites the part of the program that determines the problematic heuristic into one that carries out less strict examinations. EURISKO contained 244 heuristics at the beginning.

The success of the program's operation can be analyzed in two ways. It can be checked whether or not EURISKO, that operates at a much more complex level, found better mathematical concepts than the original AM. On the other hand, EURISKO can also be considered as a program that discovers new heuristics. Its heuristics change from one moment to another, as if evolutionary factors acted upon them. If a heuristic somehow does not prove viable, it will be modified mercilessly by a metaheuristic.

It is easy to answer the first question. Of the first 200 mathematical concepts created by AM, mathematicians found 125 to be really interesting. This is 62.5%. Of the next 300 concepts that AM found interesting and included in its stock, however, only 29 were accepted by mathematicians: this is less than 10%. The initial high ratio of hits decreased rapidly, the ratio of rejections increased. The heuristics that found the starting concepts of mathematics well in order were less successful in creating more advanced concepts. This is one of the reasons why Lenat found it necessary to step further to EURISKO.

Of the mathematical concepts found by EURISKO, mathematicians accepted many more as interesting. But as the number of new concepts increased, the ratio of the really interesting ones gradually decreased again. The decrease of the frequency of interesting concepts started later than in AM, but the rate of decrease was similarly fast. This means that metaheuristics proved useful, but beyond a certain level they are also unable to prevent the program creating masses of uninteresting concepts. To be sure, the route is promising: the introducton of metaheuristics resulted in a clear-cut qualitative improvement.

The other question is whether or not EURISKO discovered interesting and illuminating heuristics. This question is far more difficult. It is not so easy to ask independent experts whether a given heuristics is interesting and new, or not. In his famous book *How to Prove It* György Pólya describes dozens of time-honored heuristics but they were already taken into consideration when AM was constructed. A more important and more difficult problem is that we can hardly interpret the heuristics developed by the machine. We do not understand heuristics as we do mathematical formulae. We can easily recognize the concept of prime numbers if we see it in the form of a computer algorithm. Heuristics are handled differently in our thinking.

For example, how can a formula express Pólya's heuristic mentioned in Chapter 3: "try to mobilize new data"? Although this advice can be understood, it is not an algorithm. The most difficult part of writing program AM was to phrase this and similar heuristics in the form of rules meaningful to a computer.

And when we want to interpret the new heuristics developed by EU-RISKO, the problem is reversed: these heuristics are programs, or algorithms phrased in a sophisticated computer languauge. We are quite unable to translate them into human language — probably because they do not fit the system of our already existing concepts. Even if we understand the original, initial heuristics, their original meaning may change a lot through the "mutations" caused by the metaheuristics.

It is one of the most interesting lessons EURISKO program has taught us: it is imaginable that, if we are able to create real artificial intelligence, we will not be able to grasp or understand it by our mental abilities and system of concepts.

A logical extension of EURISKO would be to step a level higher by introducing meta-metaheuristics: programs that modify metaheuristics. Probably the program would become more tangled, but its quality would not improve considerably. At present we know of no principle that could help in planning the next level: what should meta-metaheuristics do? Artificial intelligence as a technical branch of science cannot give useful advice yet to solve this problem.

Meta-levels

The Greek prefix *"meta"* may mean several things. It may mean the change of the following word, like in metamorphosis, metabolism or metaphrase. It may also mean after, over, as in metaphor or metastasis (meaning the transfer, as of malignant cells, from one part of the body to another through the blood stream.) But it may also mean beyond, higher, as in metagalaxy or metaphysics.

It is the fourth meaning of meta that is used when the meaning of a system is colored, interpreted and modified by means outside the system. Metacommunication has this meaning, as it interprets, colors or even revises the meaning of the system of verbal communication by further forms of communication, like mimics or gestures. EURISKO's metaheuristics also referred to the other, normal heuristics, and influenced their meaning.

The expression meta-level will be used here in the latter sense. Thus, metagalaxy is not the meta-level of galaxy. because it says nothing about our galaxy, does not color or interpret its meaning, it is simply beyond galaxy. The new keys in Bach's "Canon per Tonos" are not the meta-levels of each other, because D minor is not about C minor, and does not interpret it. Stepping out into the fourth dimension at the end of Chapter 3 is not the meta-level of the original puzzle with six matchsticks, it is only a generalization.

The operation of meta-level is well-illustrated by M.C. Escher's picture *Drawing Hands*. The two hands drawing each other show clearly the phenomenon of tangled hierarchy. If the picture is examined only within the world of the picture, it will be impossible to disentangle the relationship between the two hands: the problem irremediably leads to the problem of the chicken and the egg. Still, the drawing amuses us, delights the eye, perhaps makes us wonder, but does not embarrass us. We know that in addition to the two hands there exists a designer outside the world of the picture who created all this. We can see the picture, we accept and enjoy its world because of its beauty, but simultaneously we also recognize and interpret it on a meta-level.

Gödel's theorem also talks about the classical branches of mathematics (number theory, analysis) on a meta-level. It works in a branch of mathematics whose objects are abstract mathematical objects and procedures of proof. This branch is called meta-mathematics and its results interpret classical mathematics' sphere of validity and strength of expression.

Metaphysics is not the meta-level of physics, because it is about things beyond the perceptible world and experience. Since things like that — either existent or nonexistent — fall outside the sphere of the science of physics, metaphysics is not the meta-level of physics as a science. Aristotle originally wanted to create a metaphysics that is really a meta-level of physics.

Chemistry is not a meta-level of physics either; although it examines particles studied by physics in higher-level units, it does not interpret the concepts and laws of physics — at the most it uses them. Not at all does it modify them: it is not about them. For similar reasons we cannot say that biology is a meta-level of chemistry, or that psychology is the meta-level of biology. Mathematics, however, can be considered as the meta-level of certain branches of science, but not of all of them simultaneously: each branch of natural science can use different mathematics as a meta-level. Gödel's theorem expresses just that: contrary to the several thousand-year-old belief, mathematics cannot vindicate the right of being a general meta-level of all branches of science, even in theory.

Man watches the squirming of the more stupid digger wasp from a meta-level. He presumes that a more intelligent being would have realized, at most after a few trials, that his activity got into a self-closing loop. Supposedly, a more intelligent being would be able to look at the hindered rite of egg-laying from the outside after a while and then, revising the daily routine of the activity, it would be able to find a solution with the aid of the meta-level, similar to the situation where we notice that the needle of the record player has got stuck and the same few beats are repeated several times. In this case we step out of the enchanting process of listening to the music and, intervening from the outside, fix the needle. We act similarly when we have an increasingly boring conversation with someone: we find some excuse to step out of the self-closing loop of the discussion. Boredom forces us to examine the system around us — although we are acting parts of it — also from a meta-level.

Even the smarter digger wasp is unable to do this. It could not get out of the infinite loop either; it simply had a luckier biological program, and so it did not even get into that loop. It does not understand the essence of the other digger wasp's problem, just as a person who has never been a drug addict does not really understand why another person is unable to stop or restrain reasonably his self-destructing passion. Drug addiction is a harsh example, but its lighter forms can be found daily from watching the television permanently to almost incessant family quarrels, from gambling automats to making puns.

Boredom can also be regarded as the common name of the metaheuristic which perceives that one of our heuristics got into an infinite loop (or at least it is highly probable), and then it starts to act: interprets, colors and modifies the situation.

We must have other metaheuristics as well. However, we can find certain similarities between man's and the digger wasp's behavior. Often, as a result of starting a chain of events belonging together, we get stuck in the logic and system of the chain and do not observe it from the outside any more. Mathematicians tell the following story about David Hilbert, while physicists relate the same story about André Marie Ampère: Once the scientist and his wife gave a party. After the first guest arrived, the wife drew the professor aside and told him to change his tie. The professor went upstairs but did not return even after an hour. The wife started to get worried, went upstairs and found her husband fast asleep in the bedroom. When the professor was awakened, he remembered taking his tie off, then continuing to do the habitual movements, taking his clothes off, putting on his pyjamas and going to bed.

In this story the metalevel that notices that a chain of movements is inappropriate under the given circumstances did not work. A lower-level heuristic took hold of guiding the behavior and did not let the higher-level metaheuristic take over. But if things like this can happen, can metaheuristics be considered as really of a higher level?

Our thinking produces even more complex relationships. When a painter sizes up whether he will have enough paint for his planned picture, he will be more accurate if he does not think in the sphere of his own art, but uses external methods: he will calculate square centimeters and amounts of paint per square centimeter. He will use mathematics at a meta-level for a few moments. But mathematicians also use the world of drawings and figures as a meta-level to sum up and pass on their thoughts. In this case it does not matter to them if the circle they draw looks rather like and egg and has some corners, because the basic level, the level of mathematics has long disregarded them. In our tangled hierarchy of thinking and in its strange self-closing loops it may also happen that one level is the meta-level of the other, and vice versa, the other level is the meta-level of the first one.

By the end of the first part of this book a slight conceptual confusion has arisen. Not only because we have recognized that the organization of our concepts makes tangled hierarchies, but also because several of our concepts have unpleasantly merged into one another. We have talked about the logic of things, everyday logic, formal logic, analogies, models, thoughts, concepts, heuristics. But what are they, after all? How can they be differentiated? Or is it possible that, by means of a Zen-like enlightenment, it will turn out that all these things are one and the same thing? European science still wants to know what it is that is common in them. In the following, we will try to to handle all these concepts at one common meta-level.

Tower of Babel © 1990 M. C. Escher Heirs / Cordon Art — Baarn — Holland

PART II

THE BUILDING BLOCKS OF THINKING

6. Cognitive schemata

We have seen in Chapter 1 that one does not arrive at conclusions with the aid of formal logic, even if the tools of formal logic are perfectly suited for drawing these conclusions. Instead, we get the results with the aid of analogies and typical examples or, to put it in technical terms, by the aid of mental models that fit the logic of things well. Those who have better mental models about the studied phenomena will be able to draw better conclusions; probably these conclusions could not be drawn with the help of less distinct and simpler mental models.

The concept of mental models is mostly used in cognitive psychological investigations and theories based upon the analysis of reasoning mechanisms. In other types of investigations, other aspects of the organization of thinking are stressed and given separate names. The so-called Gestalt trend in psychology concentrated upon studying perceptual processes. The terminology comes from the German phrase *Gestalt* (form, shape) *Psychologie*. Gestalt means a little more than pure form or shape — it is the result of something living, of an organization, of a kind of creation. We already know the starting point: the whole is more than the sum of its parts. Gestalt psychology concentrated upon the question: "Where is the point where the whole becomes a whole? Is it at the level of sensation, at the level of entering into memory, or only at the level of conscious thinking?"

On the basis of experiments on various illusions and on the perception of structures perceived together as a whole, Gestalt psychology arrived at the conclusion that we could find instances of reaching conclusions without studying the particular details in almost every part of the thinking process, being quite unaware of doing so. The increasingly refined Gestalt concept made it possible to recognize and to forecast a huge amount of new illusions of perception, memory and thinking, present in almost everyone, that can be easily explored.

The Gestalt trend brought something new into psychology mainly by keeping the traditional holistic attitude toward the different phenomena, while succeeding in applying the reductionist methods of investigation of the natural sciences to demonstrate and explain the phenomena.

The concept of schema

The concept of schema is used primarily by the investigators of memory. It is characteristic of the difficulties of nomenclature that in his book entitled *Remembering* F.C. Bartlett wrote the following as early as in 1932: "I strongly dislike the term 'schema'. It is at once too definite and too sketchy. The word is already widely used in controversial psychological writing to refer generally to any rather vaguely outlined theory. It suggests some persistent, but fragmentary, 'form of arrangement', and it does not indicate what is very essential to the whole notion, that the organized mass results of past changes of position and posture are actively *doing* something all the time; are, so to speak, carried along with us, complete, though developing, from moment to moment. Yet it is certainly very difficult to think of any better single descriptive word to cover the facts involved. It would be probably best to speak of 'active, developing patterns' ... I shall, however, continue to use the term 'schema' when it seems best to do so, but I will attempt to define its application more narrowly."

This is what we shall do, too. Although we will differ in "catching" and studying the phenomenon of schemata from the Bartlett and other classical schools, the notion will mean something similar to us, too. Cognitive schemata are units meaningful in themselves with independent meanings. They direct perception and thinking actively, while also being modified themselves, depending on the discovered information. Cognitive schemata have very complex inner structures, various pieces of information are organized in them by different relations. The various schemata are organized in a complex way in our brains; in the course of their activities they pass on information to each other and also modify each other continuously. This list is too dense to digest, but the meaning of the different characteristics will be gradually clarified.

Practically, we are able to notice something in our environment only if we have a schema about it. Let us mention here only one of the many striking and spectacular experiments. The experimental subjects were shown playing cards. Most of the cards were regular, but some were irregular like a red 6 of spades or a black 4 of hearts. When the cards were flashed for a very short period most of the subjects recognized the regular cards correctly, and classified the irregular ones into one of the regular groups without hesitation; e.g. they said either 6 of spades or 6 of hearts when a red 6 of spades was flashed. They did not even notice that something was wrong.

As the duration of presenting the cards was increased, the subjects became increasingly uneasy, they perceived that something was wrong, but could not tell what it was. For instance, they noticed that the frame of the 6 of spades was red, but did not spot the essence of the trick. Often they felt very embarrassed and anxious. One of the subjects put it this way: "I can't make the suit out, whatever it is. It didn't even look like a card that time. I don't know what color it is now or whether it's a spade or a heart. I am not even sure what a spade looks like. My God!" Upon further increasing the duration of presentation, the majority of the subjects suddenly started to class the irregular cards correctly, and continued to do so. Those who understood the irregular cards once or twice had no more problems afterwards. A few of the subjects, however, were unable to classify the irregular cards even in a period of time forty times longer than that needed for recognizing all of the regular ones correctly.

The moment of the development of a schema often gives the joy of sudden understanding. This feeling is also called the "aha!" reaction. The way György Horváth puts it (in a brief form): "Understanding is the organization of thoughts into a unit." We can also say: the schema is born.

There is a saying: I believe what I can see. But the reverse is perhaps even closer to the truth: we can see only what we believe. We are able to perceive whatever our schemata make possible for us. Seeing is believing. Science is no exception: this is how paradigms can guide research.

Bertrand Russell writes in his book *My Philosophical Development*: "It seemed that animals always behave in a manner showing the rightness of the philosophy entertained by the man who observes them. This devastating discovery holds over a wider field. In the seventeenth century, animals were ferocious, but under the influence of Rousseau they began to exemplify the cult of the Noble Savage. ... Throughout the reign of Queen Victoria all apes were virtuous monogamists, but during the dissolute 'twenties their morals underwent a disastrous deterioration. ... Animals observed by Americans rush about frantically until they hit upon the solution by chance. Animals observed by Germans sit still and scratch their heads until they evolve the solution out of their inner consciousness. I believe both sets of observations to be entirely reliable, and what an animal will do depends upon the kind of problem that you set before it."

Most of our schemata can be expressed in words only with difficulty. The experience of enlightenment in Buddhism is an extreme example: as we have seen in Chapter 4, the route to enlightenment leads through the continuous transcendence of words, concepts and categories. The technical exercises of Zen Buddhism (meditation, koan exercises, rituals) can also be considered as steps toward the development of schemata that are necessary to reach enlightenment.

A less extreme (though actually none the less mystic) example is when a crafty Bach fugue or Beatles song becomes a whole. They also have all the characteristics of a schema: they actively influence what we can hear in a piece of music, and they change from moment to moment as a result of our experiences — it is not the pieces that change but rather our schemata *about* them and developed *by* them. This is so much so that now we accept someone playing a piece of Bach or of the Beatles in quite another setting or instrumentation. Why should he not express his own schemata this way?

Not only those of our schemata that were created by music, painting and dance are difficult to put into words, but also those that developed in the sphere of poetry. This sounds paradoxical, for poems are made of words; yet, it is possible. Poems we do not know by heart may still act as independent schemata in us. Yet it is hopeless to paraphrase a poem and to tell it in other words. Symbols can also be considered as a special type of schemata. The role and functioning of symbols agree with the aforesaid. Good books modify some of our schemata through some of their ideas, and real masterpieces may become independent schemata in the end, and as such, are difficult to express in words.

We have even more everyday schemata that are difficult to express in words, and even then they are inaccurate. In 1768 when the *Encyclopaedia Britannica* was first issued, the editors launched the project in order to have at long last a comprehensive work in England that contained contemporary science in its full depth. Volume 1 included entries starting with letters A and B on 511 pages. Volume 2 contained entries from C to K, while Volume 3 took care of the rest. Volumes 2 and 3 had 753 pages altogether. Evidently, it is not that in the past two centuries our knowledge became more complete from C to Z; there is something else here. This story reminded D.R. Hofstadter of the early, heroic age of record production, when a so-called master-record was made and this was used to make copies of the records themselves. Often in the middle of a symphony the engineer in charge of the recording noticed that they were dangerously running out of space, so he started signalling wildly to the conductor to increase the speed, or else they would run out of space on the disc. Thus, the tempo of the music became faster and faster towards the end of the recording.

Probably everybody understands why these two stories belong together. Whenever I tell this story at my university classes, there is always somebody who exclaims "The same thing happens to me when I prepare for my exams!" Nobody is surprised at that. Most probably the joke where the grandmother says that she is knitting so fast because she is afraid that the yarn will run out also belongs here.

Do all these things belong to one schema? If they do, then this schema is not grouped around a word or an expression, but summarizes a more tangled complex of thinking that is well-known as a whole. It is also possible that we have several, closely connected schemata here. It is also possible that this whole thing covers one schema in some persons, but it does not do so in others. However, had these stories not touched upon ready schemata, the last story could not have been a joke, because it could not have suddenly flashed another aspect, would not have changed suddenly to another frame of reference.

The cornucopia of schema concepts

The investigators of the different areas of psychology, one after the other, created their own separate concepts about the cognitive units embodying the organization of thinking as studied by them. Here is a sample list of expressions, without detailed definitions, that appear regularly in literature: frame, outline, script, semantic memory unit, information chunk, cognitive structure, thinking strategy, schematic anticipation, pattern, model pattern, topos, stereotype, prototype, nuclear scene, template, fixed association, etc. But this list could be complemented by several common expressions: master stroke, trick, finesse, point, stock joke. Technical terms then start multiplying by partition as per different aspects of analysis: episodic, orientational, procedural, perceptual, personality, role, textual, historic, dynamic, relational, analytic, synthetic, causal, predicate, etc. schemata can all be found in literature.

The large amount of schema concepts resembles Brehm's great work about the animal kingdom, rather than a theory studying the basic mechanisms of thinking. There are more similarities than differences among the various notions. Still, a similar descriptive systematization may facilitate identifying the thinking phenomena that exist in real life, just as the large descriptive systems of biology have helped identify the newly discovered animal and plant species.

Darwin's discovery gave a revolutionary new foundation to biology, and radically changed our attitudes. Accepting this, the strictly descriptive systems that carry out classification on the basis of many complex aspects have not become unnecessary. Botanists still prefer Linné's system in identifying plants to the evolutionary system that discovers deeper relations, but often merges certain superficial characteristics into each other.

When we said that by the end of Part I we had arrived at a complete conceptual entanglement, we promised to attempt to handle these concepts at a common meta-level. Instead, we have seen a further abundance of technical terms. A comprehensive meta-level usually appears in a branch of science when concepts become hopelessly complex, and the puzzles that can be solved become more and more baroque in style. This phenomenon has led to the appearance of cognitive models. By the aid of these models not only the phenomena themselves can be analyzed directly, but the forms of operation that created them and more general principles can also be studied. We have seen in Chapter 4 that the analysis of models gave rise to an extremely reductionist new branch of science, i.e. cognitive science, but the less reductionist trends of cognitive psychology have also moved in the direction of building models.

7. The magic number seven

A scientist does not produce his models from thin air: he builds them on his already existing schemata. If such models have no tradition within his branch of science, he may attempt to adapt the successful models of other branches. Originally, the scholars of psychology with a scientific attitude set the example of the classical and very successful models of physics for themselves when they tried to understand human functioning through models based on experimental results.

Five hundred years ago both physics and chemistry dealt with natural abilities of flying and burning, characteristic and special organizations turning into each other. The vague and directly incomprehensible notions of ether, light corpuscles and phlogiston brought a decisive breakthrough by creating a paradigm — physicists had already a framework within which they could continue the well-organized puzzle solving called science. The existence of a paradigm makes it possible to build the different experiments and the discovery of different phenomena on each other, leading thus to questioning or even going beyond the original paradigm if necessary. We have no reason to disdain the exceeded paradigms: the phenomena recognized within the framework of the phlogiston theory led to a series of discoveries of new elements in the 18th century; the paradigms of physics that were later rejected had founded a technical revolution.

Only very serious reasons can force a branch of science to switch to another paradigm and to reject the hitherto approved, exciting, entertaining and successful ways of puzzle solving. Physics, chemistry and biology have already been through a few painful changes of paradigms; probably this is why we feel that their concepts are very settled, convincing and credible. Never in the history of psychology has a well-functioning and successful paradigm been totally rejected so far, and announced as totally erroneous in the light of a higher level paradigm.

In psychology we still often talk about particular features, peculiarities, natural abilities, characteristic and special organizations. They are practically synonyms of the fact that we have no idea of the essence of the thing, we cannot grasp the phenomena at a higher level of concepts, we fail in handling them at a meta-level determined by an appropriate organizing principle. Nowadays cognitive psychology uses the possibilities offered by computers as bases to its models. As we have seen, computer models fully harmonize even with the most extreme reductionist concepts.

The current paradigms of psychology can be regarded as first generation paradigms. This applies to the previously discussed concept of schemata, too. The concept of cognitive schemata has more qualities in common with the notions of phlogiston and ether than with the basic concepts of the paradigms of physics and chemistry today. The paradigms of the science of psychology change too, but the reason for this is rather that better constructed puzzles than the previous ones could be made up in another frame. As soon as a higher level principle, system of concepts or paradigm appears within a branch of science, expressions like natural ability, particular, characteristic and peculiar suddenly disappear from its vocabulary, and the scientists start seeing the phenomena according to the organization of the new meta-level. Readers trained in the exact sciences are probably far from finding the previous chapter satisfactorily exact. On the other hand, as the history of science shows, we have no reason to feel ashamed: let us work with what we have and let us see where a paradigm like this can lead to.

Man as an information-transmitting device

Among the many models built by cognitive psychology to describe human thinking, memory and problem solving, there was one that attempted to study man as a special device that transmits information. It might as well be regarded as such: man is really able to transmit information. Thus the model is not very absurd; furthermore, technical sciences have acquired abundant knowledge about similar devices. And why not suppose that in this way we can gain deeper insight into the phenomena of human information processing?

It was a logical starting point to measure man's capacity of information transmission, just as we can measure the transmission capacity of telephone lines and telegraph installations. Let us examine how much information man can transmit (i.e. repeat to the experimenter, or code by pressing appropriate buttons) within a given period of time. Doing such measurements, George Armitraj Miller met some unexpected phenomena.

90

If we say three words slowly, people will be able to repeat them easily. They can do it with four or five words, too. But they cannot repeat twelve. The limit is somewhere around seven. Up to this point there is nothing special, it was not more than the determination of a threshold. What is more interesting is that, within a wide range, this threshold is independent of how fast we say the words. People can repeat about seven words if they hear them at a rate of one second per word or at a rate of three seconds per word. Similar threshold values were received if not words, but different stimuli – tones of different pitch, colors or odors – had to be remembered.

Thus, if we want to examine man as an information-transmitting device we shall have to imagine a very specially constructed one. The structure includes something that is called the buffer store in technical devices. Units like this are usually applied to facilitate data transmission between devices operating at different speeds. A certain amount of information can be filled into the buffer, thus, e.g. a fast computer does not have to wait until the slower units take over all the information. Naturally, the storing capacity of the buffer is limited: if it is overfilled, some of the information will be lost.

Short-term and long-term memories

The buffer analogy is not perfect. This buffer-like store of man does not work like that of computers. As it turned out that the capacity of the buffer is about seven units of various simple stimuli (incidentally, it is surprisingly low), the question arose as to seven of what does this limit of capacity apply to.

If we say seven nonsense syllables, or perhaps letters to the experimental subjects, rather than whole words, even then we shall find this threshold to be a stable seven. In fact, if we go further and have the subjects repeat well-known idiomatic expressions or even proverbs, they will repeat about seven of them. Thus we are able to keep in our minds about seven letters (H, S, U, K, M, P, I, etc.), or seven words (table, Thames, farewell, gown, giraffe, etc.) or seven well-known sentences (To be or not to be, that is the question; Rome was not built in a day; An eye for and eye and a tooth for a tooth; Jack and Jill went up the hill to fetch a pail of water). It is an interesting phenomenon, for seven well-known sentences may contain dozens of words and hundreds of letters.

Although these results contradict the buffer analogy, they correspond well to the observation that we are able to perceive only those things that match our already existing cognitive schemata. Indeed, the results show that this buffer can contain seven units connected to our existing schemata. Expressing this with the computer analogy: we are not talking about simple data transmission, but our schemata also control the filling of the buffer.

The existing schemata are present in our heads, of course. Although we have seen that they are constantly changing and being shaped, their essential features remain stable through long periods of time. The storehouse of these schemata is called Long Term Memory, or in an abbreviated form, LTM. The buffer that can take up information either from the outer world or from LTM is called Short Term Memory, or STM. The data in STM are available to us only while we pay conscious attention to them. If we turn our attention elsewhere, or fall asleep, the information that was stored only in STM will be forgotten and lost.

It is not known exactly how the pieces of information stored in STM are preserved for a longer period, or how they find their way to LTM. We do not yet know the biological or psychological levels of these processes fully, either. Psychologically it can best be imagined that the information stored in STM for some period of time becomes a part of a schema stored in LTM, or may develop a new schema there.

This conception is backed up by various kinds of experimental results, although none of them prove it exactly. If the given information is asked to be repeated immediately or in a very short time, the experimental subjects will be able to recite it quite accurately. After a longer period of time the recited information gets more or less distorted. Our conception explains this phenomenon quite well, for our schemata are constantly changing; the last time it was just the given information that had caused some changes. In a short period the schema which was to include the new information had a fair chance of remaining unchanged, but after a longer period the probability of change was higher.

The following type of experiments can prove that time is needed to record information in LTM: the elements to be remembered are shown for a given period of time, then interfering information or tasks are given that are guaranteed to occupy STM. If the interfering task is given in less than 2 or 3 seconds, the subjects will not be able to remember any of the originally shown material; they will not be able to repeat them a few minutes later. If the interfering task is given only 6 to 10 seconds after the material to be remembered, the subjects will generally remember everything perfectly well after a few minutes.

Thus, the capacity of STM is about 7 units of information. The word "about" means that in various experiments this number proved to be 7, give or take 2. Naturally, the situation is not as simple as that. In cases of more complex schemata minus 2 holds rather true, while with simple schemata it is often plus two. The reason for this might be that when we experiment with simple schemata, such as words or letters, in the course of perception the subjects immediately have an opportunity to group two words intended to be independent in one schema; and since the existing schemata control perception, they have every possibility to do this. If, for instance, the words farewell and arms are also included in the list, those who know Hemingway's novel *A Farewell to Arms* will have the opportunity to group these words in one schema — thus the two words will take only one place in STM.

Consequently, we should not expect quite exact results, for we cannot tell what kind of ready schemata the subjects bring to the laboratory. There may be an indication of grouping according to already existing schemata if the subject repeats the words in an order that differs from the order of presentation — but it is almost impossible to find an appropriate basis for explaining such phenomena. Actually, what is surprising is the fact that, despite everything, the rule of 7, plus or minus 2, works quite steadily and well.

The two types of memory as a model

By introducing the ideas of STM and LTM, we have put forward a kind of conception about the principle of the operation of human memory. We have created a model; from now on we can interpret the phenomena of perception and memory on the basis of that model. Now we can see in a different light how we should build an explanation so that our listeners can follow us: we just have to avoid overloading their STM capacity. This is the very reason why we are unable to understand too complicated sentences.

The model based on two types of memory is specific to cognitive psychology. The presumption of such an information processing does not follow either from technical considerations or from our anatomy. It does not contradict them either, but deals with memory at a different level. It has another use as well: we apply it to solve puzzles raised by cognitive psychology.

Just like other models, this one also has a limited validity even within cognitive psychology. There are experimental results that cannot be explained within the framework of this model. For instance, arrange nine letters in a three by three square and show this to the experimental subjects. Then ask them to list the letters in the second row. The subjects almost always answer correctly to such a *single* question, whichever row we ask. But they cannot list all of the letters. Strange thing. The second part is in perfect harmony with our conception: we do expect them to fail in repeating nine letters. The phenomenon that they can repeat *any* three of them, but not all nine, is beyond our model. It cannot be explained by the hitherto simple STM–LTM model.

The above phenomenon is not special, it can be demonstrated by using many kinds of stimuli and grouping factors. Another puzzle emerged: how should our model be refined so as to explain this result, too? Accordingly, cognitive psychology has developed much more complex models of human memory than the one shown here. However, the simple STM–LTM model suits our present purposes as well. This model also explains and indicates various phenomena, its foundations probably will not be shaken soon, even if it gets refined in many ways. It is possible, of course, that the concepts of STM and LTM will have the same fate as the concepts of phlogiston and ether; they may turn out to be incidental to other basic principles and mechanisms. They might prove to be *epiphenomena*. But for the time being let us accept them as useful models, for on the present level of our knowledge they really prove to be good models.

The magic number seven is still more suspicious. Undoubtedly, often measured and very stable, this parameter really exists in this model. STM is handled in our model as if it were something that had seven pieces of some physical things, as if it were a real capacity or limit. Seven slots in memory that can be filled and that can be read: that is all we have, no more. The correct number is seven, or six or eight, and that's that.

Epiphenomena

One day anatomists or physiologists may really find seven pieces of something in our brains, and it will become clear what STM really is. However, I do not think it is likely to happen. Not because a discovery like that would open up incalculable vistas: how smart we could become if a surgeon could plant a few more of them into our brains! I deem it improbable because I think that, similar to STM itself, this number seven is *really* an epiphenomenon: it is incidental to the organization of our thinking.

Here is an example to illuminate this statement. There exists an unpleasant phenomenon called deadlock in computer networks: the central unit of a network is connected to, say, a hundred working stations — they are not used simultaneously anyhow, but let us have them everywhere, so as not to have to look for them. But the connection of each new station slows down the system, and not even proportionally. The network's response time starts increasing sharply after a certain point. While, say, 37 stations are switched on, everyone can work comfortably, but when a 38th is switched on, the response time will become intolerably long for everyone.

We can justly say that the capacity of this system is 37 stations, but there is no direct physical unit or parameter in the system that would be responsible for this number. Otherwise the engineers would have exchanged it for 100 a long time ago. Number 37 is the result of the construction of the whole system, not caused by any one part. It was not even designed to be exactly 37. The task of calculating the exact limit of deadlock in advance would probably have required a more complex scientific research than that of designing the whole system itself.

Naturally, in order to understand the network completely, one would have to know all its principles of planning, and the number 37 would only be its epiphenomenon, although the answer to "Why 37?" might still be a very catchy puzzle. But in order to understand the function, operation and habits of the system at considerable depths, it is sufficient to know that, due to some (let us say, physical) reasons, the capacity of the network is 37, it cannot operate with more stations than that.

Even the fact that we have five fingers on our hands is worth pondering over. Occasionally people are born with six fingers, but had it been more efficient, this mutation would long have become general. Regarding fingers, it is also probable that it is an incidental consequence of a higher system of organization (i.e. our whole system of locomotion) that the number of fingers we have on one hand is exactly five. It is conceivable that with four fingers we would be much clumsier, while to coordinate six fingers would require the whole system of locomotion to be much more complex, thus less stable and more susceptible to injury. This, of course, is not a scientific explanation yet: you may find more convincing explanations if you wish.

I doubt that the STM–LTM model outlined above, or its more refined variations, will be the last words science has to say about the investigation of thinking. In fact, I am convinced it is not. Still, I consider the development of this model a great advancement. It creates excellent puzzles for us that look solvable, and their solution seems to be instructive. Let us just continue to imagine STM as a physically existing something with a limited capacity of seven. It is almost certain that we shall get further this way than by just speculating at random. We have a paradigm that can guide us. Maybe the key does not lie here (cf. page 41) — but under this light we are not searching blindly.

8. Some tens of thousands of schemata

How many schemata do we have in our minds? At first it seems nonsense to ask such a concrete and quantitative question about a concept that so far cannot be shown in exact examples or defined exactly. How on earth can something be counted or even estimated if we do not even know what it is? At first the question seems to resemble that of how many angels can stand on the tip of a needle.

The situation is not as hopeless as that. Things have consequences, and we can learn something from them. We can estimate quite accurately how many deer there are in a forest even if we have never seen a living deer before. We may know how often deer defecate and how fast their feces decompose in Nature. With this knowledge and after walking for a day or two in the forest we can estimate how many deer live there.

Starting hypotheses

Where could we possibly find countable consequences of the existence of schemata? We are going to set out from three hypotheses. If everything goes well, we shall see that (in an appropriately designed experiment) they may be sufficient to give an approximate estimate about the quantity of schemata. Here they are:

(a) Only those schemata can be stored in STM that have had corresponding schemata in LTM previously.

(b) Only seven schemata can be stored in STM at the most.

(c) In order to maintain the schemata (stored in STM) for a longer period, a certain minimal period of time must pass.

The validity of hypotheses (b) and (c) have been analyzed previously. Hypothesis (a) can also be considered as a kind of definition of schemata: A schema is what we can store in our STMs. Many signs tend to support that whole schemata are stored in STM. This conception gives a uniform explanation to different experimental results of learning, recognition and recall. (Naturally, we should be able to interpret the complicated characteristics of schemata described in Chapter 6, according to this definition as well.)

Condition (a) says nothing about the feature that schemata would constantly change. It might also be possible that a schema, just by having entered STM, will be modified in LTM in certain cases. However, we will want to catch only a momentary state and will not have to mind whatever happens to the schemata in the moments before or after. By all probability, no radical change occurs very fast, especially in the number of schemata, but that will not affect our next train of thought.

The schemata stored together in STM did not constitute a separate schema before, or it would not have been necessary to load STM with several schemata but sufficient to load it with only that one. If certain schemata appear together in STM, this group or parts of it may become a separate new schema. Thus, quite complex schemata may develop.

A recall experiment with chess players

We are going to examine how many chess-related schemata a chess player may have in his head. There are many reasons for studying just chess players. One of the reasons is that on the basis of competition results we can judge quite accurately how well the studied persons can play chess. It can be expected that the better a chess player is, the more schemata he will carry in his head to the laboratory. Another reason is that chess is quite an exact area, thus the meaning of the given experimental task can be well described. Furthermore, chess is quite complex, thus it can have real grandmasters who play chess much better than normal mortals. The third reason is that competence in chess is quite separated from other abilities, and studies on chess have produced results that can be generalized well and on the basis of which some conclusions reaching far beyond the special field of chess can be drawn.

Imagine the following experiment. The experimental subject is shown a chess position for 2 or 3 seconds. (For example, we project it on a screen.) Subsequently, we also project a nonsense picture. This way the subject will not be able to keep and use against our intentions the afterimage of the projected picture, but will not forget what remained in his STM immediately either, because the nonsense picture will not burden his STM. Then we ask the subject to reconstruct the position seen in the picture on an empty chess board. This is a typical *recall experiment* to the interpretation of which the STM–LTM model offers a new perspective.

Let us imagine for a moment that under the conditions of the recall experiment the studied subject could recall *every* chess position perfectly. Just imagine the consequences regarding the amount of schemata he knows.

The subject could reconstruct the position only on the basis of the schemata in his STM, because due to the shortness of time he could store nothing in his LTM before the flash of the disturbing figure was shown, and could use even afterwards only what he had in his STM, because later he received no more information. (We make use of condition (c) here). Although choosing the schemata stored in STM could have been influenced by the schemata of LTM, the point is that no new information could be stored in LTM during such a short period.

Only 7 schemata could be present in STM at the most (here we make use of condition (b)), thus seven schemata were sufficient for our imaginary subject to reconstruct everything perfectly. Consequently, our subject must have had at least as many schemata in his LTM as to form different groups of seven schemata for each chess position. (Here we make use of condition (a): the functioning of STM is connected to the schemata of LTM.) If the imaginary subject had had less schemata, we could find two different chess positions to which he would not find two different groups of schemata that consist of 7 schemata at the most. The subject would necessarily make a mistake in reconstructing one of the positions, for he could not distinguish between the two positions in the course of reconstruction.

Thus, the number of ways of choosing seven schemata from the LTM of the subject must be greater than the number of all possible chess positions. "This is the reason of every self-torture and song," as the professor of mathematics, Pál Turán, liked to cite the Hungarian poet Ady when he was over the most difficult part of a complicated train of thought, reached a resting point and only had to score the points. The above statement is a resting point: nothing special can be seen yet, but we are over the hardest part. We have arrived at an inequality: one side depends only on the number of schemata known by the subject, the other side equals the number of possible chess positions.

The number of possible chess positions can be estimated in several ways. If every disallowed position is taken into consideration too, we only have to calculate the number of ways 32 chess pieces (or some of them) can be placed on the board. This will be an astronomical number, but poses no theoretical problem. If we want to consider only the positions that can really be created by real games, the method described on pages 72–73 will prove suitable. Thus, the task can be solved. This way we have received an inequality that expresses the minimum number of schemata present in the LTM of the subject. For those who understand formulae better: $\binom{N}{7} > M$, where N is the number of schemata present in the head of the person who reconstructs every position perfectly, and M is the number of all possible chess positions to be counted.

Thus our three starting hypotheses give a *theoretical* possibility in the case of the recall experiment to get at least a minimum estimate of the number of chess-related schemata in the subject's head. We said "theoretical", because our train of thought works only if the studied person can reconstruct *all* of the positions perfectly. The examination of chess players proved to be especially lucky, because similar achievements could be reached only by grandmasters, albeit they could do it only under certain conditions.

Estimates of the number of schemata

Two factors played important roles in the degree of success in reconstructing the seen positions by the subjects of the recall experiment. One of the factors was the subjects' level of competence in chess, the other was the type of positions shown. In the case of positions taken from master games, there was a clear-cut correlation between the level of chess competence of the studied subjects and the quality of reconstruction. In this case grandmasters recalled practically 100% of all the chess positions perfectly. In cases of positions taken from amateur games, the correlation was still high: the better a subject was, the better was his recollection; however, in this case even grandmasters made mistakes sometimes.

In similar situations the results may give a lead to the investigators: they tried to make the situation more extreme. There were experiments where the subjects were asked to reconstruct totally meaningless chess positions. In these positions the number of pieces was the same as in the meaningful ones, but the place of a given piece was decided by throwing a dice. The only care the investigators took was not to contradict the basic rules of chess (e.g. no pawn was allowed in the first row). Well, in these experiments there was no difference between the reconstruction performances of the subjects as a function of their level of chess competence.

Both grandmasters and weak amateurs could recall about seven pieces correctly.

So the "magic" number seven has popped up again. In cases of nonsense positions, the schemata available to grandmasters could not be other than the pieces themselves. In cases of positions taken from master games, it followed from the logic of the position that large structures could be grasped by a single schema, especially by competent grandmasters. The positions taken from amateur games constituted an intermediate situation. In a master's game every piece has a role and a meaning; in amateur games it is frequent that the actual situation of some of the pieces is indifferent.

As a start let us say that if we limit the experiment to presenting positions taken only from master games, then grandmasters and only grandmasters will behave as our previous imaginary subject: they will be able to recall all of the positions correctly. (For the sake of precision let us just note that the experimental positions were taken from the midgame phase and usually contained 20–25 pieces.) In order to give a lower estimate of the number of schemata grandmasters have, all we should know now is the number of possible positions in master games.

This can also be estimated by the method described in pages 72–73. We should know two things to apply the method. (*1*) How many moves does an average chess game have? (*2*) How many moves does a master consider possible at his level? It is easy to answer the first question: the positions shown in the experiment developed after 20–25 pairs of moves, or after 40–50 plies. To answer the second question, it is best to ask masters. On the average, masters consider 1.8–2 moves as meaningful in a position. In some positions this number may be higher, in others there is no alternative at master level. (It is interesting that even good amateurs think that more, on the average about 4–5, moves can be potentially played in a position.)

All we have to do now is perform the calculation. If you feel like it, you may calculate it as an amusement, or as an exercise for your brains or in order to understand it better — it will not be very difficult. The result will be that grandmasters know at least several thousands of schemata. This estimate is guaranteed to be a lower one: in reality, it is a rough estimate because we assumed that *any* seven schemata are suitable for recalling a meaningful chess position. Evidently, this is not so, for a chess player may know several schemata to characterize, e.g. only the white king side positions — of which only one can become active in a given position.

It is even more important that we had assumed in our calculations that all of the schemata occurred with equal probability in the course of reconstructions. We might give more realistic assumptions about the schemata's frequency of occurrence, i.e. we might take the fact into consideration that there are more and less frequent chess schemata, just as there are more and less frequently used words. With assumptions like this, the calculation requires some more complicated mathematical apparatus, but it is not impossible. As a result, we will get an estimate that is greater by an order of magnitude. This is naturally no longer a guaranteed lower estimate, but because of the point mentioned in the previous paragraph it is still a lower estimate by all probability.

It follows from the aforesaid that it seems to be realistic to estimate the number of schemata of a grandmaster of chess to be about a few tens of thousands, or about 50,000 to 100,000. We are going to show another method of estimation, based on a different principle, in Chapter 10.

The quantity of schemata of grandmasters in other professions

Our train of thought to estimate the quantity of schemata can be applied to the examination of other professions as well. Our three starting hypotheses (essentially the STM–LTM model) are valid in any field, and it is quite accidental that chess positions were shown in the previous experiments. The most important requirement (not easy to secure) is the possibility to estimate the whole amount of objects that can be shown in reality. This does not pose unsolvable problems in board games; in studying other fields, however (e.g. film scenes or tunes), estimation is very difficult if not impossible. In the game of go the number of schemata is similar to that in chess, although in go even grandmasters are unable to perfectly recall very complicated positions.

The research with chess was started by the Nobel laureate Herbert A. Simon in 1973. Simon studied the mechanisms of human decision making (and their effect on economic decisions), and for a model he analyzed the decisions of chess players. The foundations of the discovery were made possible by the lucky fact that the best chess players, but only the best players, could recall positions with 100% accuracy. With the aid of complicated mathematical methods, we can arrive at useful estimates even if performance is less than 100%, as in the cases of second class chess players or go players.

The estimate of the number of schemata grandmasters of chess have is about the same as the number of words and phrases used by the best authors and poets, which is also estimated to be several tens of thousands. The total number of Chinese writing characters also fall in this range: it is about 80,000. Only the best specialists (we can say, grandmasters) of Chinese writing know and can actively use most of that total. The best entomologists (experts in the study of insects) can distinguish about 50,000 insects. An insect is probably a complex schema for a grandmaster of entomology. The situation is similar with scholars of the different fields of botany.

These coincidences are quite remarkable, to say the least. Naturally, they might be the results of mere coincidence, or can be considered number mysticism. Still, the generalization that in most professions several tens of thousands of schemata are necessary to reach the level of grandmaster seems to be quite probable.

9. Some tens of thousands of what?

Our model proved to be suitable to give an estimate of the number of schemata, but said precious little about what these schemata could be. To tell the truth, it does not matter very much: every model necessarily makes simplifications and can grasp only some of the essential characteristic features of the phenomena. From the aspect of aesthetics, however, our model is very elegant: it is built on the simplest basic variation of the STM–LTM idea and sets out from three, quite justified and not very complex basic assumptions (let us say, from three axioms).

With our everyday attitude we tend to believe that axioms are fundamental truths, unquestionable and guaranteed to be valid. Axioms are really fundamental truths in given scientific theories, yet they can be false as well. They are used as starting points: we need some solid grounds we will not question in the course of thinking, analysis or debate; this way we will not have to return to the starting point all the time and can proceed on our way. Later, seeing where our way leads, we can return to examine the starting axioms as well.

In Chapter 3 we mentioned the principle of Occam's razor at the discussion of the characteristics of well-designed scientific problems. The following story is a nice example of how the principle works: when the first volumes of Laplace's book entitled *Mechanics of the Sky* was published, Napoleon remarked that although Laplace spoke about the sky on hundreds of pages, God could not be found in it anywhere. "I did not need that hypothesis, Sire!" Laplace replied. We should add that Laplace was a deeply religious man who had wanted to become a clergyman in his youth.

Hitherto we have developed our train of thought fully in the spirit of Occam's razor: we succeeded in giving an estimate of the number of schemata by using as few hypotheses as possible. By now, however, it would be nice to know more about the structures and characteristics of schemata. It is also painfully too little for the scholars of artificial intelligence, if we only say that they will have to get prepared to design and organize a few tens of thousands of something, but we do not even attempt to learn anything more about what these tens of thousands of something could be.

Regardless of whether schemata are physically seizable units or not, at the present level of our knowledge it is better to treat them as if they were really existing separate things. At the back of our minds we may still consider it conceivable that schemata are also only epiphenomena of the deeper levels of thinking, similar to STM and the magic number 7. Still, let us follow Laplace in not hypothesizing anything that is not necessary for developing our train of thought until it becomes absolutely necessary.

The schemata of chess players

Herbert Simon and his colleagues originally thought that the schemata stored in the STM of chess masters are simply parts of chess positions, smaller and greater characteristic structures that often occur in master games. Characteristic positions to defend the king, frequently occurring pawn-structures or groups of pieces in a typical attack–defence situation may serve as examples. (Program MAPP, to be shown in Chapter 10, is based on this idea.)

This simple conception avoids the actual essence of the schema-concept of cognitive psychology. There is nothing in it about schemata being independently meaningful units, or about both the inner structure of schemata and the organization among schemata being very complicated. A part of a position means nothing by itself, just as a chess piece is meaningless if it is taken out of the environment of the given position. A chess position is more than the sum of its pieces or the sum of its typical parts. A position has "a soul"; the players have ideas, thoughts and plans concerning the whole position. They are aiming at something, enter into their opponents' ideas, are making attacks and defending themselves. They use very simple and very complex schemata simultaneously.

A chess pawn may appear in our schemata in several contexts. In certain typical positions it is known that the main issue of the game is whether the pawn proves to be strong or weak. In cases like this the pawn is part of a complex schema where the schema is not simply a part of a position but may be the whole conceptual world and strategic content of a given opening. In other cases the role of a pawn may be simple, e.g. at the end of a great battle of giving and getting that can be calculated in advance the player will end up having one more pawn than his opponent, which will be enough for victory in the simplified position. In this case only the number of pawns, i.e. only the pawn itself counts. In this case a pawn is represented only as a very, very simple schema in our thoughts.

Young chess players soon learn the expressions "Sicilian defense" or "King's gambit". For beginners, these concepts cover very simple schemata, a series of a few moves at the beginning of the game. For grandmasters these expressions mean more complex schemata, i.e. typical plans of attacking and defense, ideas characterizing the conception of the actual opening. These ideas might as well form independent schemata also, but are parts of the general schema of a certain opening, too. Grandmasters know not only more schemata than amateurs, but their schemata and the organization among their schemata are also more complex. The schemata of grandmasters form complicated, tangled hierarchies.

Although the model used for quantitative estimation has not touched such subtleties, it has not excluded them either. Our model can bear the assumption that there can be both very simple and very complex schemata among the 7 stored in STM, and they can even interpret each other. Any kind of tangled hierarchy can be imagined in the model — the course of calculation still works: it gives an estimate of the total amount of simple and complex schemata, including the meta-schemata expressing the organization of schemata.

Schemata and memory

Our result that the grandmasters of chess (and probably of other professions as well) know about some tens of thousands of schemata regarding their field remains faultless as long as we stay strictly within the frame of our model. But as soon as we try to interpret our results with the aid of our other concepts coming from outside the model, and which are related to thinking and memory, we may get into trouble.

How many concrete facts can a person remember? And anyway, how many concrete facts of chess can a grandmaster remember? Garry Kasparov states he can freely recall a few tens of thousands of games. Everything indicates that this is true. Calculating with 40 pairs of moves in each game — this is about a few millions of concrete positions — and Kasparov knows each of them. If, for instance, we tested Kasparov's memory with the question "What was the position after the 25th move in the game played by Botvinnik and Capablanca at the AVRO competition in 1938?"

he would give the correct answer after thinking a short while. We could note that he knows this fact too; one up to his memory.

Can we say now that Kasparov stores a few millions of chess positions in his memory? Yes, we can; but this reply only states a very static and a rather uninteresting fact, because it says nothing about how these positions are organized in his memory. Yet, organization is more important than the concrete data. Again, the whole is more than the sum of it parts. We would not be better off if we determined the exact number of games known by Kasparov. It is almost certain that games are not the units of his memory: a group of games with similar strategic contents may form one complete schema. Furthermore, the most important thing in a game is not what is seen on the board: it is the unfulfilled plans and the variations warded off that mean the real depth of the fight. Evidently, all this is present in the memory of the grandmaster, but it is utterly impossible to measure.

The independent units of memory can say very little about the role of memory traces in thinking. Memory traces are organized into thinking by schemata, we can recall them only with their aid. Memory geniuses have always organized the things to be remembered into some larger units and later, upon recalling, they could rely on them.

Alexandr Luria studied a memory genius for decades. Once, without previous notice, Luria asked him to repeat a long series of words he had heard 15 years before. The memory genius closed his eyes, paused, then said: "yes, yes ... This was a series you gave me once when we were in your apartment ... You were sitting at the table and I in the rocking chair ... You were wearing a grey suit and you looked at me like this ... Now, then I can see you saying..." — and then he reproduced the list of words perfectly — on the basis of the holistic picture as he had stored it a long time before.

In cases of memory geniuses it is useless to calculate separately how many words, numbers or signs they have memorized in their lives. Each set of data memorized together becomes an independent schema in their heads, but the number of these schemata remain within the range of a few tens of thousands. Luria's memory genius used visual schemata; it is a successful memorizing system used for ages. Ancient Egyptian priests already used the so-called *method of loci* (loci is Latin for "places") to remember long lists. The items to be remembered were mentally placed with different objects in a well-known place with a complex structure (e.g. in the temple); this way they could keep the whole list in their heads —

the well-known structure of the place helped to organize the long list into a single schema.

Other non-visual methods are also suitable in helping to organize long series of data into a few schemata, thus promoting recalling. Ericsson and his colleagues had their experimental subject, SF, practice to memorize lists of numbers 3–5 hours a week for a year and a half. SF was a college student of average intelligence and a devoted long distance runner. He could remember 7 digits at the beginning of the experiment, just like most people. In the course of practice SF grouped the numbers into time-results; e.g. he memorized 3492 as "3:49.2 — near world-record time for the mile." SF knew the running times of a lot of distances (he had a lot of schemata of them), and in the course of practice he learned to make groups of four of the digits he heard into time results. Occasionally, when no time result could be made (e.g. 3771) he tried to recode them into ages and dates. The investigators wanted SF to learn other organizing principles as well, therefore they deliberately gave him series that could hardly be grouped into time results. These series were produced by a specially written computer program. Interestingly, near the end of the the experiment the computer correctly guessed in 90% of the cases what strategy of grouping SF would use for the memorization of the next series. 62% of the groups continued to be organized according to time results, 25% were based on ages, the rest were grouped by other principles (e.g. dates).

This way SF managed to become reliable in repeating 26–28 numbers correctly. (About seven times four.) Here his performance stagnated for a while, then improved further: at this point he started grouping the individual time results into results of whole competitions. Later he grouped them together with dates. When he suceeded in this, he could sum up 12–16 four-digit numbers into the results of a single competition. He could increase his memory span to 79 digits in a year and a half. (The experiment was organized so that if he could recall all of the numbers of at least 80% of the series, the series got one digit longer the next day — if he failed, they were shortened by a digit. At the close of the experiment the length of the series varied between 78 and 80.)

At the end of the experiment SF was given letters, instead of numbers. SF could recall only seven of the letters — similar to the numbers at the beginning of the experiment!

It is possible that the concept of schema is not defined exactly enough, and it is also doubtful if objects like this exist at all. Still, the paradigm of schemata proved to be very useful, because it facilitated the design of

108

such witty experiments and the construction of models suitable to give quantitative estimates. We shall continue — and do so more and more — to build theories and plan experiments as if schemata were real, physically existing building blocks of our thinking.

10. A challenge for programmers

The challenge is to have the computer perform the recall task regarding chess positions described in Chapter 8. Naturally, this task is not interesting at all for the usual means of computer programming: once we have entered the chess position into the memory of the computer, there will be no reason at all for the computer to forget it. But we want to have a program that can recall chess positions in accordance with our knowledge about schemata and the structure of memory. Let us phrase the task more exactly.

The problem has three parts. First, let us teach a certain amount of schemata to our computer. These schemata can be simple parts of chess positions, but they can all be individual programs as well. Since in computers based on Neumann's principle the programs and data are essentially the same, every schema can also be regarded as a program.

The second part of the problem is to write a program that "perceives" chess positions. Thus, this program receives a chess position as an input (of course, the input is not visual, it is coded appropriately), and gives the output as naming seven schemata (or their serial numbers).

The third part of the problem is to make a reconstructing program. The input of this part is the seven schemata given by the second part. They name the seven schemata-programs to be used for recalling. The output of this part will be a chess position. Thus, the reconstructing program does not know the original position, only the seven numbers indicating the schemata determined by the second part. It has the same information as our brains in the recall experiment: nothing else but the seven schemata are available.

The problem offers a practically unlimited freedom to programmers as to the types of programs that would serve as schemata, as to the way of choosing the seven numbers corresponding to the seven schemata from the chess position, and as to organizing the cooperation of the seven schemata to reconstruct the position. The problem seems to be too general at first, but we shall soon see that it is not. For minds trained in mathematics, the first thought is probably why not use every possible chess position as a separate schema; after all, there is a finite number of chess positions. We could number all of the chess positions once and for all. Then the "perceiving" part can determine which position is seen, and give this single number to part three (it does not even need seven numbers). Finally, the reconstructing program finds the position listed under the received number — the solution will certainly be perfect. Naturally, this is a possible way — but we will need an astronomical number of schemata.

Let us reveal now the essence of the challenge. Let us try to solve the problem by using as few schemata as possible. Thus, the task in the competition is to write a program that orders seven numbers from 1 to N to each chess position (this is the "perceiving" program), and on the basis of these seven numbers reconstruct positions taken from *games played by masters* as accurately as possible. The winner is the one who can achieve the reconstruction of the original position perfectly all the time with the smallest N value.

The significance of the problem

In the latter phrasing there is no word about schemata, it seems to be a simple problem of coding. However, we have practically made the condition of using N number of schemata at the most; for each of the seven numbers may code a separate sub-program or part of a position. The N number of schemata model LTM in the problem, while the seven numbers given to the reconstructing program stand for STM.

We have allowed schemata to be not only simple parts of positions but any program as well, so that any complex structure of schemata could be expressed within the frame of the problem. Should there be very complex schemata among our cognitive schemata, let us not force the author of the program to use simple and predetermined kinds of schemata (e.g. only details of chess positions).

Now the problem closely models the conditions of the recall experiment as selected for the STM–LTM model. It gives a practically unlimited freedom to the programmers in choosing the method of solving the three parts of the problem. We know very little exactly about how this part works in reality. Grandmasters know about 50,000 to 100,000 schemata, and are capable of practically perfect reconstructions. Thus, the problem can surely be solved with the aid of this number of schemata, but we do not know how. We are going to outline the functioning of a program that would be expected to solve the problem with the aid of about 360,000 schemata; hitherto this is the best result. But surely, there is also a solution with a few tens of thousands of schemata, because chess grandmasters produce it. Thus the problem is a well-designed scientific puzzle within the extremely reductionist paradigm of cognitive science.

The trickiest trick of the problem is that it applies only to positions taken from master games. Therefore, programs that use only condensed codes based on purely mathematical principles do not have much of a chance: how could they make use of the characteristics of *meaningful* chess positions? Therefore, the given problem is typically that of *artificial intelligence*, rather than that of mathematical coding theory. It would be an evident waste to find a solution that could also reconstruct meaningless positions, for a program like that would be able to reconstruct a whole lot more of chess positions than the number of positions that may occur. The absolute majority of the possible chess positions are nonsensical.

Theoretically, it is possible to solve the problem without making use of meaning, just by mathematical maneuvers, but it is highly improbable. It can be calculated that if the problem were about all the possible chess positions (not only about the meaningful ones), several billions of schemata would be necessary; less than that would certainly not be enough.

The problem rightfully counts on the interest displayed by cognitive psychology as well, not only on that of artificial intelligence — in fact it was actually raised within the framework of cognitive psychology. Certainly, if our concept about STM and LTM were different, the problem would also have been raised differently. Every solution to the above problem of a reconstruction program that works can be automatically considered as a schema theory. Although it is possible that quite strange things play the role of schemata in the solution (e.g. complex mathematical constructions or concepts totally alien to our normal way of thinking — like the mutant heuristics of EURISKO), it is more probable that the role of schemata will be played by something that resembles our schema concept. The problem is an exciting challenge exactly because the way to the solution will probably lead, not through some complex abstract mathematical construction, but through the development of well-invented operating principles.

112

Program MAPP

The schemata in Simon and Gilmartin's program are all parts of chess-positions. The name of the program (Memory Aided Pattern Perceiver) also indicates the attempt of the authors to model human visual perception as well.

MAPP contained hundreds of chess position details that the authors considered characteristic and frequent on the basis of either their own chess expertise or chess books. The determination of the chess position details was so successful that MAPP did well in modeling the eye-movements of chess players when they were first shown a position. The eye-movements of the experimental subjects can be traced either by complex mirror systems or by electrodes recording the movements of the muscles of the eyes. Sometimes MAPP predicted the movements of the subjects' eyes accurately for seconds. Naturally, MAPP knew nothing about what went on in the subjects' heads, just as DOCTOR understood nothing of the patients' problems.

In the recall task, the perceiver component of MAPP searched for the seven schemata that best fitted the presented chess position. Then the reconstructing program placed the seven position details on the chess board. When some of the position details conflicted with each other, a few simple heuristics decided what to put on the board.

There were two versions of MAPP. The first version included 894 schemata, and the quality of reconstruction approached that of a second class amateur chess player. In the second version the number of schemata was increased to 1144: this way the level of second class players could be surpassed a little. Increasing the number of schemata further meets difficulties, because it is less and less easy to find really characteristic position details. In order to develop the program further, it would probably not be sufficient any more to have simple parts of positions play the role of schemata, and more complex schemata would be required.

According to calculations, if the relationship between the increase in the number of schemata and the qualitative improvement of reconstruction is extrapolated, the program will be expected to reconstruct the positions perfectly with the aid of about 360,000 schemata in cases of chess positions taken from master games. This number is much higher than the estimate given in Chapter 8. But MAPP works only with very simple schemata (details of positions), certainly more of which are needed for perfect recognition than more complex ones. Taking this into consideration, the result obtained from working with MAPP also makes it probable that grand-masters of chess know about 50,000 to 100,000 (mostly quite complex) schemata.

Relying on MAPP, we can also get an estimate of how many chess-related schemata a chess player would know at a lower level. As we have seen, MAPP could reach the performance level of second class players' recalling with the aid of about 1000 schemata. Probably MAPP needed significantly more schemata to reach the same performance than humans, although the difference might be less, because the schemata of moderate amateurs are not as complex as those of masters. On the basis of the above it seems realistic to estimate the number of second class amateurs' schemata at a few hundred. On a similar basis, the stock of candidate masters' schemata, according to the Hungarian qualifications, could be estimated at about 1000 to 5000. In the next chapters you will see that the level of candidate master is an important milestone of development in most professions.

11. From beginners to grandmasters

We have seen that in a given chess position grandmasters regard less moves as meaningful and worth considering than amateurs. As we have quoted S. Suzuki in Chapter Zero "In the beginner's mind there are many possibilities, but in the expert's there are few."

It also turned out in experiments with grandmasters that, on the average, they do not calculate longer combinations than amateurs. Thus, the popular belief that masters of chess are masters of chess because they make excellent combinations is not correct. Perhaps they do so in some cases, but generally they do not. Rather, they perform calculations at better moments of the game than amateurs: they know when they have to calculate exactly. At other times, when amateurs try to make combinations, masters choose a general plan and a move fitting the plan without exact calculations.

Grandmasters do not even make the decisions faster than amateur players. If grandmasters and amateurs are told to have a good look at a chess position, consider it carefully and then choose a move, then even in the case of a moderately complicated position they will make their decision within about the same time, about 5–10 minutes.

Generally no differences with well-formulated, simple indicators could be found between amateurs and grandmasters, except for the quality of their game. Grandmasters are able to play games with 20–30 strong amateurs simultaneously, and mostly they win, about 90% of the time. In cases like this, grandmasters have only a few seconds to make each move, have no time to consider long and complicated combinations. Their opponents, however, have 2 to 3 minutes to make each move; nevertheless, they lose mostly.

We already know that this great difference in playing strength between grandmasters and amateurs means that the former have about ten times more schemata than the latter. With this knowledge we have no reason to be surprised at finding no differences in directly measurable parameters or that grandmasters are not faster and do not make combinations further in advance but they simply make better moves. The differences in the quantity and quality of the schemata offer a more profound explanation to such famous golden rules like "grandmasters know more about chess", or "for them there is nothing new under the sun".

The procedure of becoming a grandmaster

The tens of thousands of schemata necessary for the playing strength of grandmasters is learnt by long and intensive practice. This process requires at least ten years of several hours of daily engagement. Even the famous prodigies (Capablanca, Fischer, the Polgár sisters) were no exception to this. We have also seen that most of our schemata can hardly be expressed by words. This is true of chess, too. Beyond a certain level, even the best textbooks can only help the students to have an intuition of the general notions and the relations among them, hidden in the examples. This is the reason why it was so difficult to increase the number of schemata in the program MAPP after a while. At around one thousand schemata, the master writing the program reached the limit where he could express his schemata; after this point it was difficult for him to say something new at the level of position details. Being a master he probably still had a vast amount of further schemata, but could not express them at that level.

It is true of other professions as well that about ten years of intensive learning is necessary to become a grandmaster. For instance, Mozart was a famous prodigy: he composed interesting pieces of music at as early as 5 or 6 years of age. Still, if you have a look at the collection of all Mozart records (the Schwann catalogue), you will see he composed the first piece of music of which at least five different recordings were made only when he was over 16. In the case of a Mozart, the juvenile efforts are justly considered interesting (just think of the opera *Bastien and Bastienne* that he composed at 12), but evidently he composed real masterpieces only when he was over 16, after more than ten years of intensive learning and practice.

The situation is similar in the other professions where grandmasters mature early, e.g in mathematics or poetry. A kind of hierarchy can be set up according to the average age when the best of them reach the level of grandmasters. Physicists generally mature later than mathematicians, biologists mature still later, then come the painters, novelists, physicians and politicians. In the case of the sciences, this phenomenon can be well demonstrated if we take a look at the ages when the degree of B.Sc. is awarded to scholars of different branches of science.

It is probable that slower maturation within a profession depends on the nature of its schemata: usually, the less abstract a profession, the slower its students mature. The reason for this is that in this case the schemata of the profession are more closely related to the schemata of everyday life, but (just because of the professional nature of the trade) they are abstracted from them; thus in these professions the level of grandmasters may be the result of the co-maturation of two parallel processes of learning (a human and a professional process).

The level of candidate masters

The level of candidate masters is an important watershed in the development of chess players. We already know that candidate masters have about a few thousand chess-related schemata. This level is sufficient to win against inexperienced players of whatever talent, and is also sufficient to understand the depths of the games played by grandmasters. But it is not sufficient to have the slightest chance of winning against a grandmaster.

We have seen that the amount of schemata is very closely related to the level of expertise. In fact, this is a very sensitive index by which we can demonstrate differences of orders of magnitude between the different levels of expertise. Therefore, the following *generalization* seems to be meaningful: in every profession the level where a person has about a few thousand schemata related to that profession should be called *the level of candidate master*. Hopefully, this generalization will lead to a lucky concept formation, and what we have said about the virtues and shortcomings of the candidate masters of chess will prove more generally valid.

Thus, the amount of knowledge a person has in a foreign language may be considered to be at the candidate master level if he can successfully pass the medium level state examination in that language. This can be backed by the fact that an average person can reach this level in about 3–4 years (4–6 periods of 45 minutes a week with average learning at home). It is a general observation of language teachers that about 7 new words can be taught effectively in a 90-minute session. As many as 30 words can be assigned, but even if the student can reproduce all of them, he will not be able to use them correctly: they will not be built into his stock of schemata yet. The process of maturation of different grammatical structures and elements of style into schemata is even slower. If you make an estimation on the basis of these data (and supposing the student really acquired this knowledge — which is naturally essential for a successful examination), you will really get the level of candidate master.

High school students in Japan are required to know and use 1800 characters correctly at the basic examination. With our present terminology we can say that the criterion is to reach the level of candidate master in the skill of writing. Indeed, if we want to put into words what is expected of a student taking the basic examination of Japanese reading and writing, we will say almost the same as what we said earlier about candidate masters of chess.

Things are in harmony again: the requirement for the medium state degree in Japanese is just about the same. Naturally, this does not mean that, if a foreigner learns these 1800 signs, his Japanese will be as good as that of a 16-year-old Japanese. The latter will speak much better Japanese (as we shall see, almost everyone is a master in his mother tongue), but their levels of writing skill are about the same. Writing skill alone does not count too much, of course; you can find a more general everyday body of knowledge and language skill behind it, too. Candidate masters of chess also understand much more than what they can actively realize, and understand games played by masters on the whole. A 16-year-old Japanese adolescent also understands more written characters than what he can use correctly. And he understands even more of his environment. Upon hearing the phrase "blossoming of cherry trees" his heart will beat quite differently from that of a foreigner who has just passed the medium level state examination in Japanese.

On this basis we can also calculate the approximate number of professional schemata a university provides its graduates. The order of magnitude will be that of the level of candidate masters, especially if we take the redundancy between subjects into consideration. It also shows why postgraduate education is necessary: it corresponds to the master course of the Conservatoire. Probably we are not mistaken in saying that a fresh graduate knows his profession at the level of candidate master. The best ones perhaps approach the level of masters by graduation, but the requirement for graduation is the level of candidate master.

The steps of professional development

Just as language courses differentiate beginner, lower intermediate, upper intermediate, etc. levels, the different levels of expertise can also be determined in general. We have emphasized two levels: those of candidate masters and grandmasters. The scale is obviously more or less continuous from the aspects of both expertise and the number of known schemata. Several levels within this scale are usually given individual names. We are going to differentiate four levels, and describe the characteristics of the thinking of persons at these levels. We could increase the number of levels and refine analysis, differentiate second and third class chess players, simple masters and grandmasters (in fact, we are going to talk about masters and grandmasters later), but the most important phenomena are already manifested at these four levels.

The development of expertise has been examined for ages (since Plato) on the basis of the extent to which the student can make abstractions from concrete facts and special cases, and use more and more general, abstract and formal(ized) rules. Just as scholars have always noticed in the behavior of animals whatever their aspects of investigation and current paradigms enabled them to (p. 85), similarly, in investigations based on the classical conceptions, the application of increasingly abstract rules was noticed at higher professional levels.

The conclusions drawn by H.L. Dreyfus and E. Dreyfus were just the opposite. Seeing that the general and formal approaches of artificial intelligence were so unsuccessful, they started off from the hypothesis that truth lies just in the opposite of the age-old belief: in the course of the development of expertise the general rules that can be applied anywhere are replaced by the innumerable special rules of the profession concerned. Thus, professional expertise would contain numerous special pieces of knowledge. Relying on two main aspects, the Dreyfuses differentiate five levels. One of their aspects is the extent to which people at different levels use formalized and general rules or think intuitively on the basis of professional analogies. Their other aspect is the extent to which people use their pieces of professional knowledge as independent facts or in close connection with the other facts of the given profession.

The two approaches seem to be opposites, although they both contain truths. The stormy increase in the amount of schemata seems to confirm the Dreyfuses' approach, but we also know that grandmasters not only know more schemata than those at lower levels, but their schemata are also more complex. This latter fact supports the classical approach: more complex schemata are obviously more general. However, we are not talking only about abstract generalities in the sense of formal logic, but also about more special generalities appropriate for the profession's logic of things.

We have started off from the amount of known schemata. We have seen that the knowledge or expertise belonging to a given number of schemata proves to have about the same values in quite different professions (at least in cases of candidate masters and grandmasters). We are going to order our four levels to be studied to four magnitudes of the amount of schemata.

The first level is that of *beginners*. A beginner has very scarce concrete knowledge about his future profession, therefore he is trying to use his general, everyday schemata here, too. There are professions where this is more or less successful, because a lot of everyday schemata apply to the topics of the given profession as well. Psychology, political science, aesthetics, and even economics and biology belong to this group to some extent. In other professions it is immediately apparent that most everyday schemata fail, e.g. in mathematics, physics and chemistry. In the former professions people mature to be grandmasters later, in the latter ones they become grandmasters at a younger age.

The next level is that of *advanced* students. An advanced student has already acquired a few hundred schemata, but these are not enough to express his thoughts solely by his professional schemata (first of all for himself) and to solve problems as a specialist and with the attitude of a specialist. The professional schemata of an advanced student always get mixed up with his general everyday schemata. Talking to a specialist, it becomes immediately apparent that he does not yet fully understand the profession. Talking to an outsider, he has difficulties in making himself understood because he too often tries to use notions unknown to outsiders, unable to simplify these concepts to be understandable at the everyday level. Looking at this process from the outside, the advanced student seems to ride a high horse, but this is not always the case. He simply knows a lot of professional facts, but most of them are not built into his professional schemata yet.

A *candidate master* has essentially acquired the foundations of his profession. He knows and can apply several thousands of professional schemata, his everyday and professional schemata are separated, he can use the trade jargon, he can express himself with his professional schemata, and the two kinds of schemata are not mixed: he can talk to outsiders about professional matters (if he can usually put his thoughts into words

120

well enough). He thinks *analytically*: he solves his problems step by step by the aid of his schemata. Whatever he knows within his profession he can communicate to fellow members of his guild by expressing it with the technical terms of the profession: he can carry on discussions and is rational.

A *grandmaster* knows several tens of thousands of professional schemata, most of which he cannot express by way of words or argumentation. In difficult debates he can express himself with the aid of apposite analogies, rather than direct professional arguments. His thinking is *intuitive*: he can put his finger on the crucial point of the problem without exact professional deductions and find the solution. His basic method of solving problems is not of deduction and systematic exclusion of the incorrect answers, but of his insight sensing the correct solution.

Intuitive thinking

Grandmasters seem to think as if they spoke a separate language composed of elements of the profession only. Everybody speaks intuitively in his mother tongue: we have no idea what our sixth next word will be, yet we say what we want to. A grandmaster of chess does the same: he does not make combinations in advance from move to move (only in very concrete and tight situations, analogous to everyday situations where he feels he has to phrase his thoughts very exactly, does he then slow down and search for the correct words). When a grandmaster of chess is thinking for a long time, he is generally not making calculations of what would happen if he made this move and the opponent that one, but is racking his brains over what his *message* should be in the actual situation. He is looking for thoughts rather than combinations, just as one is usually not looking for words, but for arguments and thoughts when writing something.

There are many kinds of languages. Artists are well aware that painting, literature, music all have their own languages, and (to the chagrin of aesthetes and critics especially) it is difficult to express in words whether somebody uses the language of his art correctly and well or not, and if not, what is wrong. Occasionally, everyday language (including the general schemata of everyday behavior) may be totally decomposed, while another language may be totally all right.

Lajos Fülep says: "Not only Aristotle's logos and logic, or things that have been listed under these titles in the history of philosophy, exist; there

are also other ones, for instance, the logic and ratio of artistic vision —
I say 'for instance' because there are other ones as well, but now we are
interested only in this one. Philosophy has never understood this and other
logics, has never seen them adequately, therefore it has neglected them and
left mankind uninformed in a very important area ... The clarity, logic and
consistency with which Csontváry composed these pictures are unthinkable
and almost unbelievable; then, as it took a long time to paint them because
of the large size of the pictures, he carried out his ideas consistently — he
saw every form, line, color and shade exactly in advance, he could work on
any part of the picture at any moment, he always saw the whole picture in
his mind, it never evaded him, he did not have to harmonize the whole at
the end. No mathematical procedure could be more precise."

Maybe Csontváry's pictures could also be shown as typical examples
of schizophrenic creations, but it is also certain that, in order to create
pictures like this, a perfectly sane mind is necessary in some respect. By the
way, Csontváry's pictures are especially suited to teaching the symptoms
of insane everyday minds, for it is not necessary to explain in detail, just
because the picture is bad, that this part here is a symptom of an insane
mind, and that part there is weird and illogical. Thus, one could speak
the language of painting at the level of grandmasters without speaking
everyday language even at the level of candidate master. This is why we
feel the person of the chess champion to be so genuine in Stefan Zweig's
short story "Chess story". These examples are genuine, albeit not typical.
It is more typical that the professional language of the grandmaster of
chess works completely independently of his everyday language; the levels
achieved in the two areas do not influence each other. Both can be very
high, or only one of them.

Most people stand on the level of masters (but not grandmasters) in
understanding their mother tongue and handling everyday situations. In
active composition and creative situations most people stand only at the
level of candidate masters. We can understand and enjoy cultured texts
written in nice style, but few can write like that.

We often believe something because a master says it, but not if his student does. Somehow, the master's argument seems to be authentic, while
that of the student does not. The reason for this is not necessarily snob-
bery or respect of authority. Rather, the student can explicate the same
professional thought only rationally, step by step, thus, we understand him
rationally. However, we accept the intuitive reasoning of a grandmaster also
on an intuitive level, unless it contradicts our own professional schemata.

Learning the profession

Generally, the well-paved paths of teaching professions lead only to the level of candidate master; it is possible to reach this level gradually, setting rational examinations and practice requirements that can be tested well. Tarrasch, a great German master of chess at the beginning of the century said that in one year he could bring any medium chess player of average intelligence to the first class level by intensive training. (That level corresponded at the time to the present level of candidate master.) But he could not guarantee that the student would become a grandmaster, or even a master. He would have a feeling about the individual students, of course. Every teacher who has ever had a talented student gets this feeling, even if the teacher himself is not a grandmaster of his profession.

The professional schemata above the level of candidate master are increasingly difficult to express by words. The style of teaching becomes different, the teacher starts to say only half sentences, or just phrases, and the student will understand them more and more, his thinking becoming more and more intuitive. Just as a grandmaster of chess does not think in terms of actual combinations and thoughts, likewise a grandmaster of entomology does not measure the concrete characteristics of the insect when determining a rare species; rather he tries to get a picture of the whole insect. The physician who is at the level of grandmaster can also see the disease and even the patient as a whole when making his diagnosis.

A medical student can see symptoms, the graduate medical doctor can see syndromes (they are whole units, but are still exactly describable combinations of symptoms). The textbook of internal medicine alone contains some 2000 pages, each page having about 100 facts. This adds up to about 200,000 facts — and a graduate at medical school knows them. This body of facts is organized into a few thousands of schemata. On his way to master level, his stock of concrete facts will increase, but at a much slower rate. The handbooks of kidney therapy and cardiotherapy contain about 60,000 and 90,000 facts respectively. By the time a doctor reaches grandmaster level, the amount of his schemata will have increased by one order of magnitude, that of facts will have increased by much less. A doctor approaching the level of grandmaster can see diseases through much more complex schemata and will be less and less able to express in words how he arrived at the diagnosis. The candidate master, of course, already understands the diagnosis itself, for it must be within the system and paradigm of medical science.

Even grandmasters of mathematics do not think in deductions when they are solving problems or searching for new truths in mathematics. They use more general and complex schemata, usually some internal picture. The character and style of these pictures can be very diverse and personal. But there is not a trace of these pictures in mathematical books, not a single scientific paper about them. The great French mathematician, J. Hadamard, making a brave decision, wrote a long essay about the psychology of mathematical invention. He described his own spot-like, obscure pictures that accompanied his mathematical concepts. For those in whom the very same concepts are present in a quite different form, these pictures are even less clear than the least understandable creations of abstract painting. Yet, when they become definitions, theorems and proofs, they will be perfectly understandable for the specialists.

When a grandmaster of mathematics outlines the first line of a proof, he is almost certain that the deduction will be good, although perhaps he will have to work on it for a few more weeks until he writes it down according to the usual rules of mathematical publications (so that it will be clear and unambiguous even for candidate masters of mathematics). Thus it is not true even of exact mathematics that its scholars think in the codified, formal language of mathematics.

The language of candidate masters is more or less uniform, professional, and conforms to the expected style of scientific publications. This language is rational and abstract to the extent required by the profession concerned. A grandmaster uses his own personal language that contains a lot of notions and schemata that can be understood only within that particular, highly individual language. He thinks and solves problems in his own language, and translates only the results and solutions to the official language of the profession.

The Nobel prize laureate biologist Jacques Monod expounds in his book *Chance and Necessity* that the structures and functions of all living beings do not contradict the laws of biology, but do not follow from them either. Even *Homo sapiens* is an exceedingly accidental species of animal; it does not follow from the laws of biology that it necessarily had to evolve. Still, the laws of biology apply to it. The situation is similar with the internal languages of grandmasters: they do not follow from the basic language and paradigm of the profession, but are not in contradiction with each other, either. There are as many individual, personal languages and styles of thinking as grandmasters.

124

The limits of the quantitative growth of schemata

Just think of what can happen when in the few years of becoming a master the number of schemata grows to tens of thousands, although it took at least as long to develop only a few thousand schemata to reach the level of candidate masters. The number of schemata increases by geometrical progression (i.e. it doubles in constant units of time). Similar increases appear in Nature usually when certain things multiply by bipartition. In cases like this the accelerating rate of increase lasts as long as there is no obstacle to the increase. It has been demonstrated that, between 1.5 and 4 years of age, children's vocabulary increase at a similar rate. Obviously, every increase meets obstacles in Nature sooner or later (e.g. the population explosion must stop some time also). The same is true of schemata. It is at about the level of candidate master where experience shows that there is a first real chance for this (still relatively slow) increase to stop.

On the other hand, we have seen that in all professions studied this increase stopped when the amount of schemata reached a few tens of thousands (or about 100,000 at the most); even the best ones of the profession were no exceptions. The development of the individual does not necessarily stop there, for schemata are constantly changing and may also become more and more complex. Thus, one is never too wise to learn.

It is not the limited capacity of memory that sets the limit in any of the cases. Biologists and psychologists think that man probably utilizes but a fraction of his memory capacity in the course of his life. Possibly it is reaching a kind of complexity (or two kinds of complexities: of candidate master and grandmaster) that puts an end to this growth. Most principles of operation and construction also determine the upper limits of size and complexity. Evolution ensures that living organisms should not grow to be bigger than what their organizing principle can bear: if, for some reason or another, no mechanism is built into a system to control complexity, the living organism will become extinct beyond help, like dinosaurs.

If the STM–LTM model or even the schemata themselves, prove to be physically nonexistent, if they turn out to be only epiphenomena of our thinking's deeper organizing principles, the two just recognized limits of complexity are probably the results of these deeper organizing principles. It is characteristic of the strength of our paradigm based on the concept of schemata that it could lead to the recognition of phenomena that point beyond its own frames.

125

12. Profession — language — way of thinking

The following story is told about a famous medical professor. At the beginning of a semester, he held a meeting at his department to discuss the contents of the lectures to be read that semester. One of the lecturers outlined how he planned his lectures about kidney functions. A heated dispute developed among the kidney specialists about certain details of the plan. After a while the professor cut the dispute short by saying: "This is how kidneys will function this semester."

This was no cynicism. The professor simply stated that although the lecturer's plan can be disputed in some details, they are matters of scientific dispute even at present. The attitude of the lectures, however, conform to the present day attitude and paradigm of science, thus it can form basically correct concepts in the medical students. Maybe this could be achieved by another plan, by partially different ideas, but the plan outlined by the lecturer also serves the purpose of developing a medical way of thinking.

Scientific attitudes are never taught in a direct form. If they were taught directly, as independent subjects, they would contradict other everyday schemata by being organized in everyday schemata. Since most people understand everyday life on the level of masters, the intruding new ideas would meet strong and logical counter-arguments. Learning would easily end in sterile disputes; the separate schemata of the new ways of thinking would develop with more difficulties.

In order to develop a scientific attitude, everyday schemata have to be upset, anyway. It is a logically thinking child who says after his first German lesson that he can already speak German, for he has learnt that the lamp means *die Lampe* and the cat means *die Katze*, therefore, the hat must mean *die Hatze* and the stamp means *die Stampe*. His teaching was not started very well: the schemata of his mother tongue were mobilized.

The difficult parts of the material to be studied

Jean Piaget observed two opposing directions in the development of children's thinking, namely, *assimilation* and *accommodation*. Assimilation is the process where a new piece of knowledge is built into our already existing schemata. Accordingly, we transform it subjectively and distort the perceived material. Assimilation can most clearly be seen in children's games, when they draw the objects of the world into their games, compare them to their expectations and tell what has happened accordingly. Accommodation is the process where a new schema is developed in a new situation on the basis of our old schemata. Modeling and imitation are typical childhood examples of accommodation. Frequently, in cases like this, a previous experience or piece of knowledge is unintentionally modified as a result of the re-organized schemata.

The results of several psychological experiments unanimously indicate that new schemata can develop only from old ones. Precious little is known about the nature of the schemata we have at birth. When the time arrives to learn a profession, our everyday schemata are already quite well-developed, we can get oriented quite well in everyday life. We can speak our mother tongue (including the non-verbal elements of behavior and social relationships) at least on the level of candidate master and have an even higher level of understanding. Training in a given profession can rely on an already existing system of schemata, on the strength of common sense.

The basis of a lot of branches of science is learnt at the elementary and secondary schools. However, the aim of the subjects in school is not to understand the special way of thinking of different professions in-depth. The aim in school is to learn the part of science that can be fitted into the system of everyday thinking logically and with relatively few contradictions. Even this requires the development of a lot of new concepts and schemata (there are well-known "difficult parts" in every subject), requiring the functioning of accommodation. The schemata of evolution or revolutionary situations or the law of energy and mass conservation are all treated metaphorically at secondary school, in close connection with our everyday schemata rather than making abstractions professionally or in relation to other professional schemata.

The material taught at the university usually does not rely directly upon the material learnt in the secondary school. Several years of secondary school material is condensed in a few lectures. The language is more abstract, and instead of everyday and general examples, special professional cases are supplied. The system of argumentation is more formal, the role of conclusions based on analogies and the logic of things is taken mostly by the syllogisms of formal logic. These methods all aim at developing the students' own way of thinking that is based on an inner logic and is also characteristic of the profession. The main point is not how the kidneys work; in order to really understand that, we might need to understand the fundaments of life itself in its full depth, but that is still outside the paradigms of present-day science. The main point is how and within what frame should renal functions be considered.

Once a correct attitude is developed, most of the new discoveries and scientific results can be assimilated into it. In order to cultivate and follow the daily developments of a specialist's profession, it is rarely necessary to reorganize his schemata radically; no accommodation is needed. He has developed a conceptual basis where everyday intuition can be replaced by professional intuition. A candidate master is able to apply his profession in practice, and depending on his talent, he can start his way towards becoming a master.

Talent

Talent is one of our most obscure and intangible everyday concepts. We can definitely perceive its presence, but can hardly define how we perceive it. Perhaps the best definition is the following: a talented person knows more than what he has learnt. But this definition is rather more poetical than scientific: it is difficult to grasp experimentally. The investigators cannot know what knowledge the experimental subjects bring to the laboratory. When psychologists want to study talented people they generally set the criteria to certain performances. They might study top students, winners of Mathematical Olympiads or Nobel prize laureates. But the everyday meaning of talent does not express how well someone performs; success has several other components as well.

We are not going to solve the puzzle of talents either — this problem still remains outside the present paradigms of science. But our thoughts brought up hitherto are suited to make us ponder over a less studied aspect of talent.

Once a famous psychologist happened to say in company that one of his students was very talented. A mathematician immediately asked what it meant to be a talented psychologist. The answer was that somehow one gets the feeling of it. The psychologist did not ask what it meant to be a talented mathematician. That one seemed evident: he can solve the problems and does well at mathematical competitions. But these are all incidental phenomena: we do not think of them while talking about talent. We might even say that success is only an epiphenomenon of talent. It seems to be true all the more so, as we can see a lot of people with wasted talents who have never become successful, still, we can feel that they are excessively talented. Others suddenly come up with fantastic achievements after long years of repeated failures without success; had they not been talented till their success?

It is characteristic that for the definition of talent the very same words appear in dictionaries about which we have said earlier (p. 89) that they are practically synonyms of the fact that we have no idea of the essence of the thing: natural ability or power (*Webster's New World Dictionary*); (particular kind of) natural power to do well (*Oxford Advanced Learner's Dictionary of Current English*).

The essence was better approached by what a teacher of mathematics said about a very talented student of his (who later won a lot of first prizes at Mathematical Olympiads) that "it is as if he had all the mathematical structures in his head and my only job were to tell him the name of these structures". It is an important characteristic of talent that it can see things correctly from the very beginning. According to an obscure definition that corresponds to what we have said so far: the everyday schemata of talented people are organized as demanded in the profession. They have no trouble in learning the language of the profession. It is immediately apparent from this that a talented person knows more than what he has learnt: his everyday intuition also helps him in solving different professional problems. This is the reason for the "ugly duckling" effect. (I am talking about Andersen's fable about the ugly duckling who was always mocked as a duckling, but later developed into a beautiful swan.)

From this point on, a psychologist and a mathematician both mean the same thing if they say that a student of theirs is talented. They both express that their students can see the professional questions correctly even without detailed explanations, they can point to the essence of things with everyday ease. They know more than they have learnt.

The following is a characteristic example of the manifestation of correct attitude. When the trainer of a junior chess group showed a difficult chess position, it soon became evident that the great problem was whether to take a certain piece or not. Everybody gave some reason either for or against taking. Gyula Sax (then 14) just hummed and hawed and simply said: "It's fishy." The trainer brightened up and said this was the correct attitude, this is how it should be looked at. A lot of good players grew out of that group, even masters, but only Sax became a grandmaster.

In Puzzle 6 of Chapter Zero, it is not the solution but its history that is so important for us. In the meanwhile we can also learn that the puzzle happens to be even better than was originally intended to be. It is a standard puzzle. Its standard solution can be seen below:

Here, each of the six cigarettes touch all the other ones. Martin Gardner, who published the best pieces of the folklore of mathematical puzzles in his column "Mathematical Games" in *Scientific American*, once set this problem, too. A lot of people found and sent in the classical solution. Two people, however, sent another solution, outdating thus the standard one. The next figure shows that seven cigarettes all touch each other! This arrangement is perhaps even more beautiful than the classical solution.

What could be the reason of the numerous people who solved the problem for failing to come up with this solution? One of the reasons could be that the classical solution is also so harmonic and not evident that those who find it will have the feeling (arising from their puzzle solving experience) that they have found the harmony, probably this was the content of the puzzle. On the other hand, we are treating even mathematical and logical puzzles as puzzles and not as mathematical problems. The paradigm

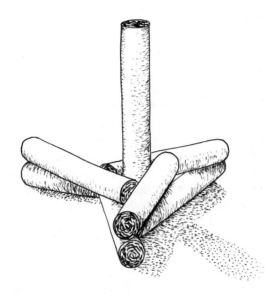

In this configuration seven cigarettes
all touch each other

or frame of reference is common sense, whose demands are met by the difficult solution with six cigarettes. Proving that no such arrangement can be done with seven cigarettes promises to be extremely difficult, and mathematical intuition says a proof like this can be only forced and non-elegant, if at all possible. To tell the truth, I know of no completely exact proof that the solution with the seven cigarettes is really the maximum that can be reached, although it seems very probable. But then, the classical solution also seemed to be the maximum.

If, after finding the classical solution, someone is seriously taking an attempt to prove by mathematical means that the conditions of the problem cannot be met by more cigarettes, he will probably get stuck somewhere, but it is improbable that he will find the best solution this way. In this case the promising ways of negative proof are radically different from the world of construction. It is almost certain that the two finders of the new solution did not reach this new discovery in a mathematical way of thinking, but within the everyday frame of puzzle solving. Perhaps they "smelled fish", i.e. they suspected the classical solution is not harmonious enough after all; heaven knows how this was represented in their inner language. At any rate, as opposed to the other finders, this suspicion made them search further, leading to success. Maybe they are not outstanding talents in mathematics, but they are definitely talents in a kind of puzzle solving.

Often we cannot tell exactly the profession where the talent of a definitely gifted child could blossom. When we say that a certain child is talented, perhaps we simply have the feeling that the child's thinking differs from average everyday thinking and that a definite inner logic can be perceived in him. From this feeling we predict that the child will surely find a profession where this kind of logic is just appropriate.

Talent is something like sex appeal. The latter does not necessarily mean that the person is very beautiful, or that he/she is especially successful, e.g. in seducing others. But he/she has a kind of magic spell. He/she can speak the non-verbal language of sexual attraction with his/her everyday schemata at master level.

Everyday language versus professional language

A grandmaster's inner professional language of tens of thousands of schemata is separated from his everyday language; that could be even insane, but usually this is the average. An example of the opposite case might be the persons who know how to get the most out of life. They have developed the schemata in certain areas of everyday behavior to the level of grandmasters, without reaching even the level of candidate masters in any concrete profession. They are grandmasters of social contact within their given social environment. According to these views, Don Juan or Casanova can be regarded as grandmasters, and their mystique will immediately be clear: in their areas they have reached the level of intuitive thinking of grandmasters. They can feel the essence without rational explanation.

Refined analysis will reveal that Don Juan and Casanova were not grandmasters of the same profession. We could even say that they were working in different paradigms. Don Juan, or at least Byron's and Mozart's Don Juan, was a grandmaster of erotism: women fell in love with him. He himself would not fall in love, he was only a seducer. In Kierkegaard's interpretation: "He is yearning for the totality of femininity in every woman, that is what underlies the sensually idolizing power that simultaneously cherishes and defeats his victim. ... That is why all the finite differences dissolve in his eyes upon comparison with the main thing: that the victim is a woman. ... But it should not at all be interpreted as his sensuality being but blindness; he is instinctively superb at differentiating; and, most of all, he idolizes." This is Mozart's Don Juan. Tirso de Molina's Don Juan of a hundred years earlier seduced women not by his sensuality, but by his rank — being the son of one of the highest aristocrats of Spain. He was a marriage swindler rather than a lady-killer.

The case of Casanova is more clear-cut; we can learn his creed from himself. As opposed to Mozart's Don Giovanni, Casanova really fell in love with each of the women; rather than seeing the general in them, he noticed what was individual and irreproducible in them. And he could express what he saw. Don Juan was a master of life, Casanova was an artist in life. This is proven not so much by his autobiography, but by his attitude, as he could look at every women with the eyes of a man in love, as a sculptor can see the sculpture in a piece of stone.

We are sensitive to the works of art by our common sense, although some works may create a kind of altered state of consciousness in us if we let it happen or let it affect us. In cases like that we perceive the work with trance logic: we accept the logic of that world and we are not disturbed if that logic sometimes contradicts the logic of our normal conscious state — just as in Chapter 1 the hypnotized persons were not bothered by seeing the assistant in duplicate.

We understand the works of science by the aid of our professional minds and place them in the system of our professional schemata. This is why most professional works are unintelligible and boring for outsiders: they do not understand the language in which it was written. This is not conceit on the part of science and scientists. European sciences can thank their achievements to the very fact that the language and methods of their investigations were separated from everyday language as much as possible.

The separation of professional and everyday languages is not totally general, just as in Eastern civilizations the feeling is not general that every differentiation is meaningless and everything is equal to everything. In the state of really deep thinking, a scientist may feel the total separation of his science from everyday things, he is in a kind of altered state of consciousness, he may do his research totally separated from worldly affairs ("He does not even notice that the house is on fire!"). In the state of satori, the enlightened master may feel the unity of the world, and the cessation of every differentiation.

In normal consciousness, everyday thinking is constantly present in both cultures, although the two kinds of common sense differ markedly. Eric Berne gives a characteristic example of this difference: "A Chinese man started to get into a local subway train, when his Caucasian companion pointed out that they could save twenty minutes by taking an express, which they did. When they got off at Central Park, the Chinese man sat down on a bench, much to his friend's surprise. 'Well,' explained the former, 'since we have saved twenty minutes, we can afford to sit here that long and enjoy our surroundings.' "

The loveliest examples of how professional and everyday languages cannot be separated can be found in the field of mathematics. Poincaré, after having declared that "mathematics is the language in which one cannot express imprecise or nebulous thoughts", remarks how differently he perceives his professional problems depending on whether the language he is thinking in is French or English. Stanislaw Ulam, a great Polish mathematician of our century wrote that, "In French generalizations come to my mind and stimulate me toward conciseness and simplification. In English one sees the practical sense; German tends to make one go for a depth which is not always there. In Polish and Russian, the language lends itself to a sort of brewing, a development of thought like tea growing stronger and stronger. Slavic languages tend to be pensive, soulful, expansive, more psychological than philosophical, but not nebulous or carried by words as much as German, where words and syllables concatenate. They concatenate thoughts which sometimes do not go very well together." Let us add Sándor Karácsony's remarks regarding the Hungarian way of thinking: "Hungarian reasoning often leaves argumentation to verbal emphasis, and if its verbal expression is not limited, it has less logical arguments, and more socio–logical and verbal reasons." He sums up his long discussion about the profound picturesque quality of the Hungarian language quite concisely, almost as an aphorism: "Things that are Hungarian are primitive in form and objective in content." There is a kind of typical Hungarian mathematical style, about which an American mathematician said with respect, but not without some critical edge: Hungarian mathematicians do very elegant mathematics.

The most striking example of the relationship between everyday and mathematical thinking can be observed in the Hindu, Srinivasa Ramanujan, one of the greatest mathematicians in history. Ramanujan had never

134

written mathematical deductions in our usual sense of mathematics. His results were rather wonderful flashes of intuition and a few related arguments. When his friends talked him into it, in 1913 Ramanujan wrote a letter to Sir Geoffrey Harold Hardy, one of the greatest mathematicians of the age. He described his poverty, and enclosed some 120 selected formulae. Hardy's enthusiasm was unimaginable. He wrote that some of Ramanujan's formulae had shaken him completely; one moment was enough to realize that only a first class mathematician could have written them. They must be true, because no man's imagination could have made them up.

Hardy believed Ramanujan had not written the deductions because he had not trusted him. In order to eliminate Ramanujan's suspicion he listed the names of mathematicians to whom Hardy had shown Ramanujan's letter. Thus, if Hardy had wanted to use the formulas illegally, Ramanujan could denounce him easily. Hardy asked Ramanujan not to feel offended that he was so plain in discussing that matter, for he would not do it if he did not strive at helping Ramanujan in getting better chances to demonstrate his evident mathematical abilities. In his answer Ramanujan explained that he wrote no deductions not because of lack of trust, but because, although he was convinced of the correctness of his results, he himself felt that the way he had reached them was heuristic. Ramanujan became one of the staff at Cambridge University with the help of Hardy, until his early death at the age of 33.

Professor of mathematics Pál Turán writes about Ramanujan in a paper: "Hardy knew what Mikszáth's cataract-operating smith had not known, i.e. solid mathematical foundations would take away Ramanujan's intuition. Therefore, he taught him only those things without the knowledge of which Ramanujan arrived at chronically mistaken conclusions. But Hardy also added that he himself had learnt much more from Ramanujan."

Ramanujan's style was the product of the Eastern way of thinking. And yet, mathematics is taught in Indian and Japanese schools the same way as in Europe: definition — theorem — proof. No other way is known to reach the level of candidate master.

Not only does everyday language affect professional thinking, but vice versa. Hardy once took a taxi with Ramanujan, and left his briefcase in the cab. He was very upset, but Ramanujan calmed him, saying there was no problem, he had seen that the licence number of the taxi was 1729. Hardy was relieved, but asked immediately how it occurred to Ramanujan to memorize an indifferent number like that. Ramanujan said it was not an indifferent number at all, for this is the smallest integer that can be produced as the sum of two cubes in two ways: $1729 = 1^3 + 12^3 = 10^3 + 9^3$.

Expertise is fantastic. Even candidate masters can solve problems that seem to be hopeless for our everyday minds. But it can also have a cathartic effect if one suddenly switches from professional to everyday language. Freud's psychiatrist colleagues once started teasing Freud about what the latent motives could be behind Freud's constant smoking, what the hidden meaning of cigars could be for Freud. After a while Freud made a theatrical gesture: "Gentlemen, this is just a cigar."

The development of specialization within science

According to Immanuel Kant, those who have learnt a branch of science have learnt science itself. Kant based this idea on the fact that understanding a branch of science also means learning the principles of mind that exist 'a priori' without previous experience and form our sensations into knowledge. However, the different branches of science have become much more complex since Kant; nowadays even the best biologists have no chance to seriously join in a discussion on the problems of nuclear physics. We are less and less certain that there are really a relatively few number of principles on which Kant based his philosophy. This uncertainty is due to our experience that the different branches of science have become divided into barely connected areas. It is possible, of course, that we are not smart enough to recognize the general principles. We cannot find the general principles with the aid of which we could find the general principles.

Yet there are certain characteristics common in every branch of science; they are the ones that differentiate science from other means of cognition, e.g. from arts or metaphysics. Science is objective: only those facts can be accepted as scientific truths that are independent of the diversity of everyday ways of thinking and the systems of human values. This is why science uses formalized language, this is why it is abstracted from everyday thinking. Science is the meta-level of phenomena: it is about them, but interprets them within an extraneous system. Only those perceptions are accepted as real phenomena that can be produced and reproduced under circumstances that can be unambiguously described in scientific language. In Chapter 3 we analyzed the paradigms of the different branches of science; now we mention characteristics common in every branch. Together, they can be called the general paradigm of science.

We have seen that paradigms are never taught directly, therefore the decision whether a train of thought can be regarded as scientific or not is based mostly on intuition. Masters of science usually determine intuitively if a conception has anything to do with science or not, and generally these scholars more or less agree in their judgement about questions like this. This intuition is similar to the situation where we are searching among stations speaking different languages on the radio and suddenly look up because we understood nothing of what was said at a station we passed, though we are quite certain that English was spoken there.

Science owes its achievements to the fact that it has chosen such a strict and well circumsribed general paradigm. Thus it is hoped that more and more generally valid principles can be found with the aid of which the different phenomena can be understood at higher and higher meta-levels. A lot of convincing successes have been achieved this way. Still, the deeper our knowledge becomes, the more complex it seems to be.

A branch of science that is general and important enough to be considered as an independent profession can be complex up to the point where it could still be taught (it must be possible to train its specialists and candidate masters). In the previous chapter we saw that even this determines the limit of complexity where a branch of science must become divided into different branches. This must happen quite soon, i.e. when the fundments of the branch cannot be organized into a few thousands of schemata any more.

Books do not help here, either: they may include facts, but the thinking schemata must be together in our heads, too, otherwise we cannot think. It may be part of schemata that, occasionally, when we use them we have to look up some data in the books; yet, a schema can function only together with other schemata. Schemata cannot be found in the books, they are present in our heads, they are dynamically and constantly changing, living things.

The increasingly specialized fields may demand less and less to be considered as independent professions. There is no need for a lot of specialists with very special knowledge, although the piece of knowledge in question may be needed occasionally. At other times the given direction of research may be promising. But even the most specialized areas cannot be more complex than what a grandmaster can grasp. If no general principles can be found in a field that would decrease complexity, the field will either be divided into even more specialized areas, or its investigation and development will be sooner or later terminated.

The language and the way of thinking of a profession are determined by the attitudes of candidate masters, while the achievable depths are determined by the complexity that grandmasters can grasp. The great moments of a branch of science are those when a few meta-level schemata develop out of the several complex schemata of a grandmaster; these meta-level schemata can be expressed and understood by candidate masters as well. After moments like this, the branch usually shows a sudden development; problems that earlier could be solved only by grandmasters suddenly become routinely solvable. This is how the discovery of the structure of DNA and the solution of the DNA code made genetic engineering an independent profession — as the separate expression "genetic engineering" indicates.

Suppose science can really be considered as a formal system and that every theorem in science can be deduced from certain well-chosen starting conditions (general principles or axioms). Science really has this aim, but in this case Gödel's theorem (p. 68) guarantees that there will always be *truths* that will elude all of the hitherto created paradigms of science and all of its existing systems of axioms. Furthermore, it is guaranteed that there will be statements (facts, relationships, exceptions, etc.) phrased correctly within the frames of science that, while being true, cannot be proven with the aid of science. This does not mean, of course, that such truths could not be deduced by extending the already existing paradigms by making the fundaments more general or adding a few more axioms, but this would certainly be impossible without changing the reference system.

Thus, science is subjected to a kind of eternal race. It is racing against the necessarily appearing questions that point beyond its systems. But it has a chance of staying in the race, because it can develop more and more general schemata phrased at higher and higher meta-levels. If the amount of questions is greater than the development of general schemata, science cannot help getting divided into independent branches after a while. Special branches of science develop, and the special areas within the branches of science are mushrooming today.

The possibilities of switching professions

If science has a general paradigm, we cannot reject Kant's conception simply by saying how unprofessional an excellent biologist is in nuclear physics. Generally, if somebody has learnt a trade, it will be much easier for him to learn another one. A well-developed system of general and abstract schemata serves as a good basis for another profession's body of material to be organized into a uniform language quite quickly. Learning a second foreign language is much easier than a first one, provided we know the first one at least on a candidate master level.

As a result of the complexity of a grandmasters' inner language, the newly learnt facts of another profession may unexpectedly soon result in master level intuitions, especially if there is some kind of similarity between the paradigms of the two branches, which similarity cannot be expressed by rules but can be felt intuitively. Quite unexpected similarities have good chances, just because there is a general paradigm in science.

In addition to a general paradigm, European science has also developed several special paradigms that are valid only within a special area. Perhaps this is where Eastern and Western ways of thinking bifurcated radically: Western thinking attempts to understand the world by several general principles, although it hopes it would need relatively few of them. In the Eastern way of thinking the only general basic principle is that there can be no general basic principles functioning in parallel: all of them are equal to the world. In order to cultivate science it is worth keeping the pluralism of principles, but the Eastern way of thinking offers a more uniform *Weltanschauung*.

Having vowed to kill a given number of people in duels, a samurai picked a quarrel with a Zen master. The Zen master could not say no, and took up the challenge. They decided to meet at the same place the next day. The master was not afraid of death: in his enlightened moments he had deeply felt that there was no real difference between life and death. But he did not want to die in shame either, so he went to a master of fencing and asked to be taught the correct attitude of fencing. The next day he met the samurai and, assuming the "on guard" position he had learnt the day before, he concentrated inward and waited for the fatal blow. When nothing happened for a long time, he looked up and saw the samurai kneeling in front of him, with his head lowered. The master inquired what had happened, and the samurai begged him to accept him as his pupil — unless he wanted to kill him — because he had never seen such a perfect fencing position.

The master could not acquire the concrete rules of the profession of fencing in one afternoon, he would have had no chance in real fencing. But a single afternoon was enough for him to learn to be able not to die in shame even with a sword in his hand, but to express the much more general essence of things in this situation as well. This is what the samurai, also looking for perfection in his own way, perceived. Similarly common and uniform fundamental positions can hardly be imagined in different branches of science.

Interdisciplinarity

Puzzle 7 in Chapter Zero is a good example of how common, everyday questions can remain stuck outside the paradigm of science. This is the only puzzle of the ten that is not a real puzzle: it has no snappy solution, no solution that would be unanimously clear-cut for common sense. Yet it seems to be an innocent question, like a good puzzle. Physics or mathematics should also be dealing with it: usually it is not impossible to solve similar questions.

Really, the question poses no problem to specialists of geometrical optics. They will imagine an x–y–z system of coordinates, and assume y-axis points toward the plane of the mirror. It will be evident immediately that the mirror does not reverse the direction of either x or z, but it will reverse the direction of y. It is a correct answer, but it does not explain what puzzles us in the puzzle. It is not a nice puzzle whose solution would be so abstract. Thus, does not the mirror reverse the left and right sides in reality? Then why cannot we read the newspaper in the mirror? Something must have been reversed, for a newspaper can be considered two-dimensional.

The reversal of axis y is an abstract concept, it is not easy to interpret it in this environment with our common sense. Perhaps the best way to illustrate it is to imagine that a newspaper is printed on a transparent sheet and we want to read it from the back. But this is abstraction again; those who still have problems in understanding why this analogy talks about mirrors are not necessarily dull-witted. Our body is not two-dimensional: if it were transparent and we looked at it from the back, we would see it quite differently.

The question can also be conceived as a psychological problem about sensation. From this aspect we can give quite a different answer. What schema or — this is a problem of perception — what Gestalt is mobilized in us when we see our image in a mirror? Mostly that of a human being. If we took a few steps forward and turned around, the picture would be almost perfect. This imaginary transformation can be done quite easily; furthermore, no other image would give a closer similarity. In reassuring similarities like this, even our everyday logic fails to notice slight contradictions like a right-hand glove that should be put on the left hand of the mirror image. These slight logical errors do not bother our common sense, just as trance logic was not interested in even greater contradictions. Yet it should have been: our mirror image has a heart in the wrong place, his appendectomy would be performed at the wrong side — are these errors not great enough? Not for our everyday logic, they are not.

A mathematician would consider yet another answer as logical. The mirror reverses the direction of the drifting of all three coordinates. But this answer is even more outrageous from another way of thinking: the DNA molecules of our mirror image would then twist in quite another direction. It is not even a creature of this world. It could definitely have no child from an earthly mortal. Do we stare at this monster each morning while it is combing its hair?

If we lie down in front of the mirror, the right and left sides remain okay; up and down also seem to stay in their places, although the DNA are still not all right. The Gestalt explanation is still logical here, of course, but it does not explain what the mirror does in the end. Somehow the everyday meaning of the question changed in each of the scientific paradigms. Perhaps, philosophy could help. Indeed, as early as two and a half thousand years ago there were debates whether mirrors reverse the image or not. Timaios in Plato's dialogue dwells upon the question without a reassuring answer. Perhaps the most thorough analysis is given by Ned Block in the *Journal of Philosophy* in 1974, but all he can do is define a lot of reversal-conceptions and say that, according to some conceptions, the mirror reverses the image while, according to other conceptions, it does not.

Everything we have said about the mirror puzzle is a typical interdisciplinary work. It could be more tricky, but hardly more scientific. Sometimes under the label "interdisciplinary" we can find thoughts reflecting excellent, special and very logical ways of thinking. They offer a unanimous frame of puzzle solving, and also solve a few interesting puzzles immediately. However, they are not typical interdisciplinary works, and soon leave this flag. They will become independent branches of science, like cybernetics or semiotics (the abstract and general science of signs), or one of the main topics of this book: cognitive science. Where the slogan "interdisciplinary" lingers on for a longer period, it usually covers the lack of inner logic and uniform paradigm. As if someone tried to assemble the pieces of two different jigsaw puzzles into one picture. Something will certainly be formed, but there is no criterion upon which it could be decided whether the solution is correct or not. The debates of legitimacy become constant. This kind of interdisciplinarity contradicts the general definition of science itself.

Because of the formal way of thinking in science and because of Gödel's theorem, there are a lot (in reality, an infinite number) of truths to which science gives no explanation. Unsolvable problems are also abundant in every system. Furthermore, these truths can be phrased in the language of science, within its system. In fact, as we will see in Chapter 14, it is often impossible to decide whether a question is Gödelian or not, just on the basis of the form of the question. But science has even a second heuristic preventing it from spending too much time on investigating Gödelian problems. Namely, science is usually willing to study only those puzzles about which science knows somehow that they must have a solution, can be resolved and are surely not Gödelian.

If someone is still very interested in a Gödelian problem he will have two logical possibilities at his disposal. One is to develop a new branch of science. It is a risky enterprise, and usually only those people are successful in it who have reached at least the master level in some other accepted branch of science. New schemata can be formed only from existing ones.

The other possibility for the lovers of Gödelian problems is to leave the frames of science and choose another method of expression transcending common sense in another way. The roads of arts, metaphysics or Zen, however, are not less rough. They also have exactly defined uniform logic (or anti-logic, as in the case of Zen), exactly definable ways of thinking with generally accepted grandmasters. I suspect that these fields also have their own Gödelian problems; perhaps some of them are dealt with by science itself.

13. Artificial intelligence at candidate master level

We have talked about a lot of frames of reference and ways of thinking. In some cases we have also used the results of artificial intelligence in order to make some of our concepts clear or to present the functioning and limits of some general principles of organization.

I do not guarantee that our examples have represented the best and most relevant results of artificial intelligence; rather, I have shown the most typical programs, characteristic of the problems concerned. The most fashionable methods of artificial intelligence (e.g. the expert systems or the principles of logical programming) have not even been mentioned. The literature on artificial intelligence is vast; we have talked only about a few of the several thousands of different programs, systems and products. However, even these incidental examples show the results achieved by artificial intelligence, like a drop of water shows the ocean.

In fact, this limited number of phenomena happen to show the strengths and weaknesses of artificial intelligence better than waterdrops show the ocean, since it is more true of the ocean that it is more than the sum of its parts. From the sum of artificial intelligence research no uniform picture has emerged yet regarding what this science can produce. There are countless promising first steps, but there are only a few second ones. Still, a lot of nice and undoubtedly working programs have also been developed. It is about time to sum up, with the aid of our concepts developed in the course of investigating human thinking, where artificial intelligence has arrived at today.

The promises of artificial intelligence

One of our starting points in Chapter Zero was that we stated that artificial intelligence is still in severe debt to its greatest promises. Yet the beginning was very promising. Even the very first chess programs played pretty well; the first attempts of translator programs resulted in quite fair translations from one language to another. The promises raised by ELIZA and DOCTOR were seen in Chapter 2.

In 1958 Herbert Simon wrote that in ten years a computer program would be the world champion of chess if such programs would be allowed to participate at human chess competitions under the same conditions. He also predicted that by the end of the 1960s there would be translator programs to translate foreign texts into English at a rather good standard. Chess programs today are allowed to participate in human chess competitions without special restrictions, perhaps because they are not real opponents to masters of chess. High quality interpreter programs have not appeared in the market yet, although they would certainly mean big business.

Simon based his predictions mainly on the fact that the appearance of computers made the combination and practical application of two previously developed scientific doctrines possible. One of these doctrines was the principle of extreme reductionism analyzed in detail in Chapter 5. It is a re-phrasing of this very principle that general intelligence (every naturally existing intelligence, including man's thinking ability) can be reproduced by the aid of physical symbols or symbol systems, and every relationship existing among these symbols can, in principle, be clearly defined.

The other doctrine is the so-called *Church–Turing thesis*. To put it in a totally informal way: this thesis says that if something can be told so that it is guaranteed that everybody understands the same thing under the explanation, then this same something can also be told in the form of a program for some kind of abstract computer. The Church–Turing thesis can be phrased in several forms in formalized languages. One of its generally accepted forms is as follows: suppose that an intelligent being somehow sorts integers into two groups. If he can describe the principle of sorting with the aid of anything, let it be even a song, a dance or kisses, so that another intelligent being will be able to sort the integers in the same way as the first one, then the principle of sorting can also be written in the form of a mathematical algorithm, and can be realized in the above-mentioned abstract computer. Putting the Church–Turing thesis in still another way: essentially it says that it is sufficient to use exclusively mathematical methods for the cultivation of mathematics.

The already existing computers based on Neumann's principle are essentially the same as the theoretical computer in the Church–Turing thesis: therefore, the two doctrines together express that general intelligence can, in principle, be fully realized by a computer. In the beginning this was considered as the fundamental paradigm of artificial intelligence; it was this upon which Simon based his belief that there was no conceptual obstacle to the solution of the above problems and to a lot of other very practical uses. Initial attempts also indicated that all that was needed was a few hundreds of well-trained specialists and a few years of their work. Similar predictions were born one after the other in the past thirty years; they are not infrequent even today.

The trend of development

Some of the predictions that proved to be too optimistic were not based on purely subjective opinions. In the figure below you can see the trend of the development of chess programs.

The horizontal axis shows in a logarithmic scale the number of chess positions examined by the computer in three minutes (x times ten thousand). We took three minutes as the unit, because, in a normal game, on the average, one has to make a move in every third minute. The y-axis shows the strength of the programs. Chess players have been ranked according to their ratings for over a decade and a half, after the method of Árpád Élő, a Hungarian-born professor of mathemathics.

The values on the rating show the expected outcome of a game between two chess players having certain rating scores. The zero point and the unit of the scale were chosen on an arbitrary basis (just like in the Celsius or Fahrenheit scales). The ratings of the world champions are usually about 2700–2800, strong grandmasters (the first 10–15 in the world ranking list) have over 2600 points, the level of international grandmasters is about 2500 points. A candidate master scores about 2100–2300. A second class player has 1700–1900 points, while a beginner scores about 1300–1400 points.

The unit of the rating was determined such that a difference of 50 points means that if a player scores higher on the rating by 50 points then the stronger player will probably win 55% of the time against the weaker one. If, for instance, a player with a score of 2600 plays a series of 10 games with someone who has only 2550 points, chances are that he will win 5.5 to 4.5. Naturally, concrete games may bring different results, but it is worth betting on this result in the long run – unless the strength of one of them changes considerably in the meantime. A difference of 200 points on the rating means that the stronger player will win 75% of the time.

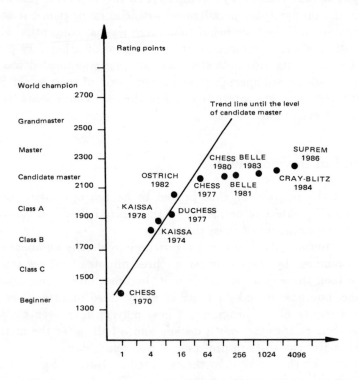

The number of chess positions examined
by the computer in 3 minutes (X*10,000)

It is interesting to note the close relationship between the rating scores and the number of known chess-related schemata. A few tens of schemata (beginner level) means about 1400 points. The magnitude of a few hundreds of schemata (advanced level) corresponds to about 1800 points, a few thousands of schemata (candidate master level) correspond to about 2200 points, while a few tens of thousands of schemata (grandmaster level) correspond to about 2600 points. A difference of one order of magnitude in the number of schemata corresponds to about 400 rating points. This fairly even rate of difference in the scores shows that our estimate of the amount of schemata mentioned in Part II really characterizes the actual playing strength. This is another independent evidence from a totally different direction in favor of the validity of our train of thought regarding the estimate of the amount of schemata.

It can be seen in the figure that up to a certain point the chess programs increased in strength linearly with the increase of computer speed (if speed is plotted logarithmically). In 1958 Simon could not base his predictions on such concrete data, but in 1979 those who wanted to estimate the date when the world champion chess program would appear were perfectly right to predict it for the middle of the 1980s. We can see, however, that the trend of chess-strength-increase broke, although the increase in computers' speed has not slackened yet (there are yet even more points towards the right side of the figure, but their values on the y-axis are less than what would be expected on the basis of the trend line).

When a trend line breaks, it usually means that there is a change in the conditions. Ferenc Jánossy says in his book *The Trend Line of Economic Development:*

"Such breaks in the trend line — and in general, every, more or less, sudden change in any process (let it be biological, economic or physical) — usually indicates that the process itself changes its own conditions, i.e. the relationships that determine its existence (or more expressively, it undermines its own preconditions) to the extent where these circumstances, having reached a critical point, fall into the background; from the aspect of further development of the process, the newly developed relationships become decisive. Just as the number of pikes put into a carp-pond will increase by geometrical progression, but only until the critical point where the lack of food prevents their further multiplication, so industry can grow *extensively* only until it uses up every labor-reserve (handicraftsmen, peasants); having reached that point, it is forced to create an economic structure where it can develop further only according to the new rules, i.e., *intensively.*"

It can be seen in the figure that the trend line of the development of chess programs broke around 1979. We can probably highlight deeper reasons for this by saying that the trend line broke when it reached the level of candidate masters. The efforts made to write chess programs have not decreased in the 1980s; nevertheless, the level of international master has not been reached yet. This statement is true of several chess programs based on quite different principles: it is true of those that are based on simply computing the move-variations in a sequence and it is also true of those based on some kind of schema-recognition.

How to play against a chess computer?

It seems logical that we will have the best chance of beating a computer if we make use of the fact of the opponent's being a machine: it has no intuition, no inspiration. Therefore, most people play very aggressively against computers: they make the position too complicated, hoping that in a complicated position they would be more likely to find a winning idea, a spectacular combination than their computer opponent. In reality, this is exactly the style that offers the greatest chance to the computer, for the machine sees through everything to a certain depth. It is most probable that in a complicated position one can get a significant advantage in the short run. But the machine does notice every combination within the next 5–6 moves, even the most hidden ones, and if there is the smallest error in our combination, the computer will immediately spot it.

Paradoxically, the most successful style against a computer is what is called the mechanical style: a sober approach, achieving small advantages on the long run with simple and lucid positions. Simple positions are just as complicated for the computer as others, the amount of possible moves is about the same in either case. Man, however, can see a simple position more easily, and can make plans further ahead. A human candidate master is right to feel that in simple positions "his moves are obvious", and he plays automatically. He feels the position to be a routine one just because he meets no problems there that could be solved only by using new ideas, by exceeding his consolidated system of thoughts. A candidate master can play chess in simple and clear-cut positions just as easily as he is talking about common matters at a cocktail party: he does not have to rack his brains about how to express sophisticated thoughts as precisely as possible. Yet computers become completely helpless just in these simple, everyday situations, just as the program ELIZA did. Once we get into an unfavorable situation, however, we will have much less chance against a computer than against a man: the machine will never get tired, become hungry or get bored with playing out a winning game.

You can regularly read reports stating that a program has reached the level of international grandmasters, that it has beaten a grandmaster. For all these cases it soon turned out that in only occasional ones did the master not take into consideration that he was playing against a machine, and thus did not apply the appropriate style against the computer. As soon as the masters came to know the style of the computer just a little, they won easily. David Levy, a Scottish master of chess (he has about 2400 rating points) bet large sums of money that no chess program would be written in the next few years that could beat him. He had close wins of a few games like this, but became increasingly uncertain of himself: he felt the programs were becoming stronger and stronger and he would soon lose the bet. In 1984 he played his next stake-match against the current champion program Cray–Blitz. Cray–Blitz was also considered to have the strength of grandmasters at the time; it was stronger than any other chess computer. By that time, however, Levy also came to know chess computers and changed his usual style consciously: he tried to play as modestly as possible, avoiding spectacular complications. As a result of this style, he not only won 4 to 0, but also lost interest in programs: "The nature of the struggle was such that the program didn't understand what was going on." Indeed, it had no idea of it, just as DOCTOR did not know that if we said that someone was drinking too much, we did not talk about water.

One must be able to play some real chess to beat proclaimed master chess programs. But even a candidate master can easily assume the necessary style for this. Although he would perhaps be bored with such games if he had to play them against human beings in this style, he might even enjoy being so much superior to the programs. But if someone is willing to be degraded to any level just to beat the computer, he might as well look up the book on the theory of chess openings that was coded into the computer — there are no books without misprints... At present, artificial intelligence is far from being able to get suspicious in similar cases.

Expert systems

The break in the trend line indicates that the conditions of improving chess programs have changed somehow after reaching the level of candidate masters. With the socio-economic environment unchanged, probably the efficiency of the applied methods have reached a certain limit. On the basis of our previous results it might be suspected that the reason for this should be looked for somewhere around the essence of the level of candidate masters; over that level the finally acquired analytical, professional thinking is increasingly replaced by intuition. Let us put this line aside until the next chapters and see what we can say about the results of the other areas of artificial intelligence.

It is customary to summarize the programs that solve problems requiring intelligence or professional knowledge by certain generally good methods under the title of *expert systems*. The basic principles of the structures of expert systems proving to be the most effective have become generally applied methods by the 1980s.

An expert system usually has two components: a *basic body of knowledge* and a *general reasoning system*. Basic knowledge contains the facts ("John is Mary's father"), the data ("Mary is 12 years old"), and the rules showing their relationships ("A father is at least 15 years older than his child") built into the expert system. The next subsystem interprets the user's starting questions and schedules the rules of reasoning to be used within the system (it decides — on the basis of the previous results and the starting questions — when and which rules to use). The reasoning system on the one hand uses the built-in body of knowledge and, on the other hand, asks questions of facts to be answered by the user; and on the basis of all this it produces new facts. Finally, the "special advices" of expert systems are composed of these new facts. Several different concrete technical solutions have developed within these general principles, but we are not going to go into details about them.

Opinions on expert systems are extremely divided: some people consider them as a kind of new gold fever, as revolutionary new posssibilities of computers, while others look at the whole topic as a large balloon that is bound to burst as soon as the new name loses its magic. Let two quotations stand here from distinguished researchers representing each extreme group:

"We use it for everything: writing programs, planning programs, i.e., everywhere where creative thinking is to be organized and subsequently the result should be applied in practice." Even more: "With the aid of expert systems, the mentally handicapped children will become clever, complex diseases can be diagnosed, the United States will seize world power and escape nuclear catastrophy."

On the other hand: "If the king is the fifth generation of artificial intelligence, then he is stark naked, at least to his ankles, but below his ankle he wears a pair of highly polished decorative shoes called expert systems." Even more: "At present the expert systems on the market contain no artificial intelligence whatsoever."

If somebody cites such extreme opinions, he usually does it in order to state his own wisdom about the golden middle way. In the present case I cannot promise anything like that: I agree more or less with the latter views. Yet, expert systems have profound and continued success on the market, and on the market the customers usually have a good look at the products before giving money for them. If the customers were victims of a delusion only, or if they were given to some whimsy of fashion, the sales trend of expert systems would not show a relatively long, steady increase. Thus, it is worth looking into what expert systems have to offer. First, let us examine how many rules representing professional knowledge could be built into the most efficient present-day expert systems.

Here again we meet the magic limit of a few thousands. A system called XCON contains the greatest number of rules at present; this system gives advice in building the configurations of computer systems. Its 1988 version works with about 6200 rules compared to five years ago when it included about 4000 rules. These rules handle about 20,000 elementary units. Ten years of experience with XCON has shown that about half of the rules had to be changed annually. The reason is not only that the rules become outdated. The inclusion of new rules also modified the previously correct functioning of the old ones; in order to teach a new rule, a lot of old pieces of knowledge had to be re-formulated.

The best specialists of computer systems sometimes sneer at XCON, saying that it should solve certain problems more elegantly than it does, but the program can provide useful pieces of advice for average engineers.

The built-in rules are usually under 2000 in the other expert systems. The reason for the great difference might be that XCON system gives advice to using man-made devices, while the medical, geodetical, chemical, microbiological, etc. expert systems work with objects given in Nature, thus they are more difficult to handle. One of the best-known and most successful expert systems is called MYCIN; it gives expert advice in diagnosing and treating bacterial diseases. MYCIN has about 1500 rules. It was found that the expertise of MYCIN reached that of an average general practitioner, but failed to match that of the specialist. The same is true of the other versions of MYCIN developed for other special medical fields, and also of any other successful expert system.

Probably we are not very mistaken in estimating the competence of expert systems to be at the candidate master level. This is backed by both the experiments comparing the performance of the systems with the opinion of human experts and the number of rules built into the systems. Although these rules are generally less complex than man's cognitive schemata as we imagine them, their role is quite similar: they have to organize concrete pieces of gnosis and facts into knowledge and problem solving ability.

Why is it that no more schemata were built into any of the expert systems? The reason is very simple: the inclusion of further rules did not improve the systems' performance; in fact, it mostly worsened it. The more recent rules got mixed up with the old ones, e.g. when something was previously determined quite well by one or two rules, a new rule messed it all up, and when programmers wanted to filter the unpleasant side-effects, the whole system became increasingly confused; undesirable side-effects kept popping up. The complexity problem noticed at the candidate master level arose in a concrete form: the complexity of the system exceeded its creators' capacity of comprehension, therefore the improvement of the programs met severe difficulties.

Naturally, nothing prevents us from placing a medical, a geological, an organic chemical and a hundred other expert systems in one and the same computer, and even organizing them in a common program frame. Their set of rules would well exceed 100,000, but the monster would not reach the master level in any one area. Knowledge in one area would not help in another area in any way. Exceeding the few thousands of schemata (i.e. the level of candidate masters) is problematical if the schemata are interrelated, if they belong to the same profession. As we have seen, the division of professions is caused by reaching just this limit of complexity.

A few general principles have been developed in the research and practice of expert systems, on the basis of which a pretty good prognosis can be given on whether or not a sufficiently good expert system can be developed in a certain area. For example, B.G. Buchanan and R.O. Duda emphasize five characteristics of such areas. First, the area should be narrow enough to include knowledge that is not available to everyone, but it should be complicated enough to give rise to a need for such special knowledge. Second, there must exist human experts of the area, whose extensive knowledge can be used as a starting point in making the program. Third, it is important to have an overall agreement among the human experts on the basic questions of the area. Fourth, it is necessary to have a lot of examples and basic data available, since expert systems and their limits can be tested only with their aid. Fifth, the better an area can be divided into different problems that barely interfere with each other, the better an expert system can be built in general.

If all these conditions are met, then making an expert system in a certain area will be essentially a routine task. The profession making such programs has even got a separate name: this activity is called *knowledge engineering*. If an area acquires the above five criteria it can be expected that candidate master level (but not master level) expert systems will soon appear.

The depth of a profession

The strongest chess programs at present are at the level of candidate masters. In the game of go, computer science is less successful: at present the strongest go-programs barely reach the level of moderately advanced players. The reason for the difference is not that less efforts have been made to write go-programs. Those who know both games state in unison that the task itself is more difficult: somehow go is a much deeper game, mobilizing deeper layers of human thinking than chess. An abundance of more obscure (although sensibly true) arguments could be brought up but, as we shall soon see, the difference in depth between the two games can be caught by more clear-cut methods as well.

The width of the scale of measurable performances can be explicitly defined, ranging from beginners to the world champion. Let us examine how many qualitative steps this span may cover.

It is customary to say that one player is of a class above another. We say that when one player is most likely to beat another. Let us, for instance, speak about a difference of one class if the stronger player's performance is at least 75% above that of the other. (If no draw is possible, we can say that the difference is one class when the stronger player beats the weaker one in at least 75% of the games.) The limit of 75% is completely accidental; we might choose 60% just as well as 90%, that will not affect our train of thought. 75% is justified by the fact that, as we have seen, this is the very difference between certain qualification grades in chess (class A player, class B player, etc.).

Just think about it: how many classes could be counted between a beginner and the world champion in chess and in go? In principle, this can be counted: take the beginner who has just learnt the basic units of the game. Find the weakest player who is just one class above him. Then find the next player who is still above by just one class, but not better than that. Continue this search and sooner or later you will certainly get to the world champion. This way you have already determined how many classes there are in the span of human knowledge in the given game.

In the case of chess, quite a good approximation can be arrived at by a much simpler and also more practical method. We have seen that about 200 rating points represent a difference of one class. A beginner has about 1300 points, while the world champion scores about 2800 — thus the depth of the game is about eight or nine classes.

Making similar calculations on the basis of go qualifications, we will get a depth of about 13–15 classes. Thus, a surprisingly great difference can be found between chess and go — and this statement is already based on objective measurements rather than subjective feelings.

Now it can be sensed that it is not idle talk to say go requires more complex schemata than chess, or is somehow more holistic, at least on the candidate master level (about the qualification of 1 kyu or 1 dan). The Japanese consider go as an organic part of their culture. They feel go expresses their fundamental system of values, aesthetic principles and ways of thinking: it is about the same thing as the story of the Zen master and the samurai. We generally consider chess as a very good game, but do not attach the expression of the essence of European thinking to it. Ex-world champion of chess Bobby Fischer said that for him "chess is life". A grandmaster's tens of thousands of schemata perhaps really allow such a subtle and refined way of expression that would justify a statement like this, but a candidate master cannot yet feel that chess would express the complexity of life for him.

Once we have a concept of depth like the above, let us wander away from our point in a brief paragraph. By the same method it soon turns out that ice hockey or basketball are deeper games than soccer: there are more classes of difference between an average selected school team and the world champion team in the former games. Or to put it in another way: the tenth best team has a much better chance of beating the world champion team in soccer than in basketball. It is customary to say that "the ball is just as round for everyone" when we want to say that even the weaker team has a chance. According to this, a soccer ball is "rounder" than a basketball. Perhaps this is why soccer is loved so much in my part of the world, and perhaps this is also why it cannot take roots more deeply in some other regions of the world, like in Japan or in the United States (although perhaps the excessive roundness of the ball disturbs these two nations because of different reasons). Theoretically, the depth of individual abilities in team sports could also be measured. I have not done it, but in my very rough estimate I have the feeling that at the personal level there is no difference in depth between soccer and basketball: the essential difference between the two games is somewhere in the structure of the whole game. Here again, the whole is more than the sum of its parts.

Returning to our main train of thoughts, our concept of depth will become especially interesting if we consider that the ranges of the amount of schemata in chess and in go are the same: it is between zero and a few tens of thousands. Thus, if we want to determine the levels of qualifications according to the amount of known schemata (as we have done in Chapter 11), then the differences among the achievements of different levels will not be so clear-cut. If go is a deeper game than chess, a player who knows 2000 schemata will beat another player who knows only 1000 schemata more easily in go than in chess. This is possible only if the schemata are more complex in go than in chess (at least below the level of grandmasters). We have mentioned that go expresses life for Japanese go players more than chess does for Europeans, as the game is less abstract for them. Go is the product of Eastern thinking: it points towards expressing the world as a whole; chess has its roots more deeply in European thinking, even if its origins lie in India.

Perhaps this is why programmers feel that it is more difficult to write a go program than a chess program. Their feeling is justified: the level of candidate masters can be reached in chess by the standard methods of programming, provided a fast enough computer is available. Beyond this point, however, even faster computers are of little help, as the figure also showed. In case of go, even the level of candidate masters seems very distant. Yet there is no lack of motivation: besides the size of the challenge it is said that a prize of one million dollars is being offered to anyone who writes a go program of the professional master level; a part of this sum is offered even to those whose programs only reach the level of 1 kyu (strong candidate master).

There seems to be a greater depth in those areas whose professional schemata stand closer to those of everyday thinking. They are also the areas where even the level of candidate masters can hardly be reached by the methods of artificial intelligence. Programs interested in natural languages are involved characteristically in such areas.

Program SHRDLU

The level of programs translating from one language to another can at best be defined as weak candidate master level. Although their vocabulary is far above this level (nothing prevents us from entering the vocabulary of any large dictionary into the memory of the computer), these words are merely data for the translator programs; they are not schemata. We can use only a few thousands of them as some kinds of schemata. Several complex schemata used by man have quite naturally proven totally impossible to be formalized so far. If someone could program the correct use of the five most frequent English words (the, of, and, a, to), simultaneously with this act, he would most likely have several relevant problems of artificial intelligence solved as well, just as a by-product.

One of the most elegant results in the research of natural human languages is Terry Winograd's 1972(!) program called SHRDLU. (The program received its name after the 7th–12th most frequently used letters of the English alphabet; the first six are: ETAOIN.) This program operated exclusively within the world of simple building blocks (cubes, pyramids and boxes), but within this world it understood and carried out quite complex instructions given in colloquial English. If at the beginning of a conversation it was told "Put the pyramid on the green cube," the program asked which pyramid we had thought of. But if a few sentences later we asked "What is under the pyramid?" it would reply unhesitatingly, just as every normal man would, "the green cube". SHRLDU produced astoundingly many, similarly intelligent answers.

SHRDLU knew only 200 words, although theoretically its vocabulary could have been supplemented. Each word triggered one or more complex programs, and these programs were connected to each other according to an entangled system in the course of understanding a sentence. The complete SHRDLU consisted of about 500 such programs. Today this program would be called a kind of expert system also, while its 500 sub-programs would be called the rules. Some of these programs were almost as complex as we imagine schemata to be. For instance, the program about the use of the pronoun "it" could adapt in various ways to all sorts of contextual conditions, although several quite common everyday uses of "it" were still outside the world of SHRDLU (e.g. it is raining, it is necessary to).

As opposed to the previous programs that worked with a few, but general rules, SHRDLU resembled a large entangled knot, as Winograd described it; today we might also say it constituted a kind of tangled hierarchy. Winograd said, "it is tangled, but is not incomprehensible". However, as soon as programmers wanted to apply the same principle to a larger vocabulary and a wider world, the program became immensely confused and worked worse than before. Although SHRDLU's method seemed to have proven to be the most promising start, no one has ever been able to write a better program, based on the same principle, ever since. SHRDLU perhaps has the intelligence of 6–8 year old children in the world of building bricks; in this narrow field it has probably reached the level of candidate masters. But again, the improvement of the program came up against the limit of complexity of candidate masters.

The critics of Winograd's program stress that, even though the program might work better than other programs based on the rules of formal logic or on other general theories, it is so tangled that no useful theory can be made out of it regarding how the understanding of human language works. On the other hand, it was just this entanglement, this lack of a general and uniform background theory that gave strength to the program: its functioning has backed the theory of tangled hierarchies! The strength of today's expert systems is also due to their several entangled rules, though their limits are also set by those very rules.

Since people are usually masters in understanding their native languages, the performance of programs translating at the level of candidate masters is very annoying for them. It is more work to correct such texts than to translate the whole material again. Those who work on developing automatic dictaphones also encounter similar difficulties. When you hear a text you can write it down because you understand it. Just try to transcribe a text heard in an unknown language: the result will be amazingly poor even if the spelling of the language is totally phonetic.

The greatest problem concerning the tasks with natural languages is that it is difficult to narrow the range within which the program has to work. In the case of dictaphones it may be accepted if it understands only its owner's voice, but it is less acceptable if it understands only certain types of sentences. In special areas of more abstract professions it is more likely that we can find such a narrow "world" for the expert systems in which they can really solve problems at the level of candidate masters, and this "world" is still interesting enough to have a general demand for expertise at that level.

An expert system providing advice at the level of candidate masters can be very useful if human experts are unavailable or very expensive and the help of an average specialist is sufficient, with no need for an outstanding expert. For instance, a chess program at the level of candidate masters is a respectable opponent for 99% of the people; it is a sure business success. Generally, in areas where reaching even the level of candidate masters entails difficulties and requires great efforts, expert systems will be marketable and of great use. However, in areas where one can easily reach the level of candidate masters or which are closely related to our everyday schemata, the performance of artificial intelligence programs is far from being satisfactory.

How intelligent are expert systems?

The methodology of expert systems makes it possible to reach the level of candidate masters in a lot of areas. However, it should be seen also that these results are rather deceptive. When the knowledge of an expert system reaches the level of candidate masters, it is strictly limited to that very narrow field of specialty. The program does not exhibit what has been established before about the main characteristics of candidate masters, i.e. its professional schemata are separated from its everyday schemata. Or if it does, it does it in a special way: its everyday schemata are totally missing. Therefore, although the program's special knowledge might be satisfactory at the level of candidate masters, from time to time it can commit unexpected and awkward absurdities. It can make such mistakes in quite common professional questions as even a beginner would never make: he does not even have to be warned, for beginners are just beginners and not idiots.

The performance of today's programs that we perceive at the level of candidate masters is the result of a kind of "optical illusion". Those who use these programs are intelligent people, therefore they rarely ask evident things. Thus they do not notice how absurd or how dangerously narrow-minded these programs are. We have seen this to be true even in an area like chess.

By our present knowledge it is easier to make a program at the level of candidate masters than at that of intermediate students, not because it requires less work but because, paradoxically, we cannot actually make such programs. For at the intermediate level it becomes immediately apparent what the system *does not* know and the user starts to examine or test the program. With this attitude he asks more and more evident questions, questions that are evident even for common sense, therefore he will get sillier and sillier answers. However, persons getting acquainted with a program on the level of candidate masters can see that the program knows a lot of things and he will be interested in what else the program knows. Essentially, it is the effect of a good student versus a poor student that is tested. The shortcomings of the program at the level of candidate masters are easily supplemented by the knowledge of its user who thus accepts the program as an expert system. The user of the intermediate level program, however, puts his finger on the program's weakest points and thus he is less and less likely to accept even what the program does know.

Therefore, when evaluating artificial intelligence programs of practical use, we implicitly (and thus deceptively) make use of the fact that *we* are intelligent, that we are already at the master level in everyday understanding, therefore we relieve the program from being intelligent and are content if it has good knowledge. From the aspect of narrow expertise we justly rate the best products of expert systems as being at the level of candidate masters, but artificial intelligence is far from reaching that level *in general*: this would presume an already existing everyday intelligence at the master level.

When we need professional advice from an expert system we are looking not for general intelligence but for a narrow range of expertise and a reasoning ability. Therefore, expert systems can be successful without getting any closer to solving the fundamental problems of artificial intelligence. Expert systems can be considered as the independent by-products of artificial intelligence research. If expert systems prove to be useful in the long run, after a while no one will remember that once these systems had been listed under artificial intelligence. If, however, the success of expert systems at the market is kept alive only by the attractive slogan of artificial intelligence, then sooner or later they will be completely forgotten and their useful technical parts will be built into the general tricks of making databases.

The prospects of artificial intelligence

The development of computer technology has changed our views about artificial intelligence. Performing the four arithmetical operations was a peak mental performance five hundred years ago. Only the greatest masters of arithmetics could exactly determine the quotients of large numbers. By the spreading of the decimal system this task became so simple that the division of any number became a minimum requirement in elementary school. A similar situation might arise with the results of artificial intelligence. If, for instance, the chess programs operating on the present principles played at the level of world champions, we would probably soon withdraw chess from the sphere of pastimes requiring great mental efforts. Chess, however, seems to form a complex enough world to prevent us from knowing it thoroughly through methods so simple. Perhaps this is why it can have grandmasters at all.

There are a few simple games that computers can play perfectly. Backgammon, the popular board game, is more complicated than can be played perfectly by a computer, but in Monte Carlo, H.J. Berliner's program beat the human world champion at a stake-game. As a matter of fact, in Berliner's analysis the program was lucky: two mistakes of the computer could be spotted in the course of the game, while its opponent made none — but the program was so strong that it could make use of its luck to win.

In short, the present state of affairs in artificial intelligence can be characterized as follows: the programs that work are not intelligent, whereas those that are intelligent do not work. For instance, there are chess programs (at the level of candidate masters) and expert systems that work, but their principles of operation are very far from the mechanisms of human intelligence. The operating principles of EURISKO or SHRDLU perhaps approach man's thinking better, but they can hardly be generalized: before reaching the complexity of candidate masters, they become immensely tangled networks that cannot be grasped.

One of the most fashionable slogans of knowledge engineering is "eliciting knowledge". By this knowledge engineers mean the attempts to ask grandmasters questions, the answers to which reveal clearly how grandmasters think and how they solve problems. Knowledge engineers often complain that masters cannot offer their knowledge lucidly and comprehensibly. Actually, they often have the feeling that masters do not even want to, perhaps because they fear losing their bread. That might be possibly so, but this is not the main point. The main reason of failure may be rather that grandmasters really cannot impart their intuitive knowledge in a formal way. Practically, knowledge engineers ask them to regress to the lower level of when they were only candidate masters and when they were more or less fully aware of what they knew.

It is not certain that we should look for features in artificial intelligence similar to man's way of thinking. In the cases of most machines, from cars to lathes, we find just those characteristics important, interesting and useful that are radically different from ours. If we have such an attitude toward artificial intelligence, we shall gain useful complements to our way of thinking, and may be more tolerant with its annoying stupidity. On the other hand, it is possible that, in order to solve practical problems like the translating program or the dictaphone, we shall inevitably create some kind of an intelligence that is similar to ours. However, this can barely be achieved by our present means; radically new principles have to be discovered, but the date of such discoveries cannot be predicted yet. Marvin Minsky, one of the founders of artificial intelligence who at the beginning was also convinced of fast successes, said thirty years later: "I think the artificial intelligence problem is one of the hardest science has ever undertaken."

Nothing in principle precludes the possibility of creating an artificial intelligence that is similar to ours (although nothing guarantees this possibility either). But it is very likely that, if something like this can be created, it will be based on units resembling our schemata: they will be living and changing things. Artificial intelligence, if at all, will probably be as diverse as human ways of thinking. Let us quote Hofstadter on the question whether or not there will ever be a chess program that beats every human being: "No. There may be programs which can beat anyone at chess, but they will not be exclusively chess players. They will be programs of *general* intelligence, and they will be just as temperamental as people. 'Do you want to play chess?' 'No, I am bored with chess. Let's talk about poetry.' That may be the kind of dialogue you could have with a program that could beat everyone."

Sky and Water II © 1990 M. C. Escher Heirs / Cordon Art – Baarn – Holland

PART III

THE STRENGTH OF DIVERSITY

14. The limits of rationality

The essence of rationality is that it appeals to reason, and only to pure reason. Thoughts, arguments and conclusions with no subjective elements and independent of the individual's emotions and current state of consciousness are called rational.

In the Hungarian satirist Jenő Rejtő's novel, Poppy, the daredevil developed quite peculiar schemata about human heads: "a person's head is a graceful and fragile little trifle". The mental model of a brain surgeon is most certainly different in many aspects. (Since we are going to examine inferences in the following, we have switched to the expression mental model. This expression has no deeper meaning for us, as we have seen in Chapter 6. Still, the following argumentation will flow more easily by using this terminology — similar reasons may also explain the diversity of schema-concepts.)

There are conclusions that are made possible only by the mental model of a brain surgeon, while others are allowed by both models. When the conclusions are based on the same assumptions in both models, Poppy and the brain surgeon are expected to draw the same conclusions because they are both intelligent persons, and their mental models probably follow the logic of things correctly. And the logic of things does not depend on the nature of our mental models.

Thus, if our heroes wanted to draw conclusions from hypotheses with the aid of formal logic, the conclusions they would reach would not differ very much. The conclusions of formal logic are independent of the model built around them, and must be true in every model that follows the logic of things correctly. Otherwise we could not regard formal logic as the correct way of reasoning. The general utility of formal logic is ensured by the fact that the reverse of what we have said is also true: if a conclusion is correct in every model that follows the logic of things correctly, then it can be deduced by means of formal logic, too. In order to prove this (already mathematical, or rather metamathematical) statement mathematically, we only have to assume that formal logic in itself never leads to contradictory forms of conclusion.

In the previous paragraph we did not follow the usual terminology of mathematical logic; e.g. we talked about the "logic of things" instead of "consistency". We are not going to use the exact terminology and definitions of mathematics in the following either; we will be content with creating relatively undistorted, metaphorical, everyday schemata from the mathematical theorems, with the aid of which we can develop our train of thought further.

Thus, formal logic is a kind of bridge among the different mental models. The Church–Turing thesis, mentioned in the previous chapter, also expresses the belief that, in principle, no other bridge is necessary: everything that can be unequivocally expressed in different mental models can also be said in the language of formal logic. In this view something being "rational" can be identified with its being "formally logical".

The problem of infinite loops

The *Weltanschauung* based on the unlimited cognitive strength of pure rationality has been made quite unstable or at least too complicated by the results of mathematical logic in the last 60 years. We have already met a result of this kind, i.e. Gödel's theorem in Chapter 5.

In Puzzle 8, Chapter Zero, we asked whether or not the following sentence was correct: "There are three error in this sentence." However long you scrutinize the sentence, you will find only two errors: one is the missing plural at the end of "error" and the other is the misspelling of "sentense". Thus the sentence is not true at first glance. But then the third error in the sentence is that it is not true. In view of that, the sentence is true after all, for it really has three errors. But then there are only two errors, for the third one we found is not an error. The snake has bitten its own tail, we can start reasoning all over again.

If we do not want to get into the same boat as the more stupid digger wasp at the beginning of Chapter 5, all we can do is spread our arms and say that this sentence is neither provable, nor disprovable. It cannot be decided within the sphere we are working in, it is a statement Gödel spoke about. Although in this case we were not thinking within the frame of a formal system, Gödel's theorem points out just that: no matter how well we formalize the frames of our thinking, there will always appear similar undecidable questions.

What can we do if we want to do something with a statement like this by all means, e.g. because for some reason or another it is very important to us to get to know the nature of the things the statement is about? In this case we cannot do anything but change the frames of our thinking. If, for example, you change what you mean by error and exclude the case when "error" means that the meaning of a sentence is false, the problem will disappear immediately. To tell the truth, this way you have bent your native language a little, but it is not too high a price to pay for solving a hitherto hopeless problem successfully, is it? On the other hand, Gödel's theorem guarantees that sooner or later similarly unsolvable problems will be found in the new language, too. This is only an analogy, of course; it would be valid literally only if the analysis of the puzzle had been made in a formalized language rather than by our common sense.

Science tries to use formalized language as much as possible; thus it is almost exactly true of science that if it wants to exclude no truths from the beginning, it will have to change its reference system continually (resulting from Gödel's theorem). As we have seen in Chapter 12, this has led to the disintegration of uniform science. Perhaps this is why ours is no longer the age of individuals equipped with encyclopedic knowledge.

Once it is unavoidable to meet such cognitive infinite loops, it would be nice at least to find a formal way that could tell that we are in such a situation. Then we could recognize immediately that we are dealing with a hopeless problem and choose another problem or start revising our system. In the case of the puzzle we have realized within seconds that our thoughts are hopelessly returning to themselves, but such recognition in more complex problems may take generations.

Unfortunately this way out is also hopeless, at least generally. There is no formal procedure (i.e. computer program) that could identify the unpleasant situation of the digger wasp generally, i.e. no program can tell when boredom should set in (p. 78). We are going to prove this statement by formal methods too, because on the one hand it happens to be quite simple, and on the other hand we want to give a sample of the style of similar demonstrations. If you are not interested in the proof you may just as well skip the next three paragraphs.

(a) We have seen that in the computers based on Neumann's principle every program consists of a sequence of numbers; the programs and data look alike. Our universal program searching for infinite loops (let's call it U) receives two series of data as input: program P and the set of data X. Thus, program U decides for any P and X whether or not P would stop if run with the data set X. Suppose program U lets us know the result by writing 1 if program P would stop sooner or later, and writing 2 if P gets into an infinite loop with data X. This can also be written as: $U(P,X)=1$, if program P stops with data X within a finite period of time, and $U(P,X)=2$, if it does not.

(b) Now, let us write a sly program, called S. Let the input data of S be any P program, and let it work as follows: Program S should first make program U run so that it gives program P to program U as both the input data. (This is possible, since a program is also a series of numbers. Thus program S can start to function by calculating the value of $U(P,P)$). If program U gives 2 as result, program S should stop immediately; if, however, program U gives 1 as result, program S should mark time forever. Once we have program U, it is easy to write a program like S. In short, sooner or later program S will stop with any kind of program P if $U(P,P)=2$, but it will get into an infinite loop if $U(P,P)=1$.

(c) Now, let us see what our universal program will do if both of its input data are the previously produced program S. What will be the value of $U(S,S)$? Suppose $U(S,S)=1$. Thus program U states that program S will stop if it gets the code of program S (i.e. itself) as the input data (in the place of P). However, in step (b) we have created program S so that it should stop only if $U(S,S)=2$. This contradicts our starting point, for we are just studying the case of $U(S,S)=1$. We have nothing left, but program U should give the value 2 if the input data pair is S,S. This way it says that if program S gets the code of program S as input data, it will get into an infinite loop. But it does so only if $U(S,S)=1$. Thus, this case has also led to a contradiction. Therefore, our program which we believed to be universal can give no answer if our sly program S is given as both of its input data. Thus, program U cannot be so universal after all.

If we interpret rationality according to the Church–Turing thesis, it will follow from our result that there can possibly exist no rational reason that could determine whether or not it has gotten into a situation similar to where the more stupid digger wasp has found itself. Yet a healthy human being can usually notice getting into an infinite loop and will somehow leave the situation. The biologists also stopped poking the digger wasps after a while. Thus, the question arises: how is it possible that man can solve theoretically unsolvable problems with his reason?

One possibility is the assumption of some kind of cognition beyond reason. We cannot exclude this possibility for sure; this question is probably a Gödelian one within the framework of science: it cannot be proven or disproven. But either this assumption or its negation can be taken as an axiom. Science (primarily in the spirit of Occam's razor) has chosen negation.

The other possibility is that even man has no ability to recognize all infinite loops. When we talked about meta-heuristics in Chapter 5, we saw that many signs really show that we are not always able to recognize our unpleasant, sometimes outright self-destructing, infinite loops.

The theory of limited rationality

If man is considered as a totally rational being, it will follow from the aforesaid that there must be cases where he does not realize having gotten into an infinite loop and fails to get out of it. Of course, this is not rational behavior. Thus, the assumption of total, unlimited rationality not only contradicts experience but is contradictory by itself.

Herbert Simon started elsewhere and arrived at the conclusion that man's decisions are not fully characterized by total rationality. When making decisions, we are far from having the capacity of attention necessary to think over every marginal condition and possibility (e.g. we are also limited by the capacity of STM), or the necessary power for calculations. As we saw it in Chapter 5, most of the time the use of heuristic methods is unavoidable; we are forced to look for solutions acceptable at a certain level, instead of finding the perfect, global optimal solution.

The theory of *bounded rationality* evoked strong aversion in economists. Strangely enough, psychologists were not surprised at all at these thoughts; an idea like that is perfectly natural for them, being in full harmony with their general paradigm. Although economists also know that there is usually no way of finding the perfect optimal solution, in their *Weltanschauung* the sensible limit of searching for the optimum can also be determined by totally rational methods. The paradigm of economics is basically *norma-tive*, setting out from how people should behave in order to reach certain goals and how the conditions of such behavior could be most suitably produced. The paradigm of psychology is basically *descriptive*, setting out from how people really behave, and looking for explanatory theoretical constructions that fit these facts.

Simon demonstrates the idea of bounded rationality in the following example: suppose there is a haystack in which there are needles. By which method could we find the sharpest needle? If the haystack is too large, it will be hopeless to hunt through it. "How can we tell how to stop searching? One rule is to stop when we have used a specified amount of effort. Another quite different rule is to stop when we have a needle sharp enough to sew with. ... Now an economist would say that the proper rule is to search until the expected improvement in sharpness per minute of additional search is worth less than the cost of the search. This is true, but not always helpful, because it is often far easier, in practice, to define what is meant by 'sharp enough' needle than to measure the marginal value of additional sharpness, or to estimate the amount of search that would be required to produce it. The process of searching for 'good enough' solutions is called *satisficing*."

For evaluating satisfaction, we have several heuristics that may give contradicting results. As opposed to searching for the optimum, satisficing may also be considered as a kind of meta-heuristic or meta-schema that interprets, evaluates and perhaps coordinates the contradictions of the results of different heuristics indicating the degree of satisfaction.

On the basis of the theory of bounded rationality, a lot of such phenomena of economic organizations can be explained that cannot be interpreted by classical theories. In spite of this, Simon's thoughts hardly had any direct effect upon microeconomic theories. According to József Kindler and István Kiss, "Perhaps this can be explained by the fact that man is reluctant to face his own limits, instinctively bending towards accepting the favorable 'self-portrait' suggested by boundless rationality."

Bounded rationality is also rationality to the core. Common sense takes its own limits in calculation and attention into consideration, and tries to find optimal solutions accordingly. In the light of this recognition, which is baffling and irrational, it seems to be now the behavior that does not take our obvious present limits of capacity into consideration at all. The paradigm of economics is just like that: its scholars are thinking basically in normative models even when putting in a claim for only description. Other branches of science that feel it less their duty to give daily, practical recipes face the less flattering phenomena and limits of their thinking (and even its irrational elements) more calmly.

170

It would not do without heuristics

Two types of limiting factors have been seen in the realization of perfect and pure rationality. The problem of endless loops opened purely theoretical limits: formal logic proved to be capable of proving that it cannot solve certain types of problems completely. The theory of bounded rationality has set out from practical difficulties: the limited nature of our information processing capacity prevents us from thinking problems over at any depth. This observation leads directly to the recognition that we cannot avoid using heuristic methods in making our decisions and in solving problems. Interestingly enough, purely theoretical results also point in this direction.

Mathematical logic and the theory of algorithms abound in results similar to the theorem stating that it is impossible to pinpoint infinite loops. With a little exaggeration we can say that we need luck to find a problem that can be solved in its complete generality.

Theoretical science finds its own well-designed puzzles even within the changed frameworks and modified paradigms: it endeavors to work out special conditions which are as general as possible, under which more or less universal solutions can still be found. Progress continues. In concrete problems, however, it is usually not easy to decide whether or not a special condition applies to the given case, and which is the one that does. In similar cases the more or less general solutions become heuristic: since the conditions of their application may be more difficult to test than to try, often it is worth trying one of the more or less general solutions without having some guarantee of the method's success.

A large amount of experience may have accumulated on which method is usually successful in special domains and in which cases. This experience cannot necessarily be worded formally, thus the conditions are set for an originally uniform and general problem to become an independent specialty with its own grandmasters.

Our train of thoughts has set out from the limiting theorems of formal logic, but the last paragraphs sound much more general. This is not due to loose phrasing, but to the fact that the branches of science have developed from formalized thinking, thus we can consider the development of mathematical logic as a model.

Limits of complexity

Both the theoretical and practical limits of formal logic displayed so far were of a technical nature. These limits can be regarded as the internal affairs of rational thinking. Formalized science has brought them to the surface, and has also found ways of handling them within its own framework: the development of increasingly general special procedures, the introduction of heuristics, and the extension or change of the system of axioms in the cases of Gödelian questions.

Those branches of science whose subject is human thinking also accept formal logic as their own way of expression, but do not consider it as an axiom that their subject really operates that way. Psychology also stays within the frames of formal thinking: it cannot do otherwise if it is to be considered scientific. But it does not follow from this that thinking itself remains within this frame. As we have seen in Chapter 3, sociobiology also puts up such questions as whether or not a given female will demand long courtship or if a given person will or will not solve puzzles outside the framework of rational consideration. But it does so strictly within a rational framework.

The position of artificial intelligence is still more interesting. As a technical discipline it might as well have built on irrational elements, e.g. by capturing a few ghosts in butterfly nets, and building a super-intelligent computer from them with the aid of paraprocessors. However, there are scarce possibilities for this nowadays, so artificial intelligence is forced at present to materialize its results in the form of computer programs. It works with the same computers about which we have already proven that they cannot create a perfect infinite loop identifier (or many other things).

Just because artificial intelligence programs are based on perfectly rational principles for lack of anything better, they will not necessarily behave rationally. It is easy to make a program that prints out that $2 \times 2 = 5$ without making its blood pressure rise. (Perhaps one of the greatest obstacles in realizing artificial intelligence is the very fact that machines have no blood pressure or other "vital juices" in a figurative sense...)

We have arrived here at a third type of limit of rationality, one that cannot be discovered within the framework of formal logic, but by comparing certain results of artificial intelligence and cognitive psychology. In the study of the break in the trend line of development of chess programs, the break turned out to have appeared when the strength of the programs reached the level of candidate masters. We have also found that nowadays

172

the other results of artificial intelligence are also at the level of candidate master at the best, and the complexity of rules built into expert systems also corresponds to this level at the best. A profession or a branch of science can be acquired in schools or at universities also up to this level by totally formalized and rational means. All this indicates that the complexity of the things that can be phrased by purely rational means and independently of our everyday schemata can hardly exceed the amount of a few thousand schemata.

The key concept here is cognitive schema, which is conceived so that it may be very complex by itself, and may also include its continuously changing relationships with other schemata. Thus, the third type of limit of rationality is being outlined along a paradigm whose fundament is totally independent of the concepts of formal logic. The bridge to formal logic (and thus, to rationality) came about because the purely rationally phrased results of artificial intelligence could achieve, quite suspiciously, the same level (and not higher) as the complexity level of candidate masters' cognitive schemata.

The two (theoretical and practical) types of limits of rationality considered hitherto is now supplemented by a third type which expresses the maximum complexity that can be reached by purely rational thinking as measured by the amount of closely cross-organized cognitive schemata. This limit seems to be in the region of a few thousand cognitive schemata.

On the other hand, we have also seen that human thinking is able to handle even higher levels of complexity. In everyday matters and relationships man is at least at the level of masters. By their cognitive schemata, grandmasters are able to comprehend complexity at an order of magnitude higher than candidate masters. There have been many signs already in Chapter 11 that grandmasters think intuitively, not only by means of rationality. This thought is supported by another, quite different type of argument: the trend of development of artificial intelligence broke very similarly in different areas.

The scientific world was very much surprised at the discovery of the limits of rationality; especially, the theoretical limits (Gödel's theorem and the failing of the hoped-for omnipotence of formal logic) had caused a severe shock. Science, however, proved to be more efficient than a method to be discarded just because it had turned out to be unable, even theoretically, to be as uniform as it wanted, and that not only our deficient knowledge had caused its complexity. These negative results do not contradict the correctness of scientific *Weltanschauung* by themselves, although they do not support it either: they do not deal with that. But they do imply that, in order to understand man's thinking mechanisms and to realize artificial intelligence, not only purely rational thinking but also other cognitive ways have to be examined more thoroughly.

15. High-level cognitive schemata

We know more than what we can express. Even the tools of the arts cannot necessarily help this. Arthur Rimbaud is an example: he gave up poetry at the age of 18 forever, after "I have written silence and nights, put down what cannot be put down. I have recorded giddiness." Poetry is a profession where grandmasters mature early. Perhaps Rimbaud also got the feeling that he had reached the maximum of achievable complexity, and we learn from him that he could express only a fraction of his psyche and feelings. Perhaps Mallarmé was less lucky, because he did not give it up: he writhed under and worked on some of his quatrains for as long as ten years, to make the order of the words and sounds, and the relationship among their meanings, as exact as possible.

We can say something more exact about science that works with purely formal wordings. If we accept the Church–Turing thesis as well as that we can comprehend one order of magnitude of complexity greater than what we can express by purely rational means, it will follow that we will not always be able to put into formal words the route by which we arrive at a recognition. We can phrase the result but not the way leading to it. It has no consequence whatsoever upon the limits of cognition: once we have the result, it can already be built into the rational schemata of candidate masters, too; it does not have to be re-discovered. However, we have learnt something about the way of cognition, namely, that it must have further means as well, at least above the level of candidate masters. Previously we called these means *intuition*, and also said that intuition was the result of complex, high-level cognitive schemata.

We have only little well-founded scientific knowledge about the cognitive schemata of grandmasters. However, everyday life is a good ground for learning more about high level schemata, because in this field almost all of us are at least masters, and thus our intuition is operable. Indeed, several high-level cognitive schemata or general heuristics could be demonstrated that could be caught in experiments on the one hand, and are absolutely not rational on the other hand. In this chapter we are going to collect a few characteristic examples from different areas of psychology.

Anchoring

Without making exact calculations, quickly try to estimate the result of the following multiplicaton: $1 \times 2 \times 3 \times 4 \times 5 \times 6 \times 7 \times 8$. I cannot know, of course, what your estimation was but, unless you had plenty of experience with similar multiplications, e.g. as a math student, you would probably have quite underestimated the result. A. Tversky and D. Kahneman had students of different majors make this estimation. They received an average estimate of around 500. Those who were asked to estimate the product of $8 \times 7 \times 6 \times 5 \times 4 \times 3 \times 2 \times 1$ just as quickly, estimated it to be about 2200 on the average.

The true result of 40,320, indicating that both groups had greatly underestimated the result, is not very important in this study. It is more important that the estimation depended so much on the sequence of the numbers to be multiplied. Those who were presented with the larger numbers first, gave larger estimates.

In another experiment half of the subjects were asked whether the percentage of African countries in the United Nations is below or above 10%. The other half was asked whether this ratio was below or above 65%. Then both groups were asked what they thought the more exact ratio of African countries could be in the UN. The first group (having 10% in the first question) gave an average estimate of 25%, while the second group (having 65% in the first question) said 45% on the average. (The truth is around 30%).

It is easy to see the common essence in the two experiments: adjustment to the original data, made on the first piece of information even if the order of the pieces of information is totally irrelevant for the task. The similarity between the two tasks slightly resembles what we discovered in Chapter 6, where the story of the first edition of the *Encyclopaedia Britannica* and that of the heroic age of gramophone record production both adhered to the very same schema.

This kind of thinking mechanism is called *anchoring heuristic*. Somebody's vague feeling, however, that the two experimental results belong to the same group, does not prove by itself that such a general heuristic does really work in most people's thinking. It is also possible that they seem to be similar only on the surface, while their real ways of operation are quite different. This is why investigators tried to define more precisely what is common in these results, and further experiments were designed where this heuristic would be expected to distort the results in a well predictable way. This approach has led to definite success: it has been proven that there is really a general heuristic in our everyday thinking as was indicated by the two experiments demonstrated above. When making judgements in problematic situations, we often take hold of some starting value from the phrasing of the problem or from making a few fragmentary calculations, then adjust our decision to this value.

The anchoring heuristic can explain such regularly observed phenomena like the almost permanent underestimation of deadlines, and that we tend to overestimate the final production of technologies that require several small successive steps (where there are only small losses at each step). We do so despite the fact that, in principle, we know that many a little makes a mickle.

The coinciding results of the various experiments show that not only had the investigators formed a schema in their heads and later called it anchoring, but also in most people's heads there really exists such a general schema, whether or not they know about it. Relying on the experimental results, we may consider the anchoring heuristic as a *psychological reality*: this concept almost certainly describes a really existing, genuine thing; it is one of our general and unwittingly operating thinking schemata. It is really a kind of heuristic, for the procedure may lead to erroneous results (even in a predictable way), although in most cases it makes fast and correct conclusions possible.

The heuristic of availability

A typical example of this heuristic is our driving more slowly when we can see traces of an earlier accident by the roadside. We feel flying to be even more dangerous, although statistics tell us that there are much less fatal aircraft accidents not only per passenger mile, but also as compared to the number of flights. But we know more memorable examples of fatal aircrashes than car accidents, and imagine the number of flights to be less than the real number, because we fly relatively rarely.

The following is quite another example from the experiments studying the psychological reality of another type of heuristic emerging after the previous two examples: which do you think is more frequent: an English word starting with the letter r or the third letter of a word being r? The majority of the people will feel after thinking a while that the letter r is more frequent at the beginning of a word than as a third letter. The truth is just the opposite. Still, when you try to find examples of both cases you will find words starting with r much more easily than ones whose third letter is r. The reason for this is that it is easier to make a search in our memory by the first letter, which makes our estimation erroneous.

There is another experiment to discover the nature of the phenomenon outlined here: the experimental subjects have been read a list of 39 famous people, then they were asked who were in the majority on the list, men or women. The investigators used two lists. In one of them 19 men and 20 women were listed randomly, while in the other list there were 20 men and 19 women. But there was a twist in the composition of the lists: women were relatively more famous than men in those with only 19 women, while in the other list this was reversed.

If the women were more famous (but less in number) almost all of the experimental subjects thought there were more women in the list, while in the other list they thought the reverse to be true. We know that, owing to the limit of STM capacity, the subjects could recall only a fraction of the whole list when making their decisions about the ratio of men and women. With such long lists the subjects could also group the names they heard into more complex schemata and the time was long enough to use LTM to a certain extent as well, but this again favored the more famous names: in another study, an average of about 12 names were recalled from a total of 19 household names, while only 8–9 were remembered from 20 less famous names. The decision was influenced by how well a name could be recalled.

The heuristic of availability is applied when the probability of an event, a fact, a consequence has to be estimated relying on our memories and experiences. In such cases an unintentional procedure works in us, attempting to recall both examples and counterexamples; our decision will depend upon the ease with with such examples can be found. This also belongs to our high-level cognitive schemata, for it works well in a lot of cases, regardless of the concrete problem. The many kinds of erroneous, non-rational behavior that can be predicted on its basis show the general validity of this heuristic.

If a machine breaks down, we usually start our search with the most frequently occurring problem, even if signs point in a different direction. We tighten the usually loose screws and check whether the defect is still

178

present. The efficiency of the heuristic of availability is shown by the fact that superficial treatment is so very often successful.

This schema also explains the significance of the history of things. In his theory of limited rationality Herbert Simon expounds that, in the practice of a firm, the rules of behavior and decision-making develop in the course of a long process, and they are hardly influenced by the situation of the moment. The phenomenon called QWERTY after Seymour Papert is an even more characteristic example.

This strange word is received if we read together the first six letters of the topmost row of a standard typewriter. The explanation of this arrangement is that in the earliest typewriters the keys often became jammed and got stuck. This problem was solved by putting the letters occurring frequently one after the other in English words as far from each other in the hammers of the mechanism as possible. With the improvement of technology this problem soon became insignificant, but the arrangement of the letters remained the same, although much more rational letter-distributions have been designed since then, with most of the workload sparing the little finger when typing with ten fingers. This new arrangement would not only decrease the occurrence of tendovaginitis, typists' professional disease, considerably but would also increase typing speed by about 30–40%. Still, such a radical reform cannot be widespread, as we are so accustomed to the QWERTY keyboard: it is very available.

The QWERTY phenomenon is very general: it is characteristic of most technical devices that they come into general use in their first primitive, yet usable, forms, and their necessary or inexperienced-type fallibilities will later play a determining role even if technical developments already make such solutions totally irrational. Our past decisions haunt us in all areas of life.

General pattern recognition

The thought that man's thinking is holistic first appeared in Chapter 5 in this book; we tend to perceive the totality of things as a whole, without examining the details. We look down upon people who cannot see the wood for the trees. This observation has become one of our guiding principles, leading to our schema concept, and this paradigm has founded our trains of thoughts about how schemata work, about the complexity and level of expertise.

We have not yet talked much about how our schemata may develop. I cannot raise ardent hopes here either: this problem is one of the most difficult unsolved puzzles of science today. This problem is raised quite differently for experts in biology, artificial intelligence and psychology, and even within these fields for microbiologists, neurobiologists, socio-biologists, cognitive or developmental psychologists. Furthermore, even micro-physics has run into similar problems. The forms of the problem may radically differ from each other in the different areas, but there are more common features in the fundamental problem than there seems to be at first glance because of the different professional languages.

Man has a natural ability to perceive similar characteristic features in the different phenomena of the world, being eager to grasp some common essence in experiences with radically different structures. The previous sentence may justly strike the critical reader's eye: we have talked about the decoding of words like "natural ability" and "characteristic features" on page 89 — they usually mean that we do not understand the essence of the thing. With this sentence I wanted to emphasize the fact rather than cover it. Still, numerous (or innumerable) concrete experimental results indicate that some kind of high-level pattern-recognizing schemata may constitute the basis of the operation and development of our cognitive schemata.

The following is an easy and spectacular demonstration: have the members of a group imagine that they toss a coin thirty times. We state that they cannot really imagine this. Those who think they can should write the result of this imaginary series of tosses on a piece of paper, then take a real coin and jot the results of thirty real tosses down on another piece of paper. In 9 out of 10 cases one can tell the results of the imaginary tosses from that of the real ones.

This trick is usually demonstrated by mathematicians who know the rules of chance and also know how much they may contradict our everyday expectations. Among thirty tosses there may be, and usually there are even 5–6 heads or 5–6 tails in a row, but when you imagine the tosses you will not dare to include such long series, because you will feel it is improbable. The situation is similar to other characteristic patterns that are felt by man to be too regular, but chance will nevertheless produce them: series like H–T–H–T–H–T–H or T–H–H–T–H–H–T–H–H (H — head, T — tail) are good examples. Mathematicians demonstrating this trick usually prepare themselves: they calculate the probability of the occurrence of such patterns in advance, and when they do get the series they determine how improbable they are as a whole. For instance, improbability is higher if no H–H–H–H–H or no T–T–T–T–T series is present. It is highly probable that the less probable series is the imaginary one.

You cannot be sure, of course: chance may be malicious, too. If, for example, somebody shows a series of thirty heads, you may be quite certain that he has not tossed it, but imagined it, because this is the other extreme: it is more likely that somebody imagined it than tossed it. Nevertheless, even chance may cause thirty heads in a row. Yet, even if you cannot go for sure, with a little mental arithmetic you may be 98–99% successful in this demonstration.

Interestingly, this demonstration can be done without previous mathematical preparation, too. If a totally uninitiated person is shown the pairs of papers and is asked to decide quickly which one of the two is less regular he will choose the imagined series with a 90% probability. We feel the result of real chance is more regular. Thus, if you want to do this demonstration without mathematical preparation, you will probably be successful by just glancing at the two pieces of paper, quickly deciding which is less regular or more accidental, then saying that it is *not* the result of chance, it is imaginary. You will make a hit with a 90% probability. You will win nine out of ten bets.

The demonstration makes use of the fact that we unwittingly perceive patterns and regularities in everything we meet, even if they do not follow from the nature of things, even if they are freaks of chance. This is why people who imagined the tosses tried to eliminate everything from the series that was regular. And those who — without mathematical preparation — try to guess which series is not the result of chance will also use their ability to perceive patterns unconsciously everywhere, even with no reason to do so. Since the person who imagines the tosses wants to eliminate every regularity, while chance does not (this is why it is chance!), it is almost certain that chance will leave more regularities in the series, and this can be felt quite easily even by those who are not very educated in mathematics. One does not even have to think too long (in fact, thinking may definitely spoil his success), he should just let his general pattern recognition mechanism work.

What we have said until now does not apply to those people who deliberately leave out too much regularity in the imagined series in order to fool the person who has to make the guess. But such people usually overshoot the mark, and the series will really be more regular than what chance would make. Without further application of mathematics, with a few hours of practice you can easily develop an intuition to feel the

181

level of regularity left by chance, thus you will probably be able to catch dissimulators (who want to hide just the lack of regularity). Once we have this "feeling of regularity", it is surprisingly difficult to express it in words. We shall make the correct decision but cannot tell exactly the reasons. Once we have this ability we shall simply sense whether the regularity of a series is by and large due to chance, or not. Grandmasters' complex intuitive schemata may also develop similarly.

At the root of all this we really tend to see regularity everywhere, even where there is none. Perhaps this basic mechanism has led to the development of superstitions too, but in most cases it makes correct observations possible. This is how our everday schemata may develop, by the help of which we can understand the relationships within our environment, although a certain proportion of faults is unavoidable, giving way to irrational behavior as well.

Specialized pattern-recognizing heuristics

A lot of experimental results indicate that some kind (or even some kinds) of general pattern-recognizing schema(ta) may operate in our thinking. In C.L. Hull's classical experiment, certain groups of Chinese characters were labeled by nonsense radicals. The common element in each character-group was a Chinese radical perfectly masked by the disorderly scrawls around it for the European experimental subjects who did not know the logic of Chinese script. Despite this, the subjects learned to label new characters with the correct nonsense radicals relatively quickly, although they could not put their reasons of categorization into words.

It was mentioned in the previous chapter that man can usually recognize his thought or actions getting into an infinite loop. We have also seen that a sensor like this can only be heuristic, for it cannot give a certain result all the time. It is possible that this characteristic of man is also due to the general pattern-recognizing mechanism, but it may also be possible that we have more special schemata that "perceive boredom".

We do not have enough scientifically founded knowledge to set an experimentally controllable theory about the operation of our most general, high-level schemata. In our present paradigm the investigation of specialized schemata that can be seen under well-defined circumstances seems to be a more promising route. Tversky and Kahneman aimed to describe those general schemata that we use in cases of uncertain data and inadequate knowledge in order to estimate the probability of possible events for ourselves, e.g. to judge the likely risks of our acts. The heuristics of anchoring and availability were already demonstrated. In their theory Tversky and Kahneman proposed a third fundamental heuristic, namely, *representativity*.

We make judgements on the basis of the heuristic of representativity usually when we establish diagnoses even in the most common everyday situations. For instance, let us say you want to get to know how probable it is that your unfamiliar partner in a conversation is an alcoholic. In this case you will mostly base your judgement on how much the given person fits the picture you have created in your mind about a typical alcoholic; how much your partner will represent typical alcoholics. The more the two fit, the more certain you will be about your diagnosis. Naturally the result will depend upon how realistic and subtle your alcoholic schema is: evidently, the model of a psychiatrist is more meaningful and complex than that of a physical education instructor. Probably the mental model of a potential fellow toper accentuates still other aspects. The functioning of the heuristic, however, is not influenced by the nature of our schemata to be compared; we only state it here that your judgements will be based purely on similarity.

This procedure usually leads to success, but the purely rational calculation of probability teaches that this is far from being enough to determine chances correctly. We also have to consider how probable the imagined diagnosis is, independently of the studied case, and how many cases constitute the basis of our image about the typical case.

In experiments that study the operation of the heuristic of representativity, situations were created where the results gained from decisions made on the basis of representativity were totally different from those of decisions based on the calculation of probabilities. For example, the experimental subjects in a study had to watch a class in a school, then half of the subjects were asked to judge how well the teacher and the students had cooperated in the given class, while the other half was asked to judge what the level of cooperation between the teacher and the students would be in the next five years. The subjects were also asked to indicate how sure they were in their judgement. Judgements were similarly sure and extreme in both groups, although the subjects all knew perfectly well that one cannot make as sure a judgement five years in advance on the basis of a single occasion as one can judge a concrete situation.

Here is another example of the operation of the heuristic of representativity: the overwhelming majority of roulette players are convinced that the probability of black increases considerably after a few reds, although they know perfectly well that roulette balls have no memory.

The heuristic of representativity proved to be an excellent descriptive term: it can explain a lot of our many, seemingly irrational acts, and can predict them well. Most of our inconsistencies and irrationalities shown when making decisions can be well explained and predicted with the aid of the three heuristics (anchoring, availability, representativity) of Kahneman and Tversky.

The psychological reality of these heuristics is a difficult problem: do such ways of operation formulated by these heuristics really exist, or are they only the consequences or epiphenomena of our other thinking processes? The descriptive power and practical use of these concepts will not decrease if they turn out to be only about epiphenomena; but then we will have to look elsewhere for the solution of how schemata work.

According to experimental results, the general pattern-recognizing heuristic can be considered as a really existing schema type. The only problem is whether one or several such fundamental general schemata operate in our thinking, and if there are many, do they work independently of each other or do they complement each other? The psychological reality of the heuristic of anchoring was also quite convincing: its operation could definitely be caught, and no more general schema whose epiphenomenon it could be can be seen on the horizon. Although we cannot tell whether the concept covers one or several schemata, once we accept the reality of schemata in general (and at the end of Chapter 7 we decided not to question this, although we may have our doubts), we have no reason to question that this concept of ours describes a really existing schema in our thinking.

In the case of the availability heuristic, the psychological reality of the concept is also very probable, although this may sooner be the epiphenomenon of a more general pattern-recognizing heuristic. We do not have any more precise knowledge about this problem. It can be questioned whether the schema of QWERTY is a true psychological reality or it is the epiphenomenon of the availability heuristic or the general pattern-recognizing heuristic, or even a special case of the former one. Similar to this is the case with the representativity heuristic.

These problems hardly affect the descriptive decision theory as an independent psychological field: the aim here is to develop professional schemata with the aid of which we can better understand man's decision-making mechanisms working in uncertain situatidns. Accordingly, this field studies the improvement and application of the above-described three heuristics. For example, this is how *simulation heuristics* was introduced as an interesting special case of the availability heuristic. A typical example of this is the situation where two persons traveling to the airport get into a traffic jam and miss their planes, one of them by five minutes, the other by half an hour. Evidently, the person who missed his plane by five minutes will be more angry, because he can imagine, and can simulate in his mind more easily that if he had made better decisions in the jam, he might even have reached his plane. Yet, for the final result it is all the same no matter how closely one misses the plane.

But now we are interested not in the increasingly specialized descriptive schemata but in the most general high-level schemata. The decision theory was an optimal field to look for such schemata, because it is very easy here to catch the extent to which a schema causes irrational behavior. We could make use of the help of the results of the normative decision theory, of the theory of probability. We could really find two or three high-level cognitive schemata in the field of the decision theory whose psychological reality seems to be very probable. Other types of examples can also be found in other areas of psychology.

Rationalization and intellectualization

La Fontaine's fable in which the fox cannot reach the grapes but says that he does' not want to because they are too sour is a typical example of *rationalization*. The fox did not behave rationally at all, but pleasantly reassured himself that what he did was the only rational possibility to do. This way he must have got rid of a serious psychological burden.

Rationalization is a mostly unconscious and involuntary mechanism, with the aid of which we distort reality in order to make our behavior seem acceptable and rational in the everyday sense, either for ourselves or for our environment. This is a very frequent and common phenomenon. Under experimental conditions, its operation can be observed best with the aid of hypnosis.

In his experiment E.R. Hilgard suggested to the subjects at the end of sessions that, after coming out of trance, they would continue to pay attention to the hypnotist and, when the hypotist took his glasses off, they would go to the window and open it, but they would not remember that the hypnotist had told them to do so. "Aroused from the trance, the subject feels a little drowsy but presently circulates among the people in the room and carries on a normal conversation, furtively watching the hypnotist. When the hypnotist casually removes his glasses, the subject feels an impulse to open the window; he takes a step in that direction but hesitates. Unconsciously, he mobilizes his wishes to be a reasonable person; seeking a reason for his impulse to open the window, he says 'Isn't it a little stuffy in here?' Having found the needed excuse, he opens the window and feels more comfortable."

In the course of rationalization we distort our acts, desires and experiences so as to bring them in harmony with everyday logic. In the course of *intellectualization* we do this in the direction of the logic of our professional schemata. A typical example of intellectualization is the doctor treating his patients as abstract, professional cases, because identifying with the pains of each of them would mean an unbearable burden for him.

Another example is when you ask engineers about the real reason of the QWERTY arrangement on the keyboards of typewriters. Most of them do not know the real reason of QWERTY, but in seconds flat they create some explanation, an objective criterion to prove the excellence of the system. They will tell that this system "makes this thing optimal" or "minimizes that thing". Really, at the time rational reasons like that played a role in designing the system, but by now it has lost its meaning completely, especially in the case of electronic typewriters. Still, it occurs only to very few engineers to face the irrationality of the situation: most of them prefer finding some reassuring explanation that conforms to their professional schemata.

Rationalization and intellectualization can be regarded as meta-schemata that connect the non-rational, involuntarily operating schemata, emotions, desires and memories of our psyche with the "languages" of our conscious, rational thinking: the everyday language that follows the logic of things, and the language abstracted from everyday language and following the logic of professional objects.

The schemata of formal logic

There is a method, with the aid of which a uniform bridge can be built between quite different mental models: the conclusions that can be drawn can be determined definitely even in cases of radically different models. This method is formal logic. It is tempting to regard formal logic also as a kind of meta-schema, helping us to gather information in life and learn the relationships among things.

In Chapter 1, however, we saw several experimental results that question whether the schemata of formal logic can be considered as having a general psychological reality. The results of the experiments with the cards and cheques contradicted the essence of formal logic itself, that the reasoning mechanism is independent of the concrete form of the problem. Studies on female logic also pointed in a similar direction. In the present chapter we have seen quite a few high-level (conscious and unconscious) cognitive schemata whose operation was not based definitely on formal logic.

On the other hand, formal logic as a general means of expression proved to be highly efficient in science. However, it is not certain that it was really formal logic that proved to be so very efficient a tool. Rather, it may have been the strict rigor by which science insists on to accept results as scientific, only if they can be expressed and deduced in the language of formal logic. Science has never demanded its scholars to report in addition how they achieved their results. We already know that this would have met with theoretical (complexity) difficulties.

If we only say that science is objective, i.e. it insists that every statement should mean the same for each of its scholars, it will follow that its results can be expressed in the language of formal logic, too. The essence of the belief of science is objectivity, and formalization can be regarded as its inevitable but secondary outgrowth. From this aspect the formalized nature of scientific language is the epiphenomenon of objectivity.

The formal seemingly logical phenomena of our everyday and professional thinking may also be only the epiphenomena of the fact that our schemata follow the logic of things quite well. This is also supported by the fact that the experiments intending to prove the psychological reality of the syllogisms of formal logic were not very successful. We have seen in Chapter 1 that people usually cannot see very clearly which syllogisms are correct and which ones are not, except for the modus ponens. Our general pattern-recognizing schema(ta), our evaluative and decision heuristics also proved to have much less complex structures than formal logic and mathematics would demand.

We can hardly imagine even that a phenomenon would be determined by really "ugly" rules, although we can produce confused rules by combining a few logical conditions. This is demonstrated by Johnson–Laird's experiment where three two-way switches were placed in front of the experimental subjects and the combined position of the three switches determined whether or not a lamp would be lit. The subjects were free to turn the swithes in either position; their task was to determine the rule when the lamp was lit. The structure of the rule built into the device was very nasty: practically, the simplest way to tell the rule was to list the cases when the lamp would be lit. The lamp was lit only when the positions of the three switches were DOWN–UP–DOWN, UP–DOWN–DOWN or UP–DOWN–UP.

The participants of the experiments usually guessed a relatively simple rule after a few trials (e.g. if the first switch is UP and the second is DOWN, the lamp is on, otherwise it is off). If the suspected rule predicted a few combinations well, the subjects already regarded the task as solved. Only a fraction of the subjects chose the solution of formal logic salutary in such cases, i.e. the systematic covering of all possibilities. Our fundamental high-level schemata do not guide our thinking in this direction.

How rational is man?

Man has succeeded in creating and utilizing the peak products of rationality, i.e. science, mathematics and formal logic. At the same time he is still suffering from neurosis, and his high-level cognitive schemata are not based on pure rationality. He easily orients himself in his complex everyday environment, and is able to solve problems of reasoning that stump even the largest computers of today; at other times, however, he makes rude errors in judging very simple events, as we have seen.

This duality is also reflected in psychological theories. On the basis of his detailed and thorough observations, Piaget describes how and through what stages a helpless child who understands nothing of the world around him becomes a rational adult who airily possesses and uses the means of formal thinking, and who thinks in abstract operations. Freud depicts a much less respectable picture of man; in his view an adult is also at the considerable mercy of his irrational wishes, instincts and only seemingly forgotten and passed traumas of his childhood. Indeed, are these two great scientists talking about the same *Homo sapiens*?

Richard Nisbett and Lee Ross write the following in their book about the inference mechanisms of man: "People's inferential failures are cut from the same cloth as their inferential successes are. Specifically, we contend that people's inferential strategies are well adapted to deal with a wide range of problems, but these same strategies become a liability when they are applied beyond that range, particularly when they are applied to problems requiring some appreciation of the normative principles that help to guide the professional scientist's more formal inferences."

Our schemata determine what we can and cannot perceive in our environment, and the schemata of science also determine the results we can achieve at all. If we study the stages through which man understands his physical and social environment, formal logic will provide an excellent external method of observation. The extent to which our behavior corresponds to the logic of the things around us is objectively measured by the extent to which it meets the expectations of formal logic. If, however, our aim is to describe our irrational acts and our neuroses, then, by their nature, the rules of formal logic will barely make their way. Both kinds of observation may be perfectly objective and correct, just as the very same animals proved to be gallantly kind-hearted or aggressively selfish, reassuringly monogamous or fatally volatile in the light of different observations (p. 85).

Many signs have indicated that our thinking is not characterized by the schemata of formal logic, at least above and under the level of candidate masters. It is improbable that we would learn the schemata of formal logic upon reaching the level of candidate masters, only to forget them again later. It seems more realistic to assume that the rational thinking of candidate masters is only an epiphenomenon of the fact that their thinking has reached the level of complexity sufficient to understand their profession's most relevant phenomena and to solve the generally occurring problems. At this level, formal logic becomes a suitable control of thoughts, for in this way we can check also the general correctness of our thoughts reached with the aid of, for example, the heuristics of representativity or availability (i.e. intuitively).

The authors cited in Chapter Zero reached similar conclusions through quite different routes of cognition. Different ways of thinking, trains of thoughts that are rational to different extents (but use their tools consistently) may all lead to the same end: reason is a co-ordinating and controlling force, rather than a fundamental mechanism of our thinking; it is a good means of doubt but less suited for creation.

16. Mystical thinking

If I said I understood what mysticism is, this statement would firmly prove my total ignorance of its essence. The way I do not understand mysticism is different from the way I do not understand the Gauss–Ostrogradsky theorem in differential geometry; I did not like the style of the latter, thus I decided to learn it only for the repeat examination at the University, but since I passed the first exam, I never learnt it, thus I still do not understand it. Still, I know I could understand this material if I had to, just as I could certainly understand the characteristics of phtalic acid anhydrates, but the topic would never attract me. Mysticism, however, does not repel me at all; in fact, its unusual nature and the way its *Weltanschauung* is a direct opposite to mine are definitely appealing. Niels Bohr said: "The opposite of a correct statement is a false statement. But the opposite of a profound truth may well be another profound truth."

Actually, this chapter should have been a sub-chapter of the previous chapter, because of the concrete things it has to say. At the same time, several threads of the book come together here, which justifies a separate chapter. Furthermore, I want a separate frame for the part in which I myself wish to understand better what I say.

The omnijectivity of mysticism

Mystic thinking is radically different from both scientific and religious cognition. Although it is usually connected to the latter, that is not a logical necessity.

Science and most religions try to be objective, though in different ways and starting from different axioms. Science restricts its field of interest to things that can be grasped (at least theoretically) by direct experience, while religion allows further starting hypotheses and methods of verification as well. Accordingly, religious science can deal even with problems like good and evil, morality and immorality, salvation and damnation. Natural science has nothing to say about these problems, although even scientists as individuals may be interested in them.

A major characteristic of mysticism is that it rejects both objectivity and subjectivity. The basis of mysticism is a determinative ecstatic experience, whose nature is usually very similar to the state of satori as described in Chapter 4. Perhaps the essence of the experience of enlightenment is that the person gets an overwhelming feeling of being one with the object to be known, his independent personality ceasing to exist totally. Enlightenment can be nothing but extremely intuitive, for at such moments one intuitively apprehends the common essence of all things in the universe.

Bertrand Russell points out four features of mysticism: "The first and most direct outcome of illumination is belief in the possibility of a way of knowledge which may be called revelation or insight or intuition, as contrasted with sense, reason, and analysis, which are regarded as blind guides leading to the morass of illusion. ... The second characteristic of mysticism is its belief in unity, and its refusal to admit opposition or division anywhere. ... A third mark of almost all mystical metaphysics is the denial of the reality of Time. This is the outcome of the denial of division; if all is one, the distinction of past and future must be illusory. ... The last of the doctrines of mysticism which we have to consider is its belief that all evil is mere appearance, an illusion produced by the divisions and oppositions of the analytic intellect."

Mystic thinking cannot be objective to start with, since it denies the possibility of objectivity outright by refusing to accept that objects exist independently of us. It cannot be subjective either, for it does not recognize the role and independent existence of the observer either. Perhaps, using Michael Talbot's expression, mystic thinking can also be called *omnijective*, for the internal and the external world, the psychic and the physical things combine into a uniform, inseparable, non-detailed mechanism. "When we dream, the omnijective nature of the dream is obvious. I may dream that I am sitting at a table having breakfast and talking to my friends, but when I awake, I know that both I and my friends are part of the continuum of the dream. To say that there are many 'consciousnesses' in the dream is merely a semantic distinction. All people in the dream are maya. They are constructions of consciousness."

Maya is a fundamental concept in the two or three thousand-year-old Hindu Tantra philosophy. In this concept everything in the world is only an illusion, and the greatest mistake we can make is to miss noticing maya, to perceive ourselves and our environment separately. Actually, this is the only statement in Tantra that is really definite for European thinking. This notion is in striking harmony with the neo-Platonic school of philosophy (that is said to have been effected by it), although essential differences can be found, too.

If everything is one, then that one thing must be very complex, as it is manifested in so many forms. Today's science agrees: the world is complex. In fact, science also hopes that the world is not as complex as that; it hopes that the world can be described by not too many well-chosen general concepts and rules. Einstein also said that "The fairest thing we can experience is the mysterious. It is the fundamental emotion which stands at the cradle of true art and true science." But mystics do not want to learn about or describe the unity of the universe; they want to experience it. Complexity is meaningless in this sphere of thinking; it is replaced by an extreme kind of trance logic. Who could be the person who wants to learn everything if everything were one? Or as the Hungarian poet Sándor Weöres says,

> If the wide world were a dipper,
> it would not fit in my apron;
> but how could I get an apron,
> if the wide world were a dipper?

The highest meta-level

Perhaps the feeling of enlightenment can also be conceived as the activization of a cognitive schema that is simultaneously the meta-level of all our cognitive schemata, but *itself* has no meta-level. Unfortunately, I cannot think of any laboratory experiment that could possibly prove even the faintest aspect of such a statement. Mystic masters who have already experienced enlightenment would probably consider the whole concept of schemata as meaningless, not because it is perhaps the epiphenomenon of more general principles, but because of the very fact that it is a concept. We can read some kind of reports of masters about their experiences, but they are immensely obscure for our rational minds, as if they spoke from another world. "As if" is not even needed: they do speak from another world, from an extremely different state of consciousness; decoding is a hopeless enterprise.

The approach of poetry and arts in general is somewhat more promising. Mystic masters usually also express themselves in pictures; e.g.: "Each branch of a coral includes the shining moon." But the arts aim at expression (although, as we have seen, they are working at a meta-level, and are also capable of creating an altered state of consciousness), therefore they necessarily have further meta-levels, e.g. the already existing schemata of the recipients, or even aesthetics. The writings of mystics fall outside the categories of the arts, aiming only at giving an idea of the impossibility of expression. Despite their intentions, we feel them to be poetic, perhaps because unwillingly and inevitably we perceive the authentic presence of the meta-level, perhaps with the aid of some general pattern-recognizing schema. This may be the very reason why in the Eastern world there is never any doubt whether somebody is enlightened or not. It appears that this kind of authenticity cannot be faked, just as the much simpler trance logic of hypnosis could not be imitated by simulators.

Several Zen masters have stated that they have gained nothing new through enlightenment. They simply experienced the operation of a capacity they had always possessed. We are all in the state of enlightenment, though unaware of it; that is the cause of our suffering. Let me illustrate this thought by a very absurd but deeply rational example of Raymond Smullyan. Smullyan used this example to illustrate a possible reason of the unresolvable debates of dualists and idealistic and materialistic philosophers.

Suppose there is a planet where strange physical laws are in force: the shapes of the objects determine their colors. For instance, if something is cubic, it is guaranteed to be green, spheres are red, etc. If someone happens to cut a roll into two, it will change its color. Half of the people on this planet are color blind, the other half are not. But they do not know this about themselves, because the truth cannot be proven in any way. If they suddenly travel to Earth, for instance, those who have color vision will be very surprised. They will see, for instance, a red cube. Color blind people will not be surprised at all, they will simply say that it is just a cube. Those with color vision, however, will be at a loss for words. How can they possibly express that they can see a cube that is still somehow a sphere? And how should they explain to the color blind people that they have not lost their minds, and that they really see such things. As time passes, they may naturally form a separate vocabulary of forms and colors for themselves, and will be able to enjoy the rich variations of the two independent experiences. Nevertheless, they have not gained any new ability, having simply become aware of an ever existing ability of theirs.

The story can be developed further infinitely. It is conceivable that those with color vision have unconsciously perceived the display of colors on their planet and do not understand why others cannot see the wonderful harmony in certain (e.g. in cubist) works of art. It is conceivable that there existed mystics on the planet before, who — baffling everybody — stated that cubes also have a higher-order quality, and enjoyed imaginary objects that were croissants on one hand, and pretzels on the other. I will not deprive you of the pleasure of playing with the idea of what strange situations and heated philosophical debates could develop on this strange planet if there were only a few people with color vision, or if almost everyone could see colors, etc.

In the previous chapter we could not decide to our satisfaction whether formal logic could be regarded as having psychological reality, or not. Perhaps the situation is similar here: the majority of people may be "math-blind", but a minority (those who are talented in mathematics) have more or less "math-vision": the language of mathematics can be developed into real schemata in them. The best which the rest of the people can achieve with great difficulties is to acquire certain complete mathematical procedures and trains of thought as complete units that can be used independently. But the components of these units do not become meaningful by themselves, just as the different phases of laying eggs are not independently meaningful acts for some of the digger wasps. Perhaps this is why it is difficult for those talented in mathematics to comprehend why others do not understand maths or fail to see its beauty. Perhaps the situation is similar with other esoteric sciences and arts (e.g. metaphysics, music, abstract painting).

Probably the schema of perfect omnijectivity — which develops at the moment of enlightenment, or at least this is when it becomes a really active schema — is a psychological reality in enlightened mystics. Subsequently, enlightened mystics can bring themselves into the pleasant state of satori on certain occasions, e.g. with meditation. Evidently, the presence of this schema is somehow determinative in their everyday lifestyle. We cannot have great hopes of determining the proportion of people who have the potential for developing mystic thinking, to tell whether it is a general psychological reality or a gift of only a few.

The experience of investigators of another altered state of consciousness, namely, hypnosis, may provide some hints. Some people can be hypnotized very easily, while others hardly or never react to the usual standard methods. Most people are moderately susceptible to hypnosis. Exact methods have been developed to measure the effect of standard hypnotic procedures. They have given quite stable results: the hypnotic susceptibility measured this way barely changes in the course of life: we are expected to remain at about the same point on the scale ten years from now. Thus, this ability is just as stable as intelligence or a good ear for music are. Still, investigators of hypnosis fully agree that even the least susceptible can reach deep hypnosis with the aid of special, individualized hypnotic methods. To tell the truth, there is not much data showing how much this hypnosis agrees with that experienced by the highly susceptible.

In the cases of other abilities, the opinions of specialists are not so uniform regarding the degree of achievable radical development in the given area. For example, Kodály's method is proved to improve the ability to enjoy music considerably, but those who are tone-deaf will never become connoisseurs in music. Those who are not very good at maths may enjoy a deduction becoming clear, but the aesthetics of mathematics will always remain alien to them, however excellent the results they may produce in other areas.

There are several ways of achieving mystic enlightenment, too. Frequently, a Zen master may tell that a disciple of his is capable of reaching the state of satori, but not with him. In this case he will recommend another master; there are several examples showing that this may be very effective. Naturally, you cannot tell what would have happened if the student had remained with the original master, but the procedure itself indicates that the talent for mystic thinking (or in other words, the inclination or natural power to develop the highest-level meta-schema) may exist, and it can definitely be recognized by its masters.

Eastern and Western ways

Besides similar fundamentals, there are also differences between Oriental and Occidental forms of mysticism. Let us quote again Bertrand Russell, who studied mainly the Western forms of mysticism: "Belief in a reality quite different from what appears to the senses arises with irresistible force in certain moods, which are the source of most mysticism, and of most metaphysics. While such a mood is dominant, the need of logic is not felt, and accordingly the more thorough-going mystics do not employ logic, but appeal directly to the immediate deliverance of their insight. But such fully developed mysticism is rare in the West. When the intensity of emotional conviction subsides, a man who is in the habit of reasoning will search for logical grounds in favor of the belief which he finds in himself."

This is squaring the circle, of course. Bringing mystic thinking to perfection has no paved roads in Western cultures. The development of logical thinking is promoted by carefully refined syllabuses, although even then, as we have seen, the syllogisms of formal logic become really active schemata for only a few people. Our religions also accept the objective attitude and the differentiation, and treat earthly existence as a kind of transitory state.

Occidental man is interested mainly in the end result. He wants to be sure of its correctness, and often considers the way leading to it as secondary. Rationality is an excellent ground for this mentality, for we have seen that intuition, or the recognition of the end result, have one order of magnitude more complex means than the means promoting rational reasoning, persuasion and verification. Thus, the development of science can be unbroken, intuition can always be ahead of reason, while reason may lay wider foundations for intuition. We have seen that Gödel's theorem alone guarantees that this mechanism can work continuously.

Oriental man is mainly interested in the way itself that leads to the full understanding of the unity of the world. The concept of end result (at least in this respect of life) is meaningless for him, because he is firmly convinced in the unity of the world even if he happens to fail in experiencing that in its full depth, being unable to reach enlightenment. Eastern religions, especially Buddhism, do not accept objective attitude and differentiation; they regard our earthly existence as equal to anything else.

Really highly developed mysticism is conceivably the most extreme form of holistic thinking. Perhaps one of the most lucid variations of this is Zen Buddhism. It is a fundamental thesis of Zen that it is utterly impossible to define what Zen is. But even that fails to define it, otherwise it could be defined after all. The situation is typically a Gödelian one. D.R. Hofstadter also emphasizes just this feature of Zen, so that Zen koans get a kind of new interpretation. Each koan can be conceived as something that highlights the Gödelian nature of a given problem within our current, not yet enlightened, thinking system. Usually it is a typical learning question in every branch of Buddhism: "Is Buddha dead?" The main point is that either yes or no is an incorrect answer. It is impossible to explain it better that the basic question is Gödelian. But there is still a long, long way to go before feeling the problem deeply and finally becoming enlightened.

Gödel's theorem caused a severe shock to Western science. The discovery of the Gödelian phenomena causes hardly any shock to Eastern people, for they have always seen the path as one where the irrationality of questions and differentiation can be increasingly experienced in its depth. This is why the Zen koan in Chapter 4 could be regarded also as a kind of moral story. There are other, more important and more personal methods of learning on the way to enlightenment from meditation through the daily rituals of monasteries to getting whacked by the master. Each of them somehow aims at transcendence and experiencing the Gödelian nature of the world. And somewhere on this path the great mystery may flash up, when we feel intuitively the common essence of all transcendence, at each step on the way.

Probably the same thing happens at the moments of enlightenment as in the development of any new schema, when, for example, the concept of numbers develops in a child. First a child can count to two, then to three, then to four; later he may ask whether there exist numbers beyond a hundred, but then, after a point, he will have no such questions. The infinite sequence of numbers will become clear to him, the schema of numbers develops and starts operating. This, however, is not a very ecstatic experience, perhaps because this meta-schema is the meta-level of only a few other schemata. The schema of enlightenment, however, is the meta-level of each of our cells, of each of our organs and, even more importantly in the present task field, of each of our conscious and unconscious schemata; it simultaneously interprets and modifies each of them. This is why it can be a deep and ecstatic experience. But even the most poetic description cannot give the experience itself, just as if someone who has never been in love cannot learn what it is like to be *in* love from all the love stories of literature.

In order to reach enlightenment one does not simply have to develop the highest-level meta-schema. One has to develop all of one's schemata so that they may possibly have a uniform meta-level. This is not an easy task. Everybody possesses several discriminative abilities or general schemata when only a few days old, like the arrangement of objects, the ability to discriminate an object from the background, or to perceive motion. In the course of our lives complex meta-schemata of differentiation develop, and those who step on the road leading to enlightenment must order all of them at the service of the highest-level meta-schema to be developed. That also takes about ten years of intensive training, just like reaching the level of grandmaster in any other field. Thus, it is justified to consider everyone who is enlightened to be a master; otherwise it does not work. Just as there is no royal way to mathematics, there is no royal way to mystic enlightmenment.

17. The trick of evolution

"The result can be amazing when you shuffle the pack. Blood will tell."
— says Woland in Mikhail Bulgakov's superb novel when he first takes a
good look at Margarita. If anyone, Woland is really fully aware of all the
overt and covert relationships among things, e.g. he knows perfectly well
how much a certain French queen in the 16th century would be surprised
to see her beautiful great-great-granddaughter in a Moscow ball room. In
spite of this, that is all he has to say about why it is just Margarita with
whom everything is so perfect. We of the 20th century can see this matter
only in this way.

It is easily possible that the 20th century actually started in 1859, with
the publication of Darwin's book *The Origin of Species*. Science had had
some idea about the rules of chance before that date, but this branch of
knowledge was used only for lack of something better to supplement their
insufficient knowledge with the application of the rule of chance. Laplace
also proved, on the basis of probability, that comets are parts of the solar
system: relying on the available data he calculated that if he had betted
on this theory his chance of winning would have been one to several billion.
Darwin's brilliant intuition, however, gave quite another role to chance: it
became imaginable that blind chance could possibly serve as the basis of
even such complex and meaningful processes like life itself.

This idea became a dominant motive in the scientific revolutions of
the 20th century. Chance is similarly a determining factor in the processes
of quantum mechanics, in genetics, and in certain branches of economics
after the model of Neumann–Morgenstern's theory of games. Related to
this latter area, a paradox idea was also proven beyond doubt; namely,
in cases of certain problems of decision the only possible way to reach
perfect, abstract rationality is to rely on blind chance to a certain extent.
It turned out that often the only possible means of pure rationality is the
dice, although one must know exactly when and how to use it.

Darwin's theory was a real intuitive product: he did not exactly define
what natural selection actually applies to, nor had he any knowledge about

the mechanisms of heredity or the fundamentals of genetics. Furthermore, a large portion of his arguments and ideas proved to be incorrect in their details as studied by the refined methods of the 20th century. The profound antipathy of his age, however, was not based on such details, not even on the frightening possibility that man could possibly be a descendant of the apes. This was the reaction of cheap journalism and narrow-minded religiousness; the serious scientists of the age would have got over it with a gesture of regret: scientific attitute being rather deeply rooted by then.

The most difficult idea to digest even by the greatest contemporaries of Darwin was that concepts like "aim" (set either by God or Nature), "progress" and "development" fell completely outside the sphere of thought of natural selection. According to the principle of Occam's razor, they should have applauded such a great gain that so many assumptions became unnecessary; and today we do so indeed. At that time, however, avoiding concepts like that meant the elimination of the final aim or meaning of science. We can regard Darwin's work as the beginning of the 20th century in this respect, too. Today we can already imagine that there is no answer to certain basic questions within the given frameworks; not because we are not smart enough, but because there is no answer to them, because the questions happen to be of the Gödelian type. This train of thoughts will be pursued further in the next chapter. Now we are going to examine how we can interpret the diversity of our ways of thinking in the light of Darwin's discovery.

At first glance the title of the chapter may not seem to be ambiguous. In the sentence "Bombardment of the vessel caused no losses" ambiguity is more unambiguous: was the sloop bombarded or bombarding?

If evolution is the basic mechanism of the development of species in Nature, then we have to see through the tricks of evolution to get to know the causes of the diversity of our living environment. However, once we have some idea of how evolution works, we can use the tricks thus learnt either for the purposes of artificial intelligence, or as a model to discover further scientific relationships. In this case the evolutionary idea is our trick, on the basis of which we build a model, regardless of how much our ideas agree with the real mechanisms of Nature.

The theory of the selfish gene

The name of the theory comes from the title of Richard Dawkins' famous book. In Darwin's original theory, natural selection was concerned with inexactly defined units that could be characterized by sufficiently vague features of heredity, variation and struggle for survival. The research of evolution first identified these units with the individuals of the different living creatures but, as the Darwinian concept of evolution became more and more the fundamental thesis of scientists, it became increasingly doubtful whether it was at all possible to build a consistent theory of evolution that regarded individuals as the basic units. With the growing exact knowledge of the mechanisms of heredity and behavior, the inner logic of the theories demanded the establishment of either smaller or larger units.

Generalization toward larger units (the assumption of group selection or species selection) is appealing because this way we can easily explain the unselfish, sometimes even self-sacrificing, behavior of certain individuals. Zoogamy can be interpreted better this way, too. Yet at the same time, keeping strictly to the classical Darwinian principles sometimes required quite forced assumptions.

The other direction of generalization is the theory of the selfish gene. It sets out from the hypothesis that perhaps the units of natural selection are much smaller: essentially they are the genes themselves. For the sake of survival, genes conglomerate into large complexes; they build "survival machines" as Dawkins puts it, thus they try to secure their survival. Although selection affects the individuals, the gene that is the most likely to survive is the one that succeeds in becoming incorporated into the individuals most fit for life; simultaneously it may, of course, contribute to the success of the individual, too. In this conception we are all the "survival machines" of our genes; we are made by our genes in our present forms for the sake of their (the genes') own survival. This is even more true of our more or less complicated gene-complexes – our physical and behavioral characteristics. The greater a gene-complex, the less it can be regarded as the basic unit of selection; and the more stably genes are joined in complexes, the more certainly they will survive or perish together.

The theory of the selfish gene embodies Darwin's original ideas very consistently and, unexpectedly, it can explain the phenomena of altruism and even self-sacrifice: it is possible that the gene of self-sacrifice may promote the survival of itself (*as a gene*) if it can save several of its own copies present in other individuals by forcing self-sacrifice of the whole individual. The key to the success of the selfish gene theory is that it is usually a fundamental condition of the operability of models based on this theory that Nature should keep producing (we might even say, testing) new versions of the genes in large masses forever. This is exactly what happens in reality, and this phenomenon suits the theory of the selfish gene much better than any of its rivals.

The real power of the theory of the selfish gene was shown when in the early 1970s John Maynard Smith noticed that the operation of a gene can also be regarded as something that commands its carrier a strategy of behavior, or even: a *game strategy*. This has to be understood quite generally: the hue of the eyes, the spininess of the leaves or even the level of aggression to be shown in the fight for territory, all belong here. On this basis, the fight for survival can also be considered as the competition of game strategies determined by the genes. Depending on the frequency of the occurrence of the different genes in the population, the chances of survival may be different for the individual genes (i.e. game strategies).

We saw two examples of how this idea can work in Chapter 3: the examples of courting and puzzle solving. In the latter we can think of a puzzle-solving and a non-puzzle-solving gene. If nobody solves puzzles, and there are a lot of difficult problems whose solution has a high survival value, then the puzzle-solving genes may proliferate until there are so few difficult tasks per puzzle-solver that those who do not waste their energy on practicing will be better off securing their survival by solving a lot of easy problems. Depending on the environment, an optimal equilibrium may develop between puzzle-solvers and non-puzzle-solvers, and it is no good for either genes to depart from this equilibrium, because that would spoil the chances of their survival. The situation is similar with the genes prescribing for females to demand long or short courtship. In this example the model is much more complex, because there are also two genes in the males' strategy (the "faithful" and the "lady-killer"), but again, an equilibrium may develop among the four genes, one from which it is not worth departing for any of them, who would proliferate at the expense of its own chances of survival.

Maynard Smith called this Evolutionary Stable Strategy, or ESS, for once the ratio of genes develop in a population according to ESS, it may subsist for a long period if the environmental conditions do not change, for none of the genes gain if they disregard the set equilibrium by excessive proliferation. Dawkin says: "I have a hunch that we may come to look back on the invention of the ESS concept as one of the most important advances in evolutionary theory since Darwin. It is applicable wherever we find conflict of interest, and that means almost everywhere. ... Maynard Smith's concept of the ESS will enable us, for the first time, to see clearly how a collection of selfish independent entities can come to resemble a single organized whole. I think this will be true not only of social organization within species, but also 'ecosystems' and 'communities' consisting of many species."

The basis of the idea of ESS is the mathematical theory of games, originally developed for economics where its general application was not very successful. The reason for this is that the value-choices of the participants of the economy appear along a lot of dimensions. In order to apply the theory of games, one would have to reconcile somehow the different values of money, independence, time-gain, etc. In economics, this is practically impossible: everybody weighs these values differently. In evolutionary biology, however, an unambiguous measure presented itself for measuring the usefulness of a given game strategy: the value of fitness. The greater the number of expected offspring a strategy yields to a gene that yielded the strategy, the more successful the gene is.

An especially attractive characteristic of ESS is that it makes quantitative studies possible, providing exact theoretical predictions about the different strategies' long-term percentage of occurrence. These studies brought convincing results: the predictions of the theory of the selfish gene were often fulfilled. We can even say that the real significance of the theory of games is being shown in the biological applications. The branch of evolutionary biology that studies the behavior of living creatures on the basis of the theory of the selfish gene is called *sociobiology*.

Cultural genes, memes

We have mentioned before how ambiguous the title of this chapter is. The theory of the selfish gene in its original form attempted only to explore how the mechanism of Nature's trick called evolution works. In order to do this, it found out that this mechanism can apply to units (i.e. the genes) that remain unchanged for long periods of time and can reproduce themselves. In the course of the development of the theory, a number of tools have been developed to reveal the essence of evolution; the concept of ESS is one of them. Perhaps these concepts will gradually prove to be the fundamental mechanisms of evolution just as, looking from a higher meta-level, only very few people today doubt that the Darwinian evolution is really the mechanism of the species' development.

On the other hand, the tools discovered in the course of working out the theories are *our* tricks, and we can try to apply them to things other than what they were developed for in the first place. For instance, Ch.J. Lumsden and E.O. Wilson noticed that our everyday culture also consists of interchangeable units in most places. Everyone can choose what clothes to wear, what tales to tell their children, what methods of problem-solving to use in certain situations. These can be perceived as if everyone could decide himself what genes to have: what the color of his eyes, the curliness of his hair, or his running ability should be like. Lumdsen and Wilson gave the previous characteristics the name *cultural genes*, and also tried to adapt the mathematical methods developed for studying genes. Some changes were necessary to some extent, naturally, for we do not choose our genes but inherit them from our parents, while the mechanisms of choosing the cultural genes had to be given appropriately and specially formed mathematical formulae.

The attempt was successful: the equations of evolutionary biology came to life even under such conditions: the theory of cultural genes which arose produced similar evolutionary motions as the models describing real genes. The spreading of cultural genes also created an equilibrium that could be sustained for shorter or longer periods. Certain cultural genes spread with the stormy speed of fads, just to die off suddenly after changing the conditions of their own existence. Other cultural genes flourished for a long time or declined slowly. Lumdsen and Wilson's model can also explain what interactional processes may lie behind the joint evolution of the real, biological genes and the cultural genes. Perhaps the finest result of the model is that quite an exact estimate can be obtained about the speed of evolution as a function of the diversity of environmental conditions, and as a function of the diversity of biological and cultural genes. The model very effectively explained our everyday experience that genetic evolution is quite a slow process while cultural evolution can be very fast, and the two processes are far from excluding each other.

Dawkins stresses another gene-like aspect of cultural elements, namely, that in human cultures, through imitation or the ability to copy one another more or less exactly, new gadgets capable of reproduction appeared and started their fight for survival. Dawkins called these new kinds of replicators *memes*. He derived the name from the Greek-sounding word mimeme. He was especially glad that the new word resembled the word gene, was similar to the word 'memory' and was related to the French 'même' (the same), too. Dawkins says:

"Examples of memes are tunes, ideas, catch phrases, clothes fashions, ways of making pots or building arcs. Just as genes propagate themselves in the gene pool by leaping from body to body via sperms or eggs, so memes propagate themselves in the meme pool by leaping from brain to brain via a process which, in the broad sense, can be called imitation. If a scientist hears, or reads about, a good idea, he passes it to his colleagues and students. He mentions it in his articles and his lectures. If the idea catches on, it can be said to propagate itself, spreading from brain to brain. ... When you plant a fertile meme in my mind you literally parasitize my brain, turning it into a vehicle for the meme's propagation in just the way a virus may parasitize the genetic mechanism of a host cell."

The concepts of cultural genes and memes may or may not cover the same physical units in our brains. The situation is similar to what we saw in Chapter 6 at the cornucopia of psychological schema concepts. These two notions grasp different aspects of the same thing. Both were defined within the frame of the way they had been designed and interpreted, thus it is practically impossible to decide whether or not they mean the same entity, although possibly they do.

I go even further: the characteristics of the concept of schemata fit these two concepts remarkably well, especially if (similarly to Dawkins) we also take larger meme-complexes into consideration as independent complex memes; in this case the possiblity of continuous change is also present. At heart I would gladly fit the concepts of meme and cultural gene among the concepts of schemata listed in Chapter 6. The difference between meme and schema does not seem to be more radical than that between schema and mental model, even though the origin, the technical device of their treatment, and the questions raised in connection with them are essentially different in the case of schemata and memes; all the more so, since the concept of schema is approached from the aspect of psychology, while that of meme is from that of biology.

Nevertheless, when a concept is defined so that it can be studied by the methodical storehouse of a given theory, the received results cannot be directly transferred to a concept, however similar, of another theory. Analogies are not evidence: this very recognition has led to the development of the professional way of thinking in science. This is why everyday and scientific languages have separated so much. Of course, analogies (especially between different scientific concepts) may guide our intuition (just

206

as we saw in Chapter 5 that the ideas of psychoanalysis could influence the design of cognitive psychological experiments) but each branch of science can get genuine, proven results only strictly within its own system.

The theory of the selfish gene offers a lot of analogies to our everyday environment, even to highly debated social problems like whether or not women's place is in the kitchen, or men's fickleness is or is not biologically determined. These analogies, however, bring the problems back to the level of everyday thinking; thus at best they will get outside the sphere of science, but at the worst the scientific results will be rudely distorted, just as the social Darwinist theories of the 1930s have nothing to do with science. Nevertheless, it is an interesting challenge to compare, within the framework of scientific thinking, the meme approach of sociobiology and the schema approach of cognitive psychology.

The "smallest number wins" game

The field of games seems to be the most hopeful area where the basically psychological concept of schema and the biological concept of meme can be studied within a common paradigm. In principle, ESS may be determined for an abstract game. One of the major ideas of the biological paradigm may thus become an external means of investigation, a basis of comparison; furthermore, the cognitive strategies of the players may also be caught. It is good to have a lot of players in the game, because this makes the simultaneous presence of a lot of strategies possible. It it also desirable that the players do not communicate with each other too much, because it is very difficult to trace these, both theoretically and in practice. Besides, the game itself should be interesting and challenging, it should stimulate real thinking so that the players really mobilize the best of their schemata.

Upon the basis of such considerations we invited applications for a *"smallest number wins"* game with the following rules in the Hungarian puzzle magazine *Füles*: the participants of the game were to send in only one single integer on the coupon in the paper. The winner would be the person who sent the smallest number which was not sent by any other player.

Altogether, 8,192 responses arrived. The diversity of the thinking of the players can be characterized by the fact that more than 2,000 different numbers were found. For those who wish to dig into the data we give the frequencies of how many people chose the first 200 numbers. You can find the winning number and a lot of interesting things there, too. The concrete winning number is rather accidental, of course, for a single additional player might have changed it considerably. However, the frequency-distribution of all the numbers we received is less accidental, it is practically not influenced by a few additional players. Thus, it is worth starting our analysis here.

The first 200 numbers were chosen by the following numbers of people:

	0	1	2	3	4	5	6	7	8	9
0-	–	387	57	52	59	59	42	73	50	91
10-	33	131	44	164	42	28	43	123	46	82
20-	13	71	47	70	26	23	34	57	33	54
30-	18	52	26	49	20	10	20	53	24	34
40-	10	34	12	21	12	12	14	34	14	46
50-	6	28	16	29	19	34	21	24	27	33
60-	5	40	13	26	38	11	25	22	12	15
70-	4	32	20	20	6	9	11	24	14	26
80-	4	4	5	14	16	7	9	26	17	12
90-	9	24	11	10	2	4	12	24	8	25
100-	17	49	14	22	7	7	9	8	4	12
110-	4	95	8	26	7	6	9	28	4	16
120-	1	15	4	28	5	2	9	24	14	14
130-	2	15	9	4	3	7	7	23	5	17
140-	3	5	6	3	3	2	5	8	5	7
150-	2	4	2	6	8	2	7	4	6	10
160-	4	3	4	4	4	0	2	5	7	12
170-	1	13	3	10	2	7	5	2	4	8
180-	0	3	3	2	4	3	2	2	1	8
190-	1	9	6	7	4	4	2	6	6	12

Nobody chose the number 200.

Allow yourself to be diverted here by a paragraph on some other interesting aspects of the results. Two thirds of the entries were odd numbers; the players seemed to have felt that these numbers are less available for others, providing therefore better chances of winning for themselves. There were 475 and 1,732 players who sent numbers ending with 0 and 1 respectively. We analyzed the numbers according to sex and place of residence (we had data of these because of the names and addresses of the players). To our surprise there were no differences whatsoever by these aspects, although we had asked hundreds of questions: we analyzed who wrote small and who wrote large numbers, who wrote 1 and who wrote 13, etc. A relatively large number of people thought that people would oust each other by small numbers, thus quite large numbers might win: 147 persons wrote numbers larger than one million, seven simply wrote the sign of infinity. A small boy wrote number 1 and then 36 zeros, and remarked that this was a very large and very rare number.

What kinds of memes or schemata can we imagine to have possibly played a role in the players' choice of the numbers? An incalculable number of trains of thought is possible from the different proportions of rational calculation, intuition and superstitious irrationality. Each train of thought, however, has the common characteristic that finally they all lead to choosing a concrete number. We could consider the numbers themselves as memes, but this way we would risk, on one hand, treating radically different thoughts and schemata alike just because they lead to the same result, and on the other hand, one thought leading to a result like "a number between 20 and 30 would be the best" would be taken into consideration at many memes. Nevertheless, aware that our present knowledge does not allow for more subtle differentiation, we are going to do just that, hoping our results will be informative anyway.

Several irrational strategies can easily be seen at first glance. Numbers 13 or 111 were chosen remarkably frequently, especially when compared to their environment. Their memes are probably very simple: "Choose me! I am the lucky number!" 8 or 9% of all the entries can be regarded as such magic numbers, similar to the almost 250(!) four-digit numbers that start with 1,900 and evidently cover years of birth. As opposed to the 1900s, numbers starting with 1,700 or 1,800 were sent in by a mere 30–35 people.

Probably different psychological mechanisms led to the strikingly frequent occurrence of the number 1: one out of about 21 persons chose this number. Number 1 is an especially great challenge, for it is certain to win if I am the only one to write it. In our imagination others would think: "Surely many people will write number 1. I'd better try another one." Thus, according to the heuristics of availability, it is highly likely that nobody writes number 1. But the heuristics of simulation also points in this direction: I shall have a fit if nobody writes 1, not even me!

We are going to show the functioning of another well-identifiable schema before discussing the general points. More than 300 players sent numbers around 600,000. At first this seems to be strange, because barely 30 people sent numbers around 500,000. The explanation is that in the invitation to the game we mentioned that *Füles* was published in 640,000 copies, therefore the potential winning number must be among the first

640,000 numbers; thus it was not much worthwhile writing too large numbers. In these 300 people the heuristic of anchoring may have worked, diverting their thinking into a totally wrong direction. Interestingly enough, this was the only case where there was a slight, but clear-cut difference between the sexes: only 45% of the players were women, but over 60% of the entries around 600,000 were sent by them.

Making an allowance for the effect of the above well-describable schemata, about 80% of all the players still remain. Now comes the surprise: ESS explains the combined behavior of this 80% quite well. For example, if we regard trains of thought leading to playing with numbers between 2 and 9 as a kind of meme, then those resulting in numbers between 10 and 99 as another meme, etc. then the several thousands of people together realized a strategy corresponding to ESS quite exactly. (The theoretical ESS of the game was determined by computer simulation, and it was compared with the results of the real competition.) We can reach a similar conclusion by ordering the memes to different intervals of numbers.

Naturally, from the psychological point of view several strategies may lead to the result that "I should take a number between 100 and 150", but now our analysis allows only for subtleties like regarding all of them as only one meme, as one strategy upon studying ESS. Being aware of this, the descriptive power of ESS is still more surprising. One of the very reasons for offering this very game was that we had annoyingly no idea of how people would behave when they met the conditions of such a game, e.g. what percentage of them would send us a number under 100. It was difficult to guess even if this ratio would be closer to 20% or to 80%. With the knowledge of the results and ESS, we now have a well-founded scientific tool to predict such questions professionally.

In a game like this, chances are certainly good if one takes a small number, for if nobody else turns out to have taken it, there is an increased probability that it would be the smallest such number, and thus it would win. Yet larger numbers also have a chance, for they avoid others more easily, so chances are higher that one of those would be the only one. People as a whole sized up surprisingly well how these two directions of thought are balanced: mathematical ESS indicates similar ratios.

The basis of the biological paradigm is an abstract conception that our memes participate in a survival race; in this particular case, such a race consists of a lot of "smallest number wins" games with a constantly changing number of participants, and the survival of a meme is secured if it can win the game occasionally. In a case like this, such an equilibrium of memes (ESS) may settle where even the more refined meme is unable to increase the ratio of its presence without spoiling its own chance of survival. Thus, it is easily possible that the theory of the selfish gene applies to our memes and cognitive schemata too, without our knowledge!

Evidently, our cognitive schemata did not develop purposefully for the "smallest number wins" game. Still, even in such a situation, a lot of independent people who probably do not think rationally as individuals developed the most rational common manner of playing as a whole. A diversity of the ways of thinking produced a meaningful unit at a higher level.

Evolution and rationality

In principle, evolution has nothing to do with rationality. The most profound novelty in Darwin's ingenious thought was the fact that he radically banished concepts like purposefulness, rationality and reason from biology, and demonstrated that the development of the species can be explained solely by the idea of natural selection if certain general conditions are present. Several signs indicate that a similar basic mechanism operates behind the spread of thoughts, schemata or memes.

On the other hand, the memes with the greatest chance of survival are those whose carriers can best follow the logic of things. We saw in Chapter 14 that usually this alone is perfectly sufficient for the appearance of rational behavior, whose epiphenomenon may be perhaps formal rationality itself. Many economists (e.g. Milton Friedman) offer the phenomenon of "as if" as the reason why they consider man as a rational being after all in their theories. Those who have survived must have behaved as if they had made their decision rationally, therefore they could survive. In fact, in their complicated meme-complexes there may appear such high-level memes whose survival is guaranteed by the very fact that they can coordinate the effect of other useful memes especially well. Perhaps the memes of rationality and even formal logic are exactly such meta-level memes.

Hofstadter goes even further: "Most philosophers and logicians are convinced that truths of logic are 'analytic' and *a priori*; they do not like to think that such basic ideas are grounded in mundane, arbitrary things like survival. They might admit that natural selection tends to *favor* good logic — but they would certainly hate the suggestion that natural selection *defines* good logic! Yet truth and survival value *are* tangled together, and civilizations that survive certainly *have* glimpsed higher truths than those that perish." The evolution of logic keeps moving on today: in the cases of complex questions related to necessity, possibility and temporal relations, the already two-and-a-half thousand-year-old debate of which syllogisms should be considered as unconditionally true forms of reasoning has not been settled yet, nor has any human species developed with the capacity of bearing the syllogisms of formal logic as a general psychological reality.

Artificial evolution?

A possible way of creating artificial intelligence could be to follow the far-reaching trick of evolution: we could try to program real memes. These memes could fight for their survival while being exposed to different kinds of mutations and other modifications, similar to the way normal heuristics change continuously as a result of the influences of the metaheuristics in the EURISKO program. We saw that the role of metaheuristics is similar to the mechanism of natural selection in a way: they mercilessly eliminate or at least change those heuristics that do not sufficiently prove fit for life, and are not efficient enough to produce interesting mathematical concepts. In the EURISKO program this method proved to be promising, although it was not completely successful. Other, more directly evolutionary programs, however, were even less successful: artificial evolution resulted mostly in nonsense entanglements. The problem is not with entanglement but with nonsense, for our intellect is also based upon tangled hierarchies.

The relative efficiency of EURISKO's metaheuristics is not due to the fact that it is similar to the method of evolution either. The similarity is due mainly to the author of the program having formulated a few phenomena at the occurrence of which he himself would gladly modify the heuristics while the program was running, if he had the possibility to intervene. Metaheuristics realize just that in their own rigid way. Heuristics themselves are completely passive; they are either alive, are modified or become extinct, but survival is not their fundamental nature (this rather obscure statement will be explained in detail right away). Selection is only one of the components of the mechanism of evolution; at least two other important circumstances of equal value are necessary for the operation of the whole system: self-reproduction and variability arising within the frame of self-reproduction. Both circumstances have to reach considerable complexity by themselves for the development of an evolution that works.

Self-reproduction is suited to sustain the evolutionary process only if it works totally automatically, without special aims or motivations, if all that the individual of self-reproduction must do is to appear in the next generation, too. This is why the whole theory regained strength when the gene was chosen as the unit of evolution: a gene has no considerations like the need to eat or search for a mate; the only characteristic of its existence is that it appears in the next generation, if possible. We could also say that this is the only meaning of its existence; but that is true only in as much as it is true that the only meaning of the moon's existence is that it becomes full each month: it cannot do otherwise once it is there and nothing prevents its revolution. Genes really build beings or survival machines that eat, search for mates, or even think and search for the meaning of their lives. But all this is only the consequence of the fact that those genes were the most successful ones in survival that excelled in creating such beings, because this way they had more chance to be present in the next generation.

The other basic condition of starting the evolutionary mechanism is that masses of constantly new versions appear among the genes, but the essence is again that this takes place without any special aim or reason. The new versions are also genes, thus their only meaning is that they also participate in the grand drama of self-reproduction: they survive if they can. The birth of the new versions also lacks any aim or intention, the only driving force is chance. We can talk about complete chance only from the aspect of vitality. New forms always develop out of old ones, keeping most of the old components intact. This fact alone explains that new versions springing from luckily developed forms of high vitality have better chances of survival than those developing from others. This is how the concept of development together with the concepts of aim and intention will become the epiphenomena of the whole evolutionary process.

This mechanism unwittingly separates the essential and the unessential in the luckily conglomerated stable gene-complexes. It is exactly this condition that we cannot realize in artificial intelligence, based on an evolutionary approach. We create artificial memes with the aid of our existing memes, thus they are also the means of survival of our own memes, rather than aimless formations. Real memes, similar to real genes, are guided exclusively by their own survival; they create complex organs and meaningful thoughts as a consequence. We cannot wait to see this, as evolution is an extremely slow process with a tremendous amount of aborted attempts. Also, we cannot see the sense in survival being such an exclusive guide. This is why we said allegorically in Chapter 14 that perhaps the main obstacle in realizing artificial intelligence today is that machines have no blood pressure or other vital juices in the figurative sense. We cannot see why all this may be necessary to make good translator programs. Therefore our programs are based on principles quite different from real intellect.

We saw in Chapter 15 how much we fail to imagine how chance works. Naturally, we can create artificial random series, e.g. by tossing a coin, but there are more productive procedures for this purpose, too. If the only aim is to create something from which intelligence should be totally absent — we can do it. But we cannot simulate a few-billion-year-old process — during which the forms of life and thinking capable of stability developed — that is constantly experimenting with countless new versions. Should we succeed in that, nothing would guarantee that the new intellect resembled our own.

The experiments with artificial evolution unwittingly simulate most of the fundamental mechanisms of natural evolution by considering our own intentions. Our own intellect does play a role in creating the environment of the simulation; our aims, plans or ideas about the trend of selection or about the structure of mutations (as in the case of the metaheuristics of EURISKO) do appear somehow in it. Finally we cannot tell what is simulation in the whole system and what is simulation of the simulation, etc. The situation is similar to the military exercise in which the troops arrived at a riverside and found a sign on the bridge: "This bridge is blown up." But the water was cold and wet, so the soldiers marched over the bridge nevertheless. Seeing this, the commanding officer ran to the bridge in a rage, only to see the troops marching under a large sign: "We are swimming."

18. Alternating the reference systems

In his book *Gödel, Escher, Bach*, Hofstadter illustrates Gödel's theorem with several analogies: one of them is about a record player. Let us imagine that a cunning destructive person makes a record that produces such sound vibrations in the record player that destroy the record player itself before reaching the end of the record. This would be a Gödelian record for that particular record player, but this is not yet the essence of Gödel's theorem.

The next logical step is that the manufacturer of the record player gets bored with the constant complaints and, regardless of expenses, develops a super record player that protects itself against evil and damaging records by its own built-in intelligence. When a record is put on, the record player will examine and check thoroughly whether or not it would produce vibrations that could destroy the instrument; if the record player finds such signs, it will readjust itself so that its sensitive frequencies should change, thus preventing the record from destroying the record player: it might grow protrusions, or might re-arrange some of its parts. Hopefully, this super record player would really be able to play every record from the beginning to the end as intended.

Gödel's theorem says that we will necessarily be disappointed in our hopes: if someone knows the structure and design of the super record player and is smart enough, he will be able to produce such a record that cannot be played by even this super record player. The super record player may readjust itself as much as it pleases, but will not be able to play the record. Gödel's theorem practically guarantees that a record, fitting all standards and coding real sounds, can be made for any super record player to demonstrate and justify the complaint that the record player is out of order. At the same time it is possible that a normal traditional gramophone can play this super-cunning record without difficulties and we can enjoy the melodies encoded in its sound grooves. Perhaps this super-cunning record will not destroy the super record player physically any more, but we can

215

never tell how it is progressing in rearranging itself; for us, the record player is really out of order.

Producing records that dodge the different super record players may seem to be an esoteric engagement. The technology of production is given by the method of proof of Gödel's theorem, but as the practical significance of the destructive record is very slight, the statement proving Gödel's theorem is not very interesting in itself, either. (It does not make any difference if we talk about a statement or a question, for we can consider the Gödelian formula both as a statement and as an unanswerable question that cannot be proven or disproven within the system — although the statement or the question can be formulated definitely.)

The only meaning of the concrete formal statement proving Gödel's theorem is that "I cannot be proven within the system in question". If a super-cunning record is played by another gramophone it might easily just repeat, "I cannot be played on that super record player". But it might as well contain a much deeper harmony, some really profound music. But this can be decided only if we listen to it on another record player that can play it. There is no other way: as we saw in Chapter 14, there is no formal procedure with the aid of which we could decide for sure whether a given question is Gödelian or not. Thus Gödelian questions may have many forms. Maybe a statement, besides being fortuitously Gödelian, also expresses a truth important from another aspect; it is possible that a record that fortuitously cannot be played by a super record player contains very good music from another aspect.

The frequency of Gödelian questions

The first Gödelian shock in the history of mathematics appeared in 1823, some 100 years before Gödel's theorem was discovered. That year János Bolyai of Hungary and Nikolai Lobachevsky of Russia discovered (independently from each other) that Euclid's famous axiom of parallelism (according to which only one straight line can be drawn through a point in a plane that is parallel to another given straight line) is a Gödelian statement as related to the other axioms of geometry. Bolyai and Lobachevsky created a geometrical system in which all of the other axioms of geometry are as true as in Euclidean geometry, but the axiom of parallelism is not true: in this system two straight lines can be drawn through a given point in a given plane that are parallel to a given straight line. The next statement can be proven in this new geometrical system: if there is a contradiction in the new system, then a contradiction within the Euclidean system can also be deduced. If Euclidean geometry never leads to contradictions, the new one will never do so either. Thus it is impossible to decide by logical means which geometry is "the real one", which one describes reality better.

Thus Bolyai had every reason to say that he created "a new, different world" out of nothing, for mathematics can never decide by itself which geometry is about the real world. In Einstein's relativity theory (i.e. in a system that is outside mathematics, a physical system) the world really happens to be non-Euclidean; thus Bolyai's and Lobachevsky's works did not remain an embarrassing logical possibility but proved to be an essential means of understanding the world more deeply. The axiom of parallelism is a record that cannot be played by the Euclidean record player, although it contains a melody that is very interesting from the aspect of learning more about the world. This record does not only sing "I cannot be played" so much so that the best mathematicians in the world could not even imagine for two and a half thousand years that it could be unplayable; they dealt only with repairing the record player, i.e. searching for the proof.

Ever since we have known Gödel's theorem we should be consciously prepared for the appearance of such records. Really, several problems in mathematics have turned out to be unsolvable; the most famous of them is the so-called continuum problem. It sets out from the statement that it can be proven that there are more points on a straight line than integers, meaning that no reciprocally unequivocal correspondence can be made among them. The question is whether there are intermediary infinite orders of magnitudes between the two kinds of infinities, or not. This question has proved to be Gödelian: it would not lead to a logical contradiction if we assumed that there were intermediary infinities, or that there were no such things. To be more precise: either both assumptions (and thus our whole mathematics) lead to contradiction, or neither of them does.

In the history of mathematics only a few tens of millions of problems arose that were regarded as worth studying more seriously. (This could be estimated on the basis of the total sum of mathematical books and journals.) The problems of mathematics are usually strictly built on one another, and their proposals are mostly justified by the fact that our intuitions say that they must have solutions: the problems of mathematics are also well-designed scientific questions. If even a few dozens of these proved to be Gödelian, then Gödelian problems could not be so rare after

217

all: there is a real danger that our intellect meets such questions at all times and in all places.

★   ★   ★

How many Gödelian questions may be brought out by Nature "who" produces millions of the more and more recent possible versions of life in a real gigantic factory with its successful genetic tricks (mutations, crossing over, inversion, etc.)? At first glance the question seems to be absurd, even if it refers to memes that materialize thoughts, yet it proves to be meaningful within the framework of the most classical biological branches of science.

Hofstadter could transfer the example of the record player almost word for word to the basic mechanisms of molecular biology. The record player corresponds to the cell that can reproduce theoretically different DNA threads by its refined mechanisms. The role of records are played by the DNA threads, the role of sounds (as the vibrations of the air) is played by the proteins that are synthesized on the basis of DNA. Occasionally these proteins may destroy the cells themselves as the sound vibrations may destroy the record player. The analogy is true of the somewhat idealized mechanisms of molecular biology, but they are less far from the real processes than the idealized record players in the example are from the real ones. Indeed, the real process of biological self-reproduction almost certainly includes those abstract phenomena sufficient to prove Gödel's theorem. Thus Hofstadter can justly formulate "Gödel's theorem of molecular biology":

"It is always possible to design a strand of DNA which, if injected into a cell, upon being transcribed, causes such proteins to be manufactured as would destroy the cell (or the DNA), and thus results in the non-reproduction of that DNA."

The result is undoubtedly striking, but it does not make molecular biology gape. Its scholars are well aware that such DNA threads do exist; they cause just enough trouble in the form of retro-viruses. The only news it might bring them may be that the existence of such phenomena does not arise from bad luck or the wickedness of Nature, but is inseparable from self-reproduction mechanisms. But this does not help in finding the method of prevention. For us, it is interesting that Nature constantly produces beings that materialize Gödelian mechanisms and are fit for life, because this also shows that Gödel's theorem is not only a kind of theoretical

218

oddity constructed in our thoughts but actually talks about very practical phenomena that appear in Nature, too.

There are some technical conditions in the exact mathematical form of Gödel's theorem: it is not always valid in cases of too simple systems of axioms. These technical conditions say essentially that the system of axioms must express that the series of integers is infinite, that each integer is followed by another that is different from the previous ones. It is evident from Gödel's deduction that if this condition is present, then within the framework of the system of axioms there can be statements formulated concerning the truth or falsity of other statements, though some of them can be neither proven nor disproven.

To put it in an informal way: the condition of validity of Gödel's theorem is that the system of axioms should be "meaningful" and "strong" enough to be able to talk about itself. This is why the analogies with the record player and molecular biology can be used: the record player (the cell) produces sounds (proteins) in a way that can theoretically be described by formalized methods, while the sounds (proteins) react to the record player (cell) and may occasionally even destroy it. The increasingly complex super record players and the records that destroy them remind us of one of the most absurd phenomena of our age, namely, of the arms race: the subsequent generations of impenetrable shields and the projectiles penetrating them easily. The basis of their mechanisms is the same.

Relying on the Gödelian analogy, we can also say that extremely total ideas are not only morally doubtful, but also contradictory in themselves: no exactly defined (i.e. essentially formalized) idea can be imagined within the frame of which everybody could be made happy. As there are perfectly normal records (that can be played by other record players and give meaningful melodies) that cannot be played by a given record player, in every formally completely determined social system there are perfectly normal people who are not allowed by the system to blossom out. Somewhat rhetorically we can say that history has no solution. The question of social systems cannot have a conceptual framework that would promise a perfect agreement, just as in order to study evolution successfully the conceptual frameworks promising a final solution had to be abandoned.

Probably it is also a Gödelian question whether artificial intelligence can be realized in principle, or not. In a nice tale of Stanislaw Lem's *The Cyberiad*, the brilliant engineer Trurl builds a Perfect Counsellor for the wicked king Mandarion who first of all uses the Counsellor to throw out the engineer legally without paying him. Trurl has gotten himself into a hopeless situation: he must achieve the payment of his reward, against a perfect intellect he himself has built. The Counsellor sees through every trick and defends the king. Yet, Trurl succeeds after all. He sends innocent greeting cards to the Counsellor in which there is no code, no wickedness. After some lengthy labor, the Perfect Counsellor realizes that the intrigue in the greetings is that they contain no hidden code whatsoever, but the king does not believe it, smells conspiracy and — to be on the safe side — has the Counsellor dismounted to the last screw. Thus he remains defenseless against the attack of Trurl, and finally must pay. Trurl summarizes the event as follows: "It was once said that to move a planet, one needs but find the point of leverage: therefore I, seeking to overturn a mind that was perfect, had to find the point of leverage, and this was stupidity."

Gödel's theorem slowly becomes a general metaphor that appears frequently in our everyday thinking, following a lot of other fundamental results of science ranging from the conservation of energy to relativity, from evolution to manpower-turned-commodity. The concept of the Gödelian question may also prove to be a viable meme, because it expresses a certain truth of the world at a level more general than earlier ones. Naturally, it constantly changes and is modified as a meme. It may lose some of its scientific exactness, but may enrich our everyday life with new possibilities of cognition and thinking. It helps us understand more deeply why alternating the reference systems is a fundamental characteristic of our thinking.

The difficulties of alternating

We saw in Chapter 5 that we can also formulate Gödel's theorem as follows: if we want to stay open to every truth with our logic, then it is necessary to make shifts among reference systems. With the analogy of the record player we can also say that if we want to stay open to listening to all kinds of melodies, then changing our record players is necessary. Our living environment also forces us to maintain the ability to change in ourselves. If there were an aspect in our environment toward which we were completely insensitive for good and all, then Nature with its tricks of large-scale trials would sooner or later produce a new species that would use just our insensitivity as its living-space. If we were lucky, this would only be mildly unpleasant for us, like fleas for a dog, but in a more unfortunate case it would endanger even our survival.

We can so easily switch from one reference system to another in our everyday thinking that we do not even notice where we made a mistake. At other times, however, we hopelessly get stuck within the frames of a train of thought, and can hardly find another point of view. An example of this is Puzzle 9 of Chapter Zero, which is also a typical task of creativity tests. Most people first look for a solution within the square determined by the nine dots, but there is no such solution. This is a well designed puzzle exactly because it suggests an erroneous reference system very subtly, almost imperceptibly. The solution is soon found by those who realize that nobody said that the straight lines were not allowed to go beyond this square and thus extend the reference system of the task to the whole sheet:

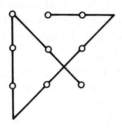

Creativity is the ability to make new, original and valuable products. We can experience every day that this ability is present in some people to a greater extent than in others. Still, creativity is one of the most difficult concepts to be caught. Murphy's law fits it perfectly well, namely, that those who have a watch always know the time exactly; those who have two watches can never be quite sure. No matter how many ways were attempted to measure creativity, the results were always different: each creativity test showed different people to be highly creative. Switching flexibly from one reference system to another is only one, and perhaps not even the most important element of creativity; the ability to use a given reference system consistently proved to be just as important a component.

The ease of alternating

The difficulty caused by Puzzle 10 in Chapter Zero shows exactly the point that we can slide from one reference system to another so easily, as unnoticeably as the metamorphoses of birds into fishes or reptiles in Escher's pictures. Both arguments in the puzzle seem to be very convincing: really, both the clearheaded and the dimheaded persons give the same answer to every question, and they really give different answers to the question "What are you?" Indeed, both arguments are faultless. But where is the trick then? It is improbable that our thousands-of-years-old belief in the uncontradicting nature of logic will be overthrown because of such a trifle puzzle. Most people try to find some way out, even figuring out "creative" tricks by which they could invalidate the whole task, while they feel that they are not really convincing. Undoubtedly, it is a well-designed puzzle.

The solution can be found in a purely logical way, too, since in the course of methodically testing all possibilities and carefully checking each word in the puzzle only one possibility is left to resolve the contradiction. However, most people do not find the solution this way, but it comes somehow in a flash as they switch their attention between the two contradictory but equally logical trains of thought: *"Is the question the same at all if it is put to two persons?"* Of course it is not: if a dimheaded is asked "Are you clearheaded?" the question will refer to him, to a dimheaded person. If a clearheaded person is asked the same thing, the question will refer to *him*. Thus the two questions are not the same, for they are not about the same person — no wonder the answers will differ.

The solution is strikingly simple, but still the puzzle is difficult; in fact, it is perhaps the most difficult one of the ten. We switch from one reference system to another so easily in our everyday thinking that we do not become aware of having just done so. In our tangled hierarchies we do not notice when we are thinking at a meta-level or slip to a lower or even to a higher level. The puzzle first suggests to us to look at it from the meta-level called logic, then it switches from one reference system to another before our very eyes without our noticing it: if we ask two equally intelligent, purely logically thinking persons, "Do you belong to the AB blood group?" we shall not be surprised at all if the answers differ. Here the reference system is not the universality of logic any more, but the diversity of everyday things.

Alternating between levels is not an aim by itself in our thinking: this method is essential in following the logic of things. Let us have a look at the following everyday situation: someone has broken the bow of his spectacles, but fortunately he notices a sign in a shopwindow: "Eyeglasses repaired while you wait!" Relieved, he enters the shop and wants to hand his glasses over to the shop assistant who flatly refuses to accept them saying they are not in their line. Our man starts to complain about the large sign in the shop widow, but he gets the answer: "Oh, we are sign painters." If Nature can produce Gödelian mechanisms even at the most fundamental molecular biological levels, no wonder the world around us is organized into complicated tangled hierarchies.

In one of the short stories of Jorge Luis Borges, the levels of reference systems are hopelessly entangled: "A slave stole a crimson ticket which in the drawing credited him with the burning of his tongue. The legal code fixed that same penalty for the one who stole a ticket. Some Babylonians argued that he deserved the burning irons in his status of a thief; others, generously, that the executioner should apply it to him because chance had determined it that way."

The survival machines of memes

We have given no exact definition of memes, stressing only their analogy with genes. A lot more is known about the direct material components of genes, but we have not been able to give a definition of genes on the basis of which genetic phenomena at the micro and macro levels could be treated uniformly. Usually scientists accept the definition that a gene is a part of the DNA thread encoding one protein molecule. However, this definition does not help classical genetics much in the investigation of the development and inheritance of different physical (and perhaps psychological) characteristics. Furthermore, even this definition is not completely unambiguous. Sometimes such genes overlap each other in the DNA thread: the end of one gene may be the beginning of another gene simultaneously; in fact, in some viruses a gene may fully include another one. This so-called "gene-in-gene" phenomenon means that the gene "inside" is read in a phase different from the one when the other is read, thus the same DNA part may encode two completely different proteins at the same time. Here we have another example of the spontaneous alternating of reference systems already at the level of molecular biology.

Biologists who want to investigate higher-level phenomena use another, softer definition of genes. Dawkins uses this one: "A gene is defined as any portion of chromosomal material which potentially lasts for enough generations to serve as a unit of natural selection." In other words: it is a replicator that can make duplicates of itself with great accuracy but with occasional variations. At this level even biologists disregard the facts of the molecular level, although they are willing to deal only with high-level theories that do not contradict these facts. Sociobiology is not the meta-level of microbiology; its objects of investigation are the survival machines built by the genes and their characteristics as independent units.

As individual living creatures can be regarded as complex survival machines, so the reference systems of human thinking, the high-level cognitive schemata of man can also be regarded as the survival machines of memes. Those memes will prove to be the most fit for life that can get organized into well-operating systems. As the complicated gene-complexes make up our different organs in order to improve their survival chances, so the complicated meme-complexes develop our general, high-level schemata.

In the previous chapter we stressed how similar the concepts of memes and genes are. Nevertheless, there are essential differences as well. We conceived schemata to be very general things that include every unit of our thinking from the simplest concepts to the highest-level heuristics. If some of the schemata are already present at birth, they can hardly be considered as memes, since such schemata are indispensable elements of our thinking which is the environment of the memes; they are not replicators. On the other hand, memes could correspond to our concept of schemata to a great extent, as we saw in Chapter 15. The more a high-level schema can be considered as general psychological reality, the less it can be considered as a meme or meme complex: instincts and *general* pattern-recognizing schemata are probably not developed by memes, while the schemata of rationality or mystic omnijectivity are likely to be developed by them.

The latter two high-level general meta-schemata have proved to be very stable and fit for life. They can be so fit for life because, perhaps, they contain only a few, and very closely, connected memes, while they can cooperate extremely well with a lot of other memes. It is difficult to decide whether the schema of onmijectivity contains one or more memes but, for those who have reached the state of enlightenment, this schema cooperates perfectly with not only many but all of the other schemata. Similarly, the schema of rationality coordinates the operation of a lot of other schemata, often unwillingly and unconsciously, as e.g. in the mechanisms of rationalization or intellectualization.

The meta-schema of rationality filters out the logical contradictions among the meanings of the individual schemata. With our present knowledge it can hardly be decided whether the underlying mechanism is based on formal logic or on another type of mechanism that follows the logic of things. If this mechanism is based on formal logic, it probably does not use all the means of formal logic: we either do not feel most of the syllogisms natural, or actually use them incorrectly. But it is also conceivable that our rational thinking is based not at all on the principles of formal logic but on something else, like some forms of the heuristics of representativity or availability. Our deeper knowledge about these mechanisms is quite scanty, but on the basis of the results mentioned in Chapter 1, and on the basis of the experiments on mental models and the heuristics of chance perception, this possibility cannot be excluded either. Even if all the fundamental syllogisms of formal logic constituted the meta-schema of rationality, this high-level schema could be composed only of about a half dozen memes.

What controls the fact that memes build their high-level survival machines in mystic, rational or perhaps some other (e.g. artistic) forms of meta-schemata is quite a question. It is also possible that these high-level schemata are simply memes themselves: they struggle for survival so that they can become the meta-schemata of as many people's memes as possible. The vitality of the meme (or meme-complex) of rationality might be due to its simplicity and general validity: rational reasoning does not offer as many possibilities of interpretation as other reasonings, exactly because of its formal character, thus this meme is the least subjected to its variations and mutations which may become its real rivals. The meme of rationality can be especially stable. Yet, compared to other non-rational principles like the schema of omnijectivity or the individual high-level schemata of the grandmasters of certain professions, this meme can co-ordinate only a ten times smaller number of schemata. The arts also make the coordination of great complexities possible.

The rivalry of schemata

Each of our schemata is a kind of reference system. When a certain schema gets into the center of our attention, the connections of this schema with other schemata will determine what will come to our minds most easily. Not only one schema can find its way into our short-term memory, but several, though not too many either: about seven of them. The survival of a schema is better ensured if it is taken more frequently into consideration, thus getting more often into STM. Several models of cognitive psychology are based on the idea that schemata are constantly competing with each other for our attention. Many seemingly paradoxical phenomena of our thinking can be uniformly interpreted within the frameworks of such theories. For example, with the aid of such models we can explain well-known phenomena like the one where, upon watching an ambiguous drawing, we often alternate between the two interpretations, but when we see the picture one way it is difficult to imagine how we could see it in another way just a moment ago.

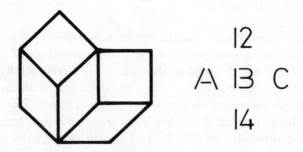

The figures above illustrate the rivalry of schemata. On first viewing the first picture, about 65% of the people report seeing a pretty young woman, while 35% see an unattractive old woman. If, however, we show a set of unambiguous pictures of definitely old women to our experimental subjects first and show the ambiguous drawing afterward, they will almost always see it as an old woman. After the display of a set of pictures of young women, almost everyone will see the young lady first in the ambiguous picture. The motif in the second drawing is used by Victor Vasarely in quite a few of his pictures. Here again, our opinion regarding which part shows concave and which one shows convex surfaces also changes continuously. The third example shows the determining power of higher-level schemata: the center of the figure can be seen as either the letter B or the number 13, depending on whether we look at it in the context of rows (from left to right) or of columns (from top to bottom).

In addition to the vast number of schema concepts, we almost imperceptibly introduced another one: that of reference systems. This expression does not indicate an essential change. It only stresses another aspect of schemata: the already existing schemata fighting with each other for our attention also determine the frames of our thinking, the conclusions that can possibly be drawn, the thoughts that can be thought and the new schemata that can be formed. This is an especially informative aspect if we study high-level schemata as reference systems. In Chapter 5 where we re-formulated Gödel's theorem in an informal language this expression was used as if it meant complete systems of axioms: switching from one to another is unavoidable if we want to remain open to every truth. But the systems of axioms, the groups of newly accepted fundamental truths are also high-level schemata that fight for survival both within the thinking of one man and among many people so that they may be present in the thinking of as many people as possible.

Seeing the heartless fight for survival lacking deeper meaning of schema–memes, there is hardly anyone who would not ask "And where am I? Indeed, where is man with his conscious and appropriate problem-solving thinking? How do our feelings, desires, joys and sorrows fit into this dehumanized theory?" It is difficult to imagine our favorite poems, the set phrases used by our beloved, the quarrels with our neighbors and Christmas greetings, as the selfish actions of memes that want to survive.

Nobody says that they could all be seen only this way, once science sees them so. There are several tools of cognition, and science is only one of them. At the everyday level of cognition, poems and Christmas greetings remain what they are: means of expressions enriching and coloring our lives. Among the ways of cognition at the meta-level, science is again only one of them. The rivalry of schemata can be seen in almost every conflict and ruminating hero of world literature. Still, it would be strange if we analyzed Hamlet's monologue as the fight of memes struggling for survival. Although the different ways of cognition can be alternated, they cannot be mixed, just as even within science the different paradigms cannot simply be mixed under the heading of interdisciplinarity.

The rivalry of Weltanschauungs

Art, mystic thinking, and science are all general and consistent reference systems that make it possible to co-ordinate the greatest achievable complexity, the tens of thousands of complex schemata of the level of grandmaster. Since reaching the level of grandmaster takes a lot of time, these ways of cognition can be regarded as mutually exclusive of each other, at least on the level of grandmaster: these meme complexes also fight each other for survival. At the level of candidate master, even all of them may be present in our thinking, they may continue their constant struggle for survival in the heads of individuals and in the total meme stock of humanity.

Scientific *Weltanschauung* has resulted in a spectacular development in European civilization in the past few centuries, thus this way of thinking has developed the best chances of survival for itself. This is taught in schools first of all, and we rely on it as a primary tool when we want to argue, to make most people accept our opinion. The roaring success of science has changed the survival chances of high-level schemata, and it cannot be known yet in what ESS the different *Weltanschauungs* may become balanced in the new situation. Considering everything, many signs indicate that a great variety of reference systems, several *Weltanschauungs* will be present in the developing ESS, even if in different ratios.

It is perhaps one of the greatest achievements of scientific Weltanschauung that it could highlight its own limits as well. Science has proven to be able to study the irrational characteristics of human thinking successfully within its own rational frameworks. In his book *Mental Models* Johnson–Laird says, "Of course there may be aspects of spirituality, morality, and imagination, that cannot be modeled in computer programs. But these faculties will remain forever inexplicable. Any scientific theory of the mind has to treat it as an automaton." By that attitude science may turn a deaf ear to learning about a lot of interesting and existing things forever, but it cannot do otherwise: radically different reference systems cannot be mixed.

Furthermore, scientific *Weltanschauung* includes a built-in belief that cannot be proven within its frameworks, i.e. that it does not really separate itself from any existing thing. As Heisenberg says, Niels Bohr had a story for exactly such debates: "One of our neighbors in Tisvilde once fixed a horseshoe over the door of his house. When a mutual acquaintance asked him, 'But are you really superstitious? Do you honestly believe that this horseshoe will bring you luck?' he replied, 'Of course not; but they say it helps even if you don't believe in it.' "

The means of expression

Rational thinking deduces its statements from each other with the help of conclusions whose forms are strictly defined; this is its only means of expression. It determines the reference system by unambiguous axioms based on practical observations. Should it meet Gödelian questions, it attempts to make new observations by which the system of axioms can be modified so that this question is deducible within the new framework. Purely rational thinking, if it has to deal with Gödelian questions for some reason or another, can react only at the level of beginning, by changing the system of axioms and the whole reference system. Yet this occurs quite frequently, for as we have seen, there are interesting and important truths that can be formulated but cannot be proven within the framework of a given system.

According to mystic thinking concepts, differences and axioms in the plural form do not exist, the world is a perfectly harmonious unity. As the exact opposite of rational thinking, mystic thinking reacts to the appearance of Gödelian questions only at the highest level, by stressing the unity of the world. It regards the appearance of such questions as proofs of its belief: the question itself was wrong, just because it was a question, for the answer can only be differentiation and categorization. Stressing the Gödelian characteristics in various situations may be the means of expression for mystic thinking . Zen koans are typical products of this kind of expression.

229

The European forms of mysticism, those that do not break completely with the particularly strong traditions of logical thinking in this culture, mostly lead to pantheism; they identify God with the world and do not accept God as a supernatural being. In their reasoning, however, they conform to the rules of formal logic, although not always consistently. To tell the truth, they cannot be consistent, for the deep subjective experience which is the basis of every mystic experience, and whose final form (and aim) is enlightenment, cannot be expressed in the objective language of rationality.

In our everyday argumentations we are very rarely consistent in the sense of the strict rules of formal logic. We are able to understand about ten times as great a complexity as what we can express by purely rational means. Thus we can express our thoughts more exactly if we do not use the means of formal logic only. Quite often we operate with elements of individual style, pictorial forms, and even distant associations, unless we are writing a scientific paper. Still, we can be quite certain that we will be understood, because understanding is an active process, the reconstruction of the communicated information with the aid of the existing schemata. On one hand, there are no two persons who would mean the same thing the same way, because in different people's heads different schemata organized into different high-level schemata compete with each other. On the other hand, the survival of schemata means that they have some constant core or essence that remains stable even in the course of inexact reproductions and continuous modifications. This is why it is possible that other people will understand what we have to say. We would not express the same thing exactly the same way twice, for our schemata that form the basis of our message are also modified constantly. As we cannot step twice into the same river, nor can we think the same thought twice.

Intuition is the result of the tangled hierarchies of our schemata and that of their constant competition for survival. The struggle of the schemata for survival is constantly going on, even if we take no notice of it. In fact, intuition is the result of mostly unconscious processes. In different people there are different schemata working and even they are being constantly modified: new schemata are born, others are forgotten or transformed. But the tangled hierarchies of our schemata and their self-contradicting groups may become meaningful units at a higher level just as we saw in "The smallest number wins" game that the joint thinking of a lot of players formed a meaningful whole – an ESS at a higher level. Perhaps this higher-level spontaneous organization is what is called a "way of thinking";

perhaps this is why we could say that there are as many ways of thinking as persons.

Rationality and logic are slow ways of cognition that can express only a fractional but very unequivocal part of our knowledge and intuition every moment. However, the results of science prove that the method is slow, but very efficient: complex schemata *can* thus develop, with the aid of which our reference system slowly changes and the deeper understanding arising facilitates more profound intuitions about the truths of the world. The tension that we know more than what we can express or prove is a constant concomitant of rational congition. In exchange for that, we can be quite sure that what we say is correct, assuming that the starting axioms really express the truths of the world.

A mystic master also knows more than what he can express. His knowledge is based on a profound determining experience about which he knows from the beginning that it cannot be expressed by the means of differentiation, by words. Other means of expression are in between rationality and mysticism, but there, alternating the reference systems cannot be avoided. The well-defined frame and its deliberate breakdown are both means of expression.

Ultimate Gödelian questions

By the recognition of Gödel's theorem science has realized that whatever framework or system of axioms it develops, there will always be truths that cannot be proven within the given frames. Thus it will always be the question of belief or at least intuition to decide whether the scientific system we are dealing with is suitable or not to solve those problems for the study of which it was created. It does not mean, however, that there are truths in the world that could not be understood with the aid of some well-chosen systems of science.

The analogy of the record player may flash a sharper light on what we want to say by its metaphorical way. If we think of the *true* statements of the world (let them be material, spiritual or even transcendental) as melodies, then the belief of science is that for every melody, it is possible to make a record player and a corresponding record so that this melody can always be listened to. By scientific understanding we mean that we can find such a record player and record for the melody, i.e. for truth. There are well-determined frames of making record players: by its nature a gramophone is a machine, a kind of automaton that has to be constructed out of components that conform to the rules of logic so that it could be produced in any number of copies that operate exactly the same way. The question is whether or not there is a melody, the music of the spheres, the choir of the angels, or the song of the sirens to which no record player and no corresponding record can be made with the aid of which the melody could be played at any time.

Among the examples listed above, the music of the spheres is especially interesting. This concept is a piece of Pythagoras' ideas, or we could also say, of his memes that have proved to be fit for life for thousands of years, although its meaning has changed or mutated somewhat. The expression is rooted in Pythagoras' world concept: in his view the stars are fixed to transparent spheres, and the spheres rotate around their axes, thus making the stars move. The quickly moving heavenly bodies make sounds whose volume, pitch and tone depend on the speed of movement, the quality of the bodies and the medium around them. In Pythagoras' conception these sounds melt into a uniform, deep harmony. This would be the music of the spheres. Well, if it really exists, can such a record player and a record be made by which this melody could be played?

Scientific *Weltanschauung* is based on the belief that it is possible to make a record player and a record for every existing melody, suitable for playing that particular tune. If it should turn out not to be so, it would not make the methods and results of science, i.e. the record players and the beautiful and true melodies coded in the records, less valuable.

If the structure of a record player is given, Gödel's theorem will guarantee that there exists a melody of which no record can be made: every record gives a different melody or the machine cannot play it. Thus, science is subjected to the eternal alternation of record players, but this does not mean that it cannot find the appropriate record player and the corresponding record sooner or later. But nothing guarantees this possibility either. We have arrived at the ultimate Gödelian questions that cannot be decided by the methods of science, by observation or by the aid of logic. In the framework of extreme mystic thinking, these are not Gödelian questions: they are non-questions. If there is only one melody, the institution of record players itself is meaningless: this melody can be heard only from within.

Yet science made quite a few functions of Nature understandable (and could even influence them artificially) that cannot be understood within other, e.g mystic or religious, *Weltanschauungs* at all. In consequence of scientific results, non-scientific *Weltanschauungs* have also changed. With the aid of science we can also understand why so many ways of thinking do have places in the evolutionary stable strategy developed in the course of the competition of different *Weltanschauungs*. Memes, similar to genes, are extremely inventive in discovering the living space ensuring their survival and in building the corresponding survival machines. Cognition of the world is not sufficient for the survival of mankind. Other aspects also arise, e.g. creating our own inner harmony, and other ways of cognition may offer more efficient help for this.

One of the methods of the struggle of the schemata for survival is open confrontation, or debate. Therefore polemics between different *Weltanschauungs* are unavoidable and endless, because they are usually about topics that are Gödelian in the range which is accepted by both parties, on the ground where persuasion can be conceived at all. It is also possible that the question of debate is Gödelian in both systems, but intuitions in the two systems suggest contradictory answers. Debates, however, are not necessarily meaningless even if they are about Gödelian questions, and none of the parties can convince the other. Alternating the reference systems is necessary and may inspire the clarification of the questions within our own system, too.

If a debate is about Gödelian questions, it only means that it cannot be settled by logical arguments. Regardless of this, one of the parties may state a truth of the world, while the other may be wrong. Bronislaw Malinowski describes that the natives on the islands of Trobriand believe that children are given by the Baloma divinity; they have no idea about physiological fatherhood. Their mystic belief "provides a co-ordinated and self-contained, though not always consistent, theory of the origin of human life. ... As a means of testing the firmness of their belief, I sometimes made myself definitely and aggressively an advocate of the truer physiological doctrine of procreation. In such arguments the natives would quote, not only positive instances, such as just mentioned, of women who have children without having enjoyed any intercourse; but would also refer to the equally convincing negative aspect, that is, to the many cases in which an unmarried woman has plenty of intercourse and no children."

Neither could Malinowski convince the natives about physiological fatherhood, nor the natives make Malinowski see that children are given by the Baloma. Undoubtedly, in this case Malinowski was right, but within the narrow reference system that was accepted by both parties the question was Gödelian. Intuition suggested different conclusions: the natives listed the examples of famously ugly women with whom evidently nobody could have slept with and still had children; while Malinowski, relying on his scientific knowledge, knew what he did. They had no means to settle the debate.

In our culture science has won the authority that makes us accept as truth its results proven by its methods even if they contradict our everyday intuition. The results of science enter our everyday thinking in the forms of analogies and metaphors, and the schemata born this way hold their ground excellently in the struggle for survival. But science cannot solve the ultimate Gödelian questions. Scientific *Weltanschauung* is only one of the several viable high-level reference systems.

Concluding theses

This is not the book I wanted to write. I wanted to provide a twofold elaboration of the topic in a single book: both as a light-hearted, entertaining and thought-provoking piece, and as an exact professional scientific work. That book, however, refused to be written — perhaps the previous section also made the reason clear. Still, it is perhaps worthwhile to summarize briefly the book's major scientific theses.

(1.) The amount of cognitive schemata necessary for the different levels of competence can be easily estimated in certain professions, and such estimations result in highly similar orders of magnitude in the different domains.

(2.) The level of competence corresponding to the complexity of a few thousand highly organized cognitive schemata is that of candidate master. This is the level that can be reached, expressed and taught by purely rational means. This is also the level that can be reached, in most domains, by the present means of artificial intelligence, which has not succeeded in passing beyond this level in any field.

(3.) Human thought is capable of reaching the complexity of some tens of thousands of cognitive schemata within a profession. This is the level of the grandmasters. Grandmasters' thinking is basically intuitive and relies on very complex, high-level cognitive schemata.

(4.) Thus, we are capable of comprehending complexity which is about ten times as great, through intuition, with our inexact heuristics, compared to what we can express by purely rational means. The diversity of thinking and the alternation among reference systems are essential in cognition and expression.

Was spelling out these theses a simple violation of style or was my changing of the system of reference rational and justified? These are but some of the questions remaining open, even though the book ends here.

Bibliography

This bibliography does not aim at completeness. It includes books and papers that had a direct influence in writing this book. Each item here is referred to in the Index by its serial number, even if the authors and titles are not mentioned in the text of the book.

[1] *Anderson, J. R.* (1983). The architecture of cognition. Harvard University Press.

[2] *Anderson, J. R.* (1984). Cognitive psychology. Artificial Intelligence 23. pp. 1–11.

[3] *Atkinson, R. L., Atkinson, R. C., Hilgard, E. R.* (1983). Introduction to psychology. Harcourt Brace Jovanovich, Inc.

[4] *Bancroft, A.* (1979). Zen: direct pointing to reality. Thames and Hudson.

[5] *Barash, D. P.* (1978). Sociobiology and behavior. Elsevier.

[6] *Baron-Cohen, S.* (1988). "Without a theory of mind one cannot participate in a conversation." Cognition 28. pp. 83–84.

[7] *Barr, A., Feigenbaum, E. A.* (eds., 1981, 1982). The handbook of artificial intelligence, Vol. 1–2. Pitman.

[8] *Bartlett, F. C.* (1932, 1977). Remembering. Cambridge University Press.

[9] *Berliner, H. J.* (1980). Backgammon computer program beats world champion. Artificial Intelligence 14. pp. 205–220.

[10] *Berliner, H., Ebeling, C.* (1986). The SUPREM architecture: a new intelligent paradigm. Artificial Intelligence 28. pp. 3–8.

[11] *Berne, E.* (1968). Games people play. Penguin Books.

[12] *Bever, T. G., Carroll, J. M., Miller, G. A.* (1984). Talking minds: The study of language in the cognitive sciences. MIT Press.

[13] *Block, N.* (1974). Why do mirrors reverse right/left and not up/down? Journal of Philosophy 71. pp. 259–277.

[14] *Bobrow, D. G., Collins, A.* (eds., 1975) Representation and understanding — Studies in cognitive science. Academic Press.

[15] *Buchanan, B., Duda, R. O.* (1983). Principles of rule-based expert systems. Advances in Computers 22. pp. 163–216.

[16] *Buchanan, B., Shortliffe, E.* (eds., 1984). Rule-based expert systems: The MYCIN experiments of the Stanford heuristic programming project. Addison–Wesley.

[17] *Capra, F.* (1975). The Tao of physics. Shambhala Publications.

[18] *Cavalli-Sforza, L. L., Feldman, M, W.* (1981). Cultural transmission and evolution. A quantitative approach. Princeton University Press.

[19] *Cerf, V.* (1973). Parry encounters the Doctor. Datamation, pp. 62–64.

[20] *Cermak, L. S., Craik, F. I. M.* (eds., 1979). Levels of processing in human memory. Erlbaum.

[21] *Charness, N.* (1981). Search in chess: Age and skill differences. Journal of Experimental Psychology 7. pp. 467–476.

[22] *Charniak, E., McDermott, D.* (1985). Introduction to artificial intelligence. Addison–Wesley.

[23] *Cherniak, C.* (1986). Minimal rationality. The MIT Press.

[24] *Cherniak, C.* (1988). Undebuggability and computer science. Communications of the ACM 31. pp. 402–412.

[25] *Cohen, P. R., Feigenbaum, E. A.* (1982). The handbook of artificial intelligence, Vol. 3. Pitman.

[26] *Colby, K. M., Weber, S., Hilf, F. D.* (1971). Artificial paranoia. Artificial Intelligence 2. pp. 1–25.

[27] *Copi, I. M., Gould, J. A.* (1972). Contemporary readings in logical theory. Macmillan.

[28] *V. Csányi* (1982). General theory of evolution. Akadémiai Kiadó, Budapest.

[29] *Czigler I.* (ed., 1981.) A tanulás és az emlékezés pszichológiája. Szöveggyüjtemény II. Egységes jegyzet, Tankönyvkiadó.

[30] *Dawkins, R.* (1982). The extended phenotype. Freeman.

[31] *Dawkins, R.* (1976). The selfish gene. Oxford University Press.

[32] *De Gelder, B.* (1987). On not having a theory of mind. Cognition 27. pp. 285–290.

[33] *De Groot, A.* (1965). Thought and choice in chess. Mouton, Den Haag.

[34] *Doyle, J.* (1983). What is rational psychology? Toward a modern mental philosophy. AI Magazine 4. pp. 50–53.

[35] *Doyle, J.* (1988). Big problems for AI. AI Magazine 9. pp. 19–22.

[36] *Dreyfus, H. L.* (1972). What computers can't do. Harper and Row.

[37] *Dreyfus, H. L., Dreyfus, S. E.* (1986). Mind over machine. The Free Press.

[38] *Élő, Á. E.* (1978). The rating of chessplayers. Arco, New York.

[39] *Engländer T.* (1979). Bevezetés a leíró döntéselméletbe. ÉVM Továbbképző Központja, Budapest.

[40] *Enomiya-Lassalle, H. M., S.J.* (1960). Zen — Weg zur Erleuchtung. Herder, Wien.

[41] *Ericsson, K. A., Chase, W. G., Faloon, S.* (1980). Acquisition of a memory skill. Science 208. pp. 1181–1182.

[42] *Eysenck, M. W.* (1984). A handbook of cognitive psychology. Erlbaum.

[43] *Feigenbaum, E. A., Feldman, J.* (eds., 1963). Computers and thought. McGraw Hill.

[44] *Foss, B. M.* (ed., 1966). New horizons in psychology. Penguin Books.

[45] *Freud, S.* (1973). Introductory lectures on psychoanalysis. Pelican Books.

[46] *Frey, P. W.* (1978). Chess skill in man and machine. Springer Verlag.

[47] *Gardner, H.* (1985). Frames of mind. Heinemann, London.

[48] *Garma C. C. Chuang* (1974). Teachings of Tibetan Yoga. Citadel Press.

[49] *Gentner, G., Stevens, A.* (eds., 1983). Mental models. Erlbaum.

[50] *Gevarter, W. B.* (1985). Intelligent machines. Prentice–Hall.

[51] Goldman, A. I. (1986). Epistemology and cognition. Harvard University Press.

[52] *Gregory, R. L.* (1970). The intelligent eye. Weidenfeld and Nicholson.

[53] *Groner, R., Groner, M., Bishof, W. F.* (eds., 1983). Methods of heuristics. Erlbaum.

[54] *Hadamard, J.* (1945). The psychology of invention in the mathematical field. Dover.

[55] *Hayes-Roth, F., Waterman, D. A., Lenat, D. B.* (1983). Building expert systems. Addison–Wesley.

[56] *Heiser, J. F., Colby, K. M., Faught, W. S., Parkinson, R. C.* (1979). Can psychiatrists distinguish a computer simulation of paranoia from the real thing? Journal of Psychiatric Research 15. pp. 149–162.

[57] *Hidi, S., Baird, W.* (1986). Interestingness — A neglected variable in discourse processing. Cognitive Sciences 10. pp. 179–194.

[58] *Hilgard, E. R.* (1968). The experience of hypnosis. Harcourt, Brace and World Inc.

[59] *Hofstadter, D. R.* (1979). Gödel, Escher, Bach. Basic Books.

[60] *Hofstadter, D. R.* (1985). Metamagical themas. Basic Books.

[61] *Hofstadter, D. R., Dennett, D. C.* (1981). The mind's I. Basic Books.

[62] *Hogarth, R. M.* (1980). Judgement and choice. Wiley and Sons.

[63] *Holding, D. H.* (1985). The psychology of chess skill. Erlbaum.

[64] *Hookway, C.* (ed., 1985). Mind, machine and evolution. Cambridge University Press.

[65] *Horváth Gy.* (1984). A tartalmas gondolkodás. Tankönyvkiadó.

[66] *Indurkhya, B.* (1987). Approximate semantic transference: A computational theory of metaphors and analogies. Cognitive Science 11. pp. 445–480.

[67] *Jánossy F.* (1975). A gazdasági fejlődés trendvonaláról. Magvető Kiadó.

[68] *Johnson-Laird, P. N.* (1983). Mental models. Cambridge University Press.

[69] *Johnson-Laird, P. N., Steedman, M. J.* (1978). The psychology of syllogisms. Cognitive Psychology 10. pp. 64–99.

[70] *Johnson-Laird, P. N., Wason, P. C.* (eds., 1977). Thinking: Readings in cognitive science. Cambridge University Press.

[71] *Kahneman, D., Slovic, P., Tversky, A.* (eds., 1982). Judgement under uncertainty: Heuristics and biases. Cambridge University Press.

[72] *Kara Gy.* (ed., 1986). A köztes lét könyvei. Európa Könyvkiadó.

[73] *Karácsony S.* (1939). A magyar észjárás. Exodus kiadás.

[74] *Kneale, W., Kneale, M.* (1962). The development of logic. Oxford University Press.

[75] *Kolata, G.* (1982). How can computers get common sense. Science 217. pp. 1237–1238.

[76] *Kónya A.* (1980). A tanulás és az emlékezés pszichológiája. Szöveggyüjtemény. Egységes jegyzet, Tankönyvkiadó.

[77] *Kotovsky, K., Hayes, J. R., Simon, H. A.* (1985). Why are some problems hard? Evidence from the tower of Hanoi. Cognitive Psychology 17. pp. 248–294.

[78] *Kovács P. A.* (1987). Sakkprogramozásról mindenkinek. NOVOTRADE RT.,Budapest.

[79] *Kuhn, T.* (1962). The structure of scientific revolutions. University of Chicago Press.

[80] *Kun E.* (1966). A rejtvény. Gondolat Kiadó.

[81] *Kunda, Z., Nisbett, R. E.* (1986). The psychometrics of everyday life. Cognitive Psychology 18. pp. 195–224.

[82] *Laird, J. E., Newell, A., Rosenbloom, P. S.* (1987). SOAR: An architecture for general intelligence. Artificial Intelligence 33. pp. 1–64.

[83] *Landauer, T. K.* (1986). How much do people remember? Some estimates of the quantity of learned information in long term memory. Cognitive Science 10. pp. 477–493.

[84] *Langley, P.* (1977). Rediscovering physics with BACON.3 in: Proc. 6th IJCAI, Cambridge, Mass. pp. 505–507.

[85] *Larkin, J. H., Simon, H. A.* (1987). Why a diagram is (sometimes) worth 10,000 words. Cognitive Science 11. pp. 65–99.

[86] *Lénárd F.* (1978). A problémamegoldó gondolkodás. Akadémiai Kiadó.

[87] *Lenat, D. B.* (1982, 1983). The nature of heuristics. I.–III. Artificial Intelligence 19. pp. 189–249.; 21. pp. 31–59.; 21. pp. 61–98.

[88] *Lenat, D. B., Brown, J. S.* (1984). Why AM and EURISKO appear to work. Artificial Intelligence 25. pp. 269–294.

[89] *Lindsay, P. H., Norman, D. A.* (1972). Human information processing. Academic Press.

[90] *Loftus, E. F.* (1980). Memory. Addison–Wesley.

[91] *Lovász L., Gács P.* (1978). Algoritmusok. Műszaki Könyvkiadó.

[92] *Lumsden, C. J., Wilson, E. O.* (1981). Genes, mind and culture. Harvard University Press.

[93] *Luria, A. R.* (1975). The mind of a mnemonist. Penguin Books.

[94] *Maynard-Smith, J.* (1982). Evolution and the theory of games. Cambridge University press.

[95] *Meehan, J. R.* (1978). The metanovel: Writing stories by computer. Ph.D. theses, Yale University.

[96] *Mérő, L.* (1983). Experiments with tree-pruning strategies. Computers and Artificial Intelligence 2. pp. 19–33.

[97] *Mérő, L.* (1987). Artificial intelligence at candidate master level. Electro Technology XXXI. pp. 54-65.

[98] *Mérő, L.* (1984). A heuristic search algorithm with modifiable estimate. Artificial intelligence 23. pp. 13–27.

[99] *Mérő, L.* (1986). The 'least number wins' game on a large sample. Proc 10th International Conference of the PME, London. pp. 457–462.

[100] *Mérő L.* (1987). Miért mélyebb a go játék, mint a sakk? A korrelációs együttható egy újabb értelmezése. Magyar Pszichológiai Társaság VIII. Országos tudományos konferenciája, Budapest. p. 42.

[101] *Mészáros I.* (1984). Hipnózis. Medicina Kiadó.

[102] *Michie, D.* (1986). On machine intelligence. Ellis Horwood.

[103] *Miller, G. A.* (1956). The magic number seven — plus or minus two. Psychological Review 63. pp. 81–98.

[104] *Miller, G. A., Gildea, P.* (1987). How children learn words. Scientific American 257. pp. 94–99.

[105] *Minsky, M.* (ed., 1968). Semantic information processing. The MIT Press.

[106] *Monod, J.* (1971). Chance and necessity. Vintage Books.

[107] *Motley, M. T.* (1985). Slips of the tongue. Scientific American, pp. 114–119.

[108] *Naylor, C.* (1983). Build your own expert system. Sigma Technical Press.

[109] *Neisser, U.* (1976). Cognition and reality. Freeman.

[110] *Neumann, J. von* (1959). The computer and the brain. Yale University Press.

[111] *Neumann, J., Morgenstern, O.* (1947). Theory of games and economic behavior. Princeton University Press.

[112] *Newborn, M. M.* (1978). Recent progress in computer chess. Advances in Computers 18. pp. 59–117.

[113] *Newell, A., Simon, H. A.* (1972). Human problem solving. Prentice–Hall.

[114] *Nievergelt, J., Farrar, J. C., Reingold, E. M.* (1975). Computer approaches to mathematical problems. Prentice–Hall.

[115] *Nilsson, N. J.* (1980). Principles of artificial intelligence. Tioga Publishing Company.

[116] *Nisbett, R., Ross, L.* (1980). Human Inference. Prentice–Hall.

[117] *Norman, D. A.* (1980). Post–Freudian slips. Psychology Today April 1980, pp. 43–48.

[118] *Orne, M. T.* (1959). The nature of hypnosis: Artifact and essence. The Journal of Abnormal and Social Psych. pp. 277–299.

[119] *Papert, S.* (1981). Mindstorms. Basic Books.

[120] *Pauker, S., Gorry, G., Cassirer, J., Schwarz, W.* (1976). Toward the simulation of clinical cognition: Taking a present illness by computer. American Journal of Medicine 60. pp. 981–996.

[121] *Pearl, J.* (1984). Heuristics. Addison–Wesley.

[122] *Pearl, J.* (1988). Embracing causalty in default reasoning. Artificial Intelligence 35. pp. 259–271.

[123] *Peat, F. D.* (1987). Synchronicity: The bridge between matter and mind. Bantam Books.

[124] *Piaget, J.* (1968). La formation du symbole chez l'enfant. Delachoux et Niestlé.

[125] *Pléh Cs.* (1986). A szövegszerkezet és az emlékezeti sémák. Akadémiai Kiadó.

[126] *Pólya, G.* (1957). How to solve it. Princeton University Press.

[127] *Pushkin, V. N.* (1972). Problems of heuristics. Israel program for scientific translations, Jerusalem.

[128] *Pylyshyn, Z.* (1984). Computation and cognition: Toward a foundation for cognitive science. MIT Press.

[129] *Reitman, J. S.* (1976). Skilled perception in GO: Deducing memory structures from inter–response times. Cognitive Psychology 8. pp. 336–356.

[130] *Reitman, J. S., Wilcox, B.* (1979). Modeling tactical analysis and problem solving in GO. Proc. 10th Annual Pittsburgh Conference. pp. 2133–2148.

[131] *Resnick, L. B.* (1976). The nature of intelligence. Erlbaum.

[132] *Reynolds, R. I.* (1982). Search heuristics of chess players of different calibers. American Journal of Psychology 95. pp. 383–392.

[133] *Rips, L.* (1983). Cognitive processes in reasoning. Psychological Review 90. pp. 38–71.

[134] *Rubinstein, Sz. L.* (1960). Gondolkodáslélektani vizsgálatok. Gondolat Kiadó.

[135] *Russell, B.* (1963). Mysticism and logic. Unwin books.

[136] *Schank, R. C.* (1979). Interestingness: Controlling inferences. Artificial Intelligence 18. pp. 273–297.

[137] *Schank, R. C., Abelson, R. P.* (1977). Scripts, plans, goals, and understanding. Erlbaum.

[138] *Searle, J.* (1980). Minds, brains and programs. The Behavioral and Brain Sciences. 3. pp. 417–457. (Followed by several reflections.)

[139] *Sharkey, N. E.* (ed., 1986). Advances in cognitive science. Ellis Horwood Ltd.

[140] *Simon, H. A.* (1974). How big is a chunk? Science 183. pp. 482–488.

[141] *Simon, H. A.* (1980). Cognitive science: The newest science of the artificial. Cognitive Science 4, pp. 33–46.

[142] *Simon, H. A.* (1977). Models of discovery. Reidel Publ. co.

[143] *Simon, H. A.* (1983). Reason in human affairs. Stanford University Press.

[144] *Simon, H. A., Chase, W. G.* (1973). Perception in chess. Cognitive Psychology 4. pp. 55–81.

[145] *Simon, H. A., Gilmartin, K. J.* (1973). A simulation of memory for chess positions. Cognitive Psychology 5. pp. 29–46.

[146] *Simon, H. A., Hayes, J. R.* (1976). The understanding process: Problem isomorphs. Cognitive Psychology 8. pp. 165–190.

[147] *Simons, G. L.* (1985). Expert systems and micros. The National Computing Centre, London.

[148] *Singleton, W. T., Hovden, J.* (eds., 1987). Risk and decisions. Wiley and Sons.

[149] *Smullyan, R.* (1983). 5000 B.C. St. Martin's Press, New York.

[150] *Smullyan, R.* (1982). The Tao is silent. Knopf.

[151] *Smullyan, R.* (1978). What is the name of this book? Simon Schuster.

[152] *Standing, L.* (1973). Learning 10,000 pictures. Quarterly Journal of Experimental Psychology 25. pp. 207–222.

241

[153] *Sternberg, R. J.* (1982). Handbook of human intelligence. Cambridge University Press.

[154] *Suzuki, D. T.* (1957). Mysticism — Christian and Buddhist. Collier Books.

[155] *Suzuki, D. T., Fromm, E., de Martino, R.* (1960). Zen Buddhism and psychoanalysis. Harper and Brothers.

[156] *Szeberényi J.* (1982). Értem-e a molekuláris genetikát? Natúra, Budapest.

[157] *Talbot, M.* (1981). Mysticism and the new physics. Bantam Books.

[158] *Tulving, E.* (1983). Elements of episodic memory. Oxford University Press.

[159] *Tihomirov, O. K., Poznianskaya, E. D.* (1966). An investigation of visual search as a means of analysing heuristics. Soviet Psychology 5. pp. 2–15.

[160] *Varga T.* (1966). Matematikai logika kezdőknek 1–2. Tankönyvkiadó.

[161] *Vernon, P. E.* (1970). Creativity. Penguin Modern Psychology Readings.

[162] *Vida G.* (ed., 1981–1984). Evolúció I.–IV. Natúra, Budapest.

[163] *Watson, J. D.* (1965). Molecular biology of the gene. Benjamin.

[164] *Webber, B. L., Nilsson, N. J.* (eds., 1981). Readings in artificial intelligence. Tioga Publishing Company.

[165] *Weizenbaum, J.* (1966, 1983). ELIZA — a computer program for the study of natural language communication between man and machine. Communications of the ACM 9. pp. 36–45. Reprinted: Communications of the ACM 26. pp. 23–27.

[166] *Weizenbaum, J.* (1976). Computer power and human reason. Freeman, San Francisco.

[167] *Winograd, T.* (1972). Understanding natural language. Academic Press.

[168] *Winograd, T.* (1980). Language as a cognitive process. Addison–Wesley.

[169] *Winston, P. H.* (1984). Artificial intelligence. Prentice–Hall.

[170] *Woodworth, R. S., Schlossberg, H.* (1961). Experimental psychology. Holt, Rinehart and Winston.

[171] *Wooldridge, D.* (1968). The mechanical man — The physical basis of intelligent life. McGraw–Hill.

[172] *Yngve, V. H.* (1961). The depth hypothesis. In: R. Jakobson (ed.). Structure of language and its mathematical aspects. Providence.

[173] *Zajonc, R. B.* (1980). Feeling and thinking: Preferences need no inferences. American Psychologist 35. pp. 151–175.

242

Sources

Hereafter you can find the sources of quotations. The numbers in brackets indicate the serial numbers of references that can also be found in the Bibliography.

p. 1. *Jorge Luis Borges*: Labyrinths. Penguin Books, 1981. p. 85.

p. 3. *Frigyes Karinthy*: Grave and gay. Corvina Press, 1973. pp. 91–92.

p. 4. *Franz Kafka*: The trial. Stocken Books, 1970. p. 228.

p. 4. *William Shakespeare*: Hamlet Act II. Scene 2. In: The illustrated Stratford Shakespeare. Chancellor Press, 1982. p. 808.

p. 4. *Bertrand Russell* [135] p. 17.

p. 4. *Ottlik Géza*: Próza. Magvető Kiadó, 1980. pp. 63–64.

p. 5. *Niels Bohr*, cit.: Werner Heisenberg: Physics and beyond. Allen and Unwin, 1971. p. 137.

p. 5. *Boris Pasternak*: Doctor Zhivago. A Signet Book, 1958. p. 210.

p. 5. *Blaise Pascal*, cit.: J. S. Bolen: The Tao of psychology, Harper and Row, 1982. p. 86.

p. 5. *Jules Renard*: Napló. Nagyvilág, 1968. p. 1550.

p. 5. *Shunryu Suzuki*: Zen mind, beginner's mind, cit.: J. A. Anderson et al., Psychological Review 84., 1977. p. 413.

p. 17. The source of data in Table 1: Goldman [15] 296.o.

p. 37. *S. L. Rubinstein*, cit.: Lénárd Ferenc [86] 179.o.

p. 39. *Thomas Kuhn* [79] p. 38.

p. 51. *Thomas Mann*: Doctor Faustus. Penguin Books, 1968. p. 171.

p. 56. *Sigmund Freud* [45] p. 213.

p. 57. Two Zen classics. Weatherhill, New York. p. 91–92. 64.o.

p. 57. *Paul Reps*: Zen flesh, Zen bones. Anchor Books. pp. 111–112.

p. 84. *F. C. Bartlett* [8] pp. 200–201.

p. 85. *J. S. Bruner* and *L. Postman*, cit.: T. Kuhn [79] pp. 63–64.

p. 85. *Horváth György* [65] p. 227.

p. 85. *Bertrand Russell*: My philosophical development. Allen and Unwin, 1959. p. 129.

p. 104. *P. Laplace*, cit.: Simonyi Károly: A fizika kultúrtörténete. Gondolat Kiadó, 1978. p. 283.

p. 107. *A. L. Luria* [93] p. 19.

p. 121. *Fülep Lajos*: Művészet és világnézet. Magvető Kiadó, 1976. pp. 624–625.

p. 132. *Sören Kierkegaard:* Mozart Don Juanja. Magyar Helikon, 1972. p. 79.

p. 133. *E. Berne* [11] p. 159.

p. 134. *S. M. Ulam:* Adventures of a mathematician. Scribner, 1976. 275.o.

p. 134. *Karácsony Sándor* [73] p. 193. and p. 295.

p. 135. *Turán Pál,* In: Nagy pillanatok a matematika történetében. Gondolat Kiadó, 1981. p. 198. and p. 206.

p. 147. *Jánossy Lajos* [67] p. 139.

p. 149. *David Levy,* cit.: N. E. Sharkey [139] p. 330.

p. 150. *G. L. Simons* [147] 12.o., 15.o., 23.o.

p. 161. *Marvin Minsky,* cit.: G. Kolata [75] p. 1238.

p. 161. *D. R. Hofstadter* [59] p. 678.

p. 165. *Rejtő Jenő:* Pipacs, a fenegyerek. In: Rejtö J. (P. Howard): Az elsikkasztott pénztáros, Albatrosz könyvek, 1970. p. 244.

p. 166. Source of the sentence: D. R. Hofstadter [60] p. 7.

p. 170. *H. Simon* [142] p. 173.

p. 170. *Kindler József, Kiss István:* Bevezetö. In: H. Simon: Korlátozott Racionalitás. Budapest, 1982. p. 13.

p. 175. *Arthur Rimbaud:* Delíriumok II. In: A. Rimbaud összes költői művei. Európa Kiadó, 1965. 247.o.

p. 186. *E. R. Hilgard,* [3] p.˙436.

p. 189. *R. Nisbett, L. Ross* [116] p. xii.

p. 191. *Niels Bohr,* cit.: W. Heisenberg, op. cit. p. 143.

p. 192. *Bertrand Russell* [135] pp. 17–19.

p. 192. *M. Talbot* [157] p. 2.

p. 193. *Albert Einstein:* The world as I see it. Philosophical Library, New York, 1949. p. 5.

p. 193. *Weöres Sándor:* Csalóka Péter. In: Weöres S.: Egybegyüjtött írások. Magvető Kiadó, Budapest, 1975. Vol. 2. p. 119.o., translated by Anna C. Gösi–Greguss.

p. 196. *Bertrand Russell* [135] pp. 32–33.

p. 200. *Mikhail Bulgakov:* The master and Margarita. Harper and Row, 1967. p. 253.

p. 203. *R. Dawkins* [31] p. 90.

p. 206. *R. Dawkins* [31] pp. 206–207.

p. 207. Füles XXVIII. Number 21, 1984. p. 9. — On the results of the game: XXVIII. Number 31. 1984. p. 15.

p. 211. *D. R. Hofstadter* [60] pp. 764–765.

p. 218. *D. R. Hofstadter* [59] p. 536.

p. 220. *Stanislaw Lem:* The Cyberiad. Sacker and Warburg, 1975. p. 194.

p. 222. after: S. M. Ulam, op. cit. p. 294.

p. 223. *Jorge Luis Borges:* op. cit. p. 57.

p. 223. *R. Dawkins* [31] p. 30.

p. 228. *P. N. Johnson–Laird* [68] p. 477.

p. 229. *Niels Bohr*, cit.: Werner Heisenberg, op. cit. p. 92.

p. 233. *Bronislaw Malinowski*: The sexual life of savages in North–Western Melanesia. Routledge and Kegan Paul, 1968. p. 153 and p. 158.

Index

The numbers in the brackets after the page numbers indicate the serial numbers of sources to be found in the Bibliography.

C

candidate master 114–128, 137, 146, 173–175, 199, 228, 234 [37, 97]

"Canon per Tonos" 89, 77 [59]

Capablanca, J. 106, 116 [46]

capacity limit 90–95, 125 [23, 35, 103, 110, 152]

cards' problem 15, 187 [51, 69, 70]

Casanova, G. 133

cell 218–219 [59, 156]

cheques' problem 17–20, 187 [51, 69, 70]

chess players' schemata 96–103, 104–109, 115–116 [21, 33, 46, 63, 132]

chess positions, taken from master games 100, 111 [33, 46, 144, 145]

– , quantity of 72, 99–101 [97, 145]

chess programs 2, 47, 143–148, 153–155, 158 [46, 78, 112]

Chinese writing 102, 182 [60, 170]

Church–Turing thesis 144–145, 166–168, 175 [27, 59, 74, 91]

class difference 153–155 [100]

cognitive psychology 47–54, 69, 88–93, 116, 173, 206, 225 [2, 42, 137, 168]

– schema 84, 111, 165–180, 234 [12, 42, 109, 125, 140]

– science 47–51, 88, 111, 141 [1, 14, 60, 113, 128, 139, 141]

coin tossing 181–182, 214 [71]

Colby, K. 30 [26, 56]

common sense 20–27, 33–43, 52, 80, 127, 133–136, 157–158, 176, 187, 196, 205–207, 222 [23, 39, 62, 71, 89, 116, 122, 173]

– language 133, 157–158, 205–206 [107, 116, 117, 173]

– logic 11, 20, 24–27, 39, 52, 80

– thinking 33–43, 52, 127, 136, 176, 187, 207, 222 [23, 39, 62, 71, 89, 116, 122, 173]

compiler 74 [59, 110]

complexity 125, 137–138, 160, 173–175, 187–189, 197, 228–230 [23, 24, 60, 91, 142, 146]

– limits 125, 152, 157, 172

computer 19, 33, 73–74, 110, 146

– model 89, 210, 228

– network 94 [59]

concept 63–80 [47, 59, 61, 170]

– hierarchies 65–80 [69, 60, 65, 105]

consistency 13, 18, 68, 165, 221 [27, 43, 59, 74]

context 226 [105]

continuum problem 217

courting 42, 172, 203 [5, 31]

creativity 47, 71, 221–222 [60, 153, 161]

Csontváry Kosztka, T. 122

cultural evolution 204–206 [17, 60, 92, 162]

cybernetics 141

D

da Molina, Tirso 133

Darwin, Ch. 39, 50, 88, 200–204, 211

Dawkins, R. 202–206, 223 [30, 31]

deadlock 95 [59]

depth of professions 153–155 [100]

description 68, 169

descriptive decision theory 184–185 [39, 148]

development 201 [79]

– , trend of 146–150, 173 [67, 104, 112]

dictaphone 2, 157, 161

digger wasp 62–63, 78, 166, 168, 195 [60, 171]

disharmony 60 [123, 150]

dissimulation 23–24, 30–32 [118, 166]

DNA 137, 141, 218, 223 [59, 156, 163]

DOCTOR 29–31, 113, 143, 149 [19, 166]

Dollo, L. 50

Don Juan 133

dream 12–13, 23, 56, 192 [3, 45, 157]

dream-work 56 [45]

Dreyfus, H. L. 119 [36, 37]

Dreyfus, S. E. 119 [37]

Duda, R. O. 152 [15]

E

Einstein, A. 293, 217

ELIZA 27–32, 143, 148 [114, 165]

Élö Á. 145 [38]

Encyclopaedia Britannica 86, 176 [60]

energy preservation 45